BRIAN'S SONG

On November 30, 1971, television sets in 48 million American homes were tuned to the most successful made-for-television movie in history, **Brian's Song**, starring James Caan as Brian Piccolo and Billy Dee Williams as Gale Sayers. Based on Gale Sayers's **I AM THIRD**, **Brian's Song** told the honest, moving story of brotherhood and friendship on the playing field and off—the story of gifted, doomed Brian Piccolo of the Chicago Bears and his friend, co-player and roommate Gale Sayers.

Brian's Song is now a legend.

I AM THIRD, the book that inspired **Brian's Song**, became one of the most talked-about books of the year. Acclaimed as a remarkable autobiography, it soared—at $6.95 in hardcover—to a prominent place on bestseller lists.

Now, for the millions who loved **Brian's Song**, here, in paperback, is

I AM THIRD

"THE LORD IS FIRST,
    MY FRIENDS ARE SECOND,
    AND I AM THIRD."
            —*Gale Sayers*

I AM THIRD
Gale Sayers

With AL SILVERMAN
Introduction by Bill Cosby

BANTAM BOOKS · TORONTO · NEW YORK · LONDON

A NATIONAL GENERAL COMPANY

I AM THIRD

*A Bantam Book / published by arrangement with
The Viking Press, Inc.*

PRINTING HISTORY

*Viking edition published 1970
2nd printing .... February 1971*

Bantam edition published April 1972

2nd printing .... April 1972	5th printing .... April 1972
3rd printing .... April 1972	6th printing .... April 1972
4th printing .... April 1972	7th printing .... May 1972

8th printing

Published simultaneously in the United States and Canada

*Bantam Books are published by Bantam Books, Inc., a National
General company. Its trade-mark, consisting of the words "Bantam
Books" and the portrayal of a bantam, is registered in the United
States Patent Office and in other countries. Marca Registrada.
Bantam Books, Inc., 666 Fifth Avenue, New York, N.Y. 10019.*

PRINTED IN THE UNITED STATES OF AMERICA

Introduction

by Bill Cosby

When I was a very small kid I played a lot of football on the asphalt of Philadelphia. In those days I often wound up on the hoods of cars, or almost spliced in half by a fire hydrant, or hickeyed by a light pole because I happened to be a bad judge of distance. My own pitiful personal football triumphs have helped heighten my appreciation for the author of this book. I have two special memories of Mr. Gale Sayers. Both will remain in my mind, I think, forever.

The first thing I saw was in, of all places, Hugh Hefner's house. If you can believe it, there was one day when I was looking for something to do in the Playboy mansion and a fantastic thought crossed my mind: have Hefner's secretary call the Chicago Bear office and ask them to send over some films on the Bears and Gale Sayers.

The Bear office responded quickly, and I had a beautiful time. While watching the movie I saw Dick Butkus eating up as many people as he could and I saw Gale Sayers get in and out of quite a few predicaments. But I'll never forget one play. Gale Sayers was sweeping to his right, moving around right end, and this hole opened up. I don't remember if it was made by a blocker or whatever, but it just opened up. And my feeling while watching was that Gale would never make the cut in time. Because, number one, he wasn't looking in that direction. And, number two, he was moving in another direction.

And the man made the cut.

And I just exploded. I mean, my arms fell off, my legs fell off, and my head rolled on the floor—that's how excited I got about it. Sometimes when you get excited about watching a beautiful thing happen before your eyes, your arms fall off . . . and your legs fall off . . . and your head falls off. And I turned around to the projectionist after I recovered myself and I said to the cat, "Back that up!" And he backed it up. And I said, "Now run it again." And he ran it again. And Gale did the same thing. And this time my legs fell off . . . my arms fell off . . . and my head fell off. And I sat there telling the projectionist, who must have thought I was crazy, to run it over and over. And I saw that thing, I swear to you, twelve times. And I still cannot believe that Gale made that cut.

Then there was the Pro Bowl game in January 1970, the National Football League All-Stars from the East vs. the NFL All-Stars from the West. And this time Gale Sayers was coming around his left end.

I was standing on the sidelines because I'm a celebrity and there are some groovy cats in Los Angeles who let me stand on the sidelines. I was standing there and Gale was coming around this left end. And there are about five or six defensive men ready, waiting for him, you know. And I saw Gale Sayers split. I mean, like a paramecium. He just split in two. He threw the right side of his body on one side of the field and the left side of his body kept going down the left side. And the defensive men didn't know who to catch. They just stood there. Then they looked to the referee for help, because there's got to be a penalty against splitting yourself. But there is not. Tony Quinn was with me and we both looked it up in the rule book and there's no rule against splitting yourself in half.

I know all of this doesn't have anything to do with Gale's book in particular—but it does have to do with Gale Sayers. He was too modest to explain in this otherwise splendid autobiography how he splits himself in two, but I did see it and I was there.

So it gives me great pleasure and pride to say to the reader that as you turn this page you will now get into the life story of the man responsible for a new rule being put into professional football: no splitting yourself in two.

Beverly Hills, California

The Game Plan

I think I know me, but in this book I'm taking no chances. There are a lot of people who at least know sides of me. I figure, the more sides I show the better and truer and more honest a picture you'll get of Gale Sayers, football player and man.

All these people—their names are scattered throughout the book—were kind enough to sit down, sometimes in the vicinity of a tape recorder, and tell what they know about me. And I thank them all. Because I don't have the strongest memory in the world, and without their help, without their own memories of me, we would have had a little thinner book—and, I think, a far less interesting book.

There is one person who knows more about me than anyone—who probably knows me better than I know myself. That is my wife, Linda, and, as she has enriched my life, so has she enriched my life story, with her observations, her recollections, her emotions about the things that have mattered in our life.

So it is that you will find Linda intruding in many chapters, telling, in her own words, aspects of my life that I would find difficult to express myself. If Linda is an extension of me—and I think she very much is— then I feel it important for her to exercise a woman's prerogative—get in her licks. In a couple of spots, as you will see, we even go at it together, in the form of a home playlet. This happened when we forgot the tape recorder was running and just started talking out things that had been hidden in our minds. And so I mean it when I say I doubt that this book could have been written without the help and cooperation and concern of my wife.

I have divided my book into three sections because this is the way my life seems to have fallen. Part I is mainly concerned with the events surrounding my knee injury in 1968, which really shook me up more than I had ever been shaken up in my life. Part II covers my childhood, my growing up, my high-school and college days, and the people and events that touched my life the most and pointed me in the direction to where I am today. Part III deals with my life as a professional football player, from the beginning of my career in 1965 to the present. It deals also with the developments in my life off the field. Taken as a whole, my book is, I think, more than anything else, the story of change— how it is possible for a man to change from a nothing to a something.

I write this just before my twenty-seventh birthday. I have to wonder where a twenty-seven-year-old gets off writing his autobiography, his life story. But I better leave the final judgment to you.

Contents

Introduction by Bill Cosby   v

The Game Plan   ix

Part One

1. "You Wouldn't Lie to Me"   3
2. How's Your Marlin?   11
3. The Loneliness of Being by Yourself   20
4. I Am Third   32
5. A Season of Strange, Crazy Things   48
6. Pick   63

Part Two

7. Santa Claus, Go Straight
   to the Ghet-to   85
8. Going for the Pookie-Burger   95
9. Linda   112
10. I Say Yes to Seventeen Colleges   122
11. A Place That Was Not Home   132
12. "Look at You, Sayer!"   143
13. Exploding Inside   155
14. Caught in the Middle   169

Part Three

15. Who Needs Seven Touchdowns?   187
16. Looking Somewhat like a Man   201
17. The Subject Is Relaxation   210
18. Paying the Price   216
19. A New Day   232

Appendix   241

Part One

1

"You Wouldn't Lie to Me"

It's gone! When Kermit Alexander hit my knee those two words flooded into my mind. It's gone! As soon as I hit the ground I knew it was gone. When I got up, did I turn to Alexander and say, "It's gone!"? It seems that I did. I do remember bouncing right up and trying to put weight on the right leg. I couldn't.

It hurt at that moment, but it wasn't that much of a hurt. At least I didn't think it was. Later I saw photographs of me screaming when I hit the ground, but I don't even remember that. I just remember jumping back up and trying to walk on the leg . . . and the knee wobbling back and forth, and buckling on me. And that's when I motioned to the bench, telling them to come and get me. I put my arms around my teammates, and as they lifted me off the ground I passed out.

It was just an ordinary, basic play against the San Francisco 49ers. In the huddle our quarterback, Virgil Carter, called, "Twenty-eight toss, south Lin." The south formation is when we are in a strong side right and the tackle pulls out, and I run back to the weak side behind his block.

Carter flipped me the ball and I broke left, hoping to go outside the defense behind the blocking of our tackle, Randy Jackson. But the 49ers' right linebacker, Harold Hays, was stringing Jackson along the line, keeping his hands on Jackson in order to control him and prevent me from breaking to the outside. And their right corner-back Kermit Alexander, who must also try to turn the play inside, had come up fast to try and strip the blocker. I saw him coming. I figured if Jackson could hit him, I would cut inside of him, something I have

3

done a million times before. But not this time. Alexander had submarined under the blocker, and at the instant I planted my foot he hit me with a rolling low shoulder block. The cleats of my right shoe were anchored in the turf, preventing give, and the knee took the full shock of the blow.

I have photos of the injury being inflicted, and you can see that my knee was bent to about a ninety-degree angle. It wasn't bent at the hinge as it would be normally; it was bent sideways, bent ninety degrees from the long axis of the thigh.

I remember the fellows coming up to me on the bench and telling me they were going to get Alexander—and me shaking my head. It wasn't Alexander's fault. It was a clean tackle. Alexander was getting paid to do his job on defense—to stop me. And I was getting paid to get by him. On that particular play he did his job to perfection, and I didn't do my job. He just submarined under my blocker and hit my knee at the right place, at the right moment; my foot fixed to the ground as I was trying to twist away from him. I could have had on tennis shoes, I could have been on the ice, or Astroturf, or foam rubber, and I still would have torn up my knee. Because he hit my knee just right. The knee is made to bend only one way and Alexander's shot forced it to bend the wrong way.

I must have been out for just a few seconds, because I remember reaching the sidelines and Dr. Theodore Fox, our bone specialist, coming over to me.

"It's gone, doc," I said, the only two words I could think of, the only words that made sense to me at the moment.

Dr. Fox bent over and felt the knee. He didn't feel it long. He got up and, very casual, said, "It's O.K." And he started to walk away.

"Come back here!" I screamed. "Tell it to me straight."

Then he came out with it. "Gale, I'm terribly sorry to have to tell you this, but the knee is gone, the ligaments are gone."

At that moment I was racked by self-pity. I asked

myself, Why me, why did it have to be me? I think my
whole life passed in front of me. Briefly, I thought of
my family, of my wife, Linda, up in the stands, wondering what she was thinking. But mostly I was thinking
only of myself. . . . Why me, why did it have to be me?
And then I put my head in my hands and started to cry.

*For two weeks, I had had a premonition about Gale.
I don't know why. Before then I always had the normal
fear of injury, the unspoken fear that every player's wife
has. But somehow I kind of felt it wouldn't happen to
Gale. And I felt that way until the Minnesota game,
two weeks before this disaster. Bobby Joe Green, our
punter, tore up his knee in that one. That was the first
time I think a knee injury really affected me, because
at that moment I had kind of a cold feeling like, God,
it really strikes close to home. It really was a strange
thing because suddenly I had this excessive fear that I
had never felt before. The next week, against Green
Bay, Gale had that great game when he gained 205
yards. But even in that game I was scared for him, I
don't know why.*

*The minute Kermit Alexander hit Gale I knew it was
bad. In his four years of professional football, Gale has
always gotten up lazily after being tackled, taking his
time getting back to the huddle. This time it was like he
was panicky. He jumped up and discovered he couldn't
put his foot down. And I knew it was something bad
because I had never seen this reaction out of him.*

*But my immediate reaction was just as strange. I
really wasn't upset. I was talking to all the wives—
jibber, jabber—and then it happened and, still, I was
relatively calm. Until I borrowed somebody's binoculars
and I looked at Gale through the binoculars and saw
he was crying. Well, I just couldn't stand that. I had
seen him cry only once before. That was when we were
dating in his senior year in high school. He was supposed to take me to the movies one night, but he said
he didn't want to go. And he just started crying. Then
he told me that his mother had left home again.*

But here he was, sitting and crying in front of forty-five thousand people. I have always felt that Gale puts me second, his family second, during the football season. It's like he's having an affair, an affair with football. But it really didn't hit me how important football was to him until the moment that I saw him sitting there and pride and nothing mattered. He was sitting there and crying in front of everybody. And I started crying, too.

I stayed on the bench until half time. Then they carried me on a stretcher into the dressing room and they got my clothes off. And Dr. Fox said he'd see me at the hospital after the game, that he'd want to operate right away. People kept coming by and telling me they were sorry and asking what they could do. *Well, what could they do?* I was trying to figure out what *I* could do, where I was going from here. Then Linda came in and the first thing she said to me was, "Well, it could be worse."

"Linda," I said, "I don't know what in the hell could be worse than this."

"Shoot," she said, recovering fast, "I can't think of a thing right now."

And I guess I used every profane word I had heard in my life. Not against Linda, but against fate, against what had happened to me.

They dressed me, handed me a pair of crutches, and helped me into the ambulance. They wanted me to lie down in the back and I said I wanted to sit up front, I'm going to sit up front. And they started to turn the siren on and I told them, "Turn the damn siren off."

Oh, I was in a beautiful mood. The trouble was I wasn't feeling that much pain. So I was more angry than anything else. We got to the hospital and this photographer came up behind us and wanted to take my picture. And I threatened to hit him with my crutches if he did.

Linda said, "It's the public demand."

I snarled, "The public isn't going to do anything for me right now; you just get him out of here."

The first thing I did when I got into my room was

take off my clothes, put on the white gown, and wash my hands. I don't know why I washed my hands, except that they were dirty. And still I couldn't believe what had happened. I kept trying to pace the floor, kept trying to stand on the leg. Like maybe it wasn't true, maybe it isn't what's happening. I waited impatiently for Dr. Fox. I kept asking, "Where is Dr. Fox? Where is Dr. Fox?" Until the last minute I kept saying, "Well, maybe when Dr. Fox comes he's going to find it's something else."

They gave me a couple of hypodermics, tranquilizers I guess, but I was so keyed up it didn't do a thing to me. Heck, I was wide awake on the operating table until they finally put me to sleep.

While we waited, I kept asking for the score of our game (we beat the 49ers 27–19) and I said to Linda, "Why couldn't it have happened next year?"

Linda said, "Why are you so worried?"

"Well, this is my year to get a new contract." When I joined the Bears in 1965 I signed a four-year contract. They got me cheap, considering I made All-Pro for three years (and, as it turned out, a fourth, too, even though I missed the Bears' last five games of 1968). So I was in line for a very big salary jump. But that really wasn't what was bothering me. I just didn't think something like this would ever happen to me. In my entire football lifetime up to then, I had missed only one game—high-school, college, or pro—and that one game caused such a commotion it will have to be explained fully later on. I kept thinking of Jim Brown, who had played nine years without serious injury. Conveniently, I blocked out of my mind all those who had suffered serious injuries in their pro careers. Why did it have to happen to me? That's what I wanted to know.

I asked Dr. Fox that before he took the knife to me. "Now, look, Gale," he said, "you've been playing football for four years in high school, four years in college, and four with the Bears. That's twelve years right there. Except for one game, you haven't had one injury which has kept you out of a ball game. So you've been fortunate. The law of averages has caught up with you, that's all. Consider how fast you run, how hard you run, the number of times you've been hit. When you've got two forces running at each other like two locomotives, the impact is fantastic. You've been lucky.

"Now I'm telling you this: I will make your knee as good as, if not better than, it was before. That I promise you."

I said, "Don't bull me, doctor, don't tell me this if it isn't true."

"Gale," he said, "you have my promise."

Dr. Fox started cutting into me at five-forty-five that Sunday night. I was on the operating table for three hours. Later the doctor told me it was the worst kind of knee injury you can get. I had what he said was about fifty per cent of a total situation. A total situation would be when all of the ligaments on both sides of the joint were gone. In my case, the ligaments on the inner, or what is called the medial, side of the joint (the big-toe side) were gone.

Torn were all the ligaments and all the supporting structure on the inner side of the knee, plus the anterior cruciate ligament. The medial collateral ligament was torn in three places. The medial meniscus, which acts as a washer between the thighbone and the shinbone, was torn loose. The anterior cruciate, which acts to stabilize the knee and also functions as a fulcrum of rotation, was torn. In addition, all of the capsule, which is the enveloping structure of the knee joint and where the muscles attach, was torn from the kneecap to the back of the knee.

When I came to, I found myself lying in bed in the intensive-care unit with a fifteen-pound cast covering my right leg from the toe to the top of the hip.

Dr. Fox was there and he kept reassuring me, "Everything's O.K."

I was still groggy from the anesthesia and not very reassured. I said, "You wouldn't lie to me, you wouldn't lie to me." I kept repeating this. Desperately, I lifted

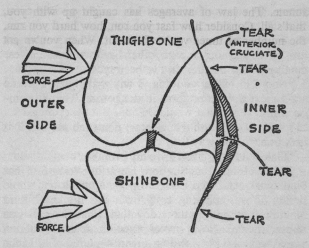

myself up and started screaming at him: "YOU WOULDN'T LIE TO ME!"

He hadn't lied to me. The operation took place on Sunday night. I began to walk with crutches on Tuesday. On Wednesday I threw away the crutches. "I don't want to use crutches," I said. "I'm going to show that I can walk on the leg." I started walking on the leg.

Friday they held a press conference at the hospital, and I was discharged. Before I left, Dr. Fox and I talked alone.

"You're doing fine," he said.

"When do you think I'll be ready again?"

"Not this season, of course. Maybe in three months."

"Thank you, doctor." I was overwhelmed.

"Don't thank me," he said, "this is my job."

I started to cry again, I don't know why. But it was the last time I cried for myself. Linda and I went home together, and she knew what I had to do, and I knew what I had to do. As soon as I got out of the hospital I more or less accepted my injury and determined to get my knee back in shape so that I could play next year. I had read in the newspapers all that garbage about how running backs with knee injuries rarely come back to top form, that I might have to spend the rest of my playing career as a flanker or a pass receiver only. I vowed to come back as a running back. I was determined to come back all the way. And not because I was out to prove anything to anybody. Sure, I would set an example for others if I showed I could come back in a year. That would be fine. But everything I try to prove is to myself and not to anyone else. It has always been that way with me.

That first night home I didn't do any dreaming about my knee. I read once where Emerson Boozer of the New York Jets, who also had a knee operation, would dream he was spinning away from tacklers and his leg would fall off and lie there downfield. Now isn't that an idiotic dream? No, I never once dreamed about my knee, because I very seldom dream—period. Oh, Linda got me one time when I was dreaming about playing basketball one-on-one with Bill Russell. He must have been killing me because I kept hollering in my sleep, "Damn it, there he goes again."

But I never dreamed about my knee, and that first night home I *know* I didn't dream, because I didn't sleep. I couldn't get comfortable.

Along about three in the morning I woke Linda. "Call Dr. Fox," I said, "ask him if I can lie on my stomach."

She said, "I'm not calling Dr. Fox at three o'clock in the morning."

It was five after three when she called. The doctor was very good about it all. "Tell Gale he can sleep in any position he wants."

That made me feel better, though I don't know how it made Dr. Fox feel. But it wouldn't be the last time he heard from me late at night.

2

How's Your Marlin?

We took five hundred telegrams and about seventy-five hundred letters back home from the hospital. It was certainly good of people to care that way. A lot of letters came from old friends and coaches and owners around the league, but I would say a majority of them were from kids. My favorite was from a boy in the South. This was just after the 1968 Presidential election, you know, and the boy wrote:

> I was sorry to see you get hurt, Mr. Sayers. I was talking to my father. He heard that George Wallace, when he became President, was going to send all the Negroes back to Africa. I didn't want George Wallace to become President because I didn't want to see you go back to Africa.

For a while during my recuperation period I thought it might not be a bad idea to go over to Africa and hide. I told my friend, Tommy Dare, "I'm going to Johannesburg, South Africa, and be homecoming king of Johannesburg U." People cared about me and I appreciated that, I was grateful for that. But as I went along I found that they were driving me crazy with the same question all over again: How's your knee? Everywhere I went, that's all they asked: How's your knee? I mean, there was one time when a fellow really double-teamed me. First he said, "Hey, I thought you were O. J. Simpson." Then: "How's your knee?"

It got to a point where when people would ask me about my knee I'd say, "It's killing me, I can hardly walk." I know they all meant well, and maybe part of it was me—especially since that was my first real injury

11

ever. Maybe if I get another one I'll take it a little bit better (though I would rather not be tested, thank you). But it just got to be so bad. A person would ask me one day, "How's your knee?" and then come back the very next day and ask me the same thing again.

I think the situation reached a climax the day a gentleman stopped at my desk at Paine, Webber, Jackson & Curtis, where I work in the off-season as a stockbroker. I don't think he really knew what he was saying, but he said, "Congratulations on your injury." I didn't know what to do—say thank you or what.

Finally, late in the spring, after I had gone marlin fishing with football commissioner Pete Rozelle for the American Sportsman television show, my friends came up with the answer. The first thing they greeted me with when I returned from that trip was "How's your marlin?" "How big did you say it was, baby?" From then on they'd all look at the knee and say, "How's your marlin?"

By that time, my marlin was making good progress. It was those early days after the injury that were the worst, the days when the leg was still in a cast and I was powerless to help myself. I was as unpleasant a person as you could find. I mean, I couldn't be around people. I put a strain on all my personal relationships, especially my family. It was rough for our little girl, Gale Lynne, who was two at the time, and very rough for Linda. It had to be one of the worst periods of our married life, rivaled only by the time in my senior year in college when I signed with the Bears and then refused to attend classes any more. Linda really hated me then.

But now we couldn't get along for two minutes. We were at each other's throats all the time. She kept saying I was feeling sorry for myself, and I guess I still was. She wanted me to take her out and I wouldn't, but only because I couldn't get around like I wanted. She finally went back to mother in Omaha for a week, thinking maybe it would be better when she returned. But it was worse. I was jumpy and kind of depressed and I felt all caged up.

The only thing that kept me going right after the injury was that the football season was still on. The Bears were fighting for a division title and I was still a member of the team, as I found out when I went to Los Angeles with them for the next-to-the-last game of the season. The night before the game Ed McCaskey, who is the Bears' treasurer, and his wife, took me to the Factory, a discotheque in Hollywood. That night they held a bed check and I hadn't returned yet. They fined me $250. It was the first fine of my life, but it was right for them to do it. We went out and beat the Rams the next day 17–16, and that almost made the fine worthwhile.

Really, the big regret about that 1968 season was not being able to play, because we had a good chance to win our division. In fact, we could have won it had we beaten Green Bay in the last game of the season. They beat us 28–27.

Another regret about missing the last five games was that I was headed for the best year of my life.

We lost our opener against Washington at home 38–28. I gained 105 yards that day, but that was nothing. Sonny Jurgensen came into Wrigley Field and he could do no wrong. I mean, he wasn't missing anything. To top it off, he hit Gerry Allen for a ninety-nine-yard touchdown pass near the end. But, oh, I tell you, he was hot, Lord he was hot. He was a pleasure to watch from the sidelines.

The big thing about the game was that they had jumped off to a fourteen-point lead. Then it was 14–7, then 21–14, 28–21. We were scoring, but Jurgensen was so hot the defense couldn't do anything. If they could have held him we would have won the game. But the way he was firing the ball nobody could have stopped him that day. In my time, I think Jurgensen has been, without a doubt, the best quarterback in the league.

It didn't look like we were going to do anything that year, because we lost our second game to Detroit 42–zip, and I think I got about forty yards. But finally we cracked open against Minnesota. We beat them 27–17, and they weren't even in the game, we just dominated the whole game. I remember a lot of runs I should have broken, but I was just getting hit on the leg, or falling or something. I ended up with 108 yards.

Then we went to Baltimore and they beat us 28–7, but I had a fifty-seven-yard touchdown run that I think was the best run of my professional-football career.

It was supposed to be an end run to the right. I did go to the right as far as I could, to the sidelines. But there was no blocking on the play whatsoever and there were quite a few people there. They had me hemmed in, so I stopped and came toward the middle and they were coming in from the other way. Then I caught this flow and there was this little bitty hole showing and I shot through it and went back toward the right sidelines, which I had been supposed to do all along.

Three times I passed Bubba Smith, who was playing defensive left end. It was like one of those old silent-movie chase scenes where the farmer trying to cross the road gets knocked on his rear by the bandits' car whizzing by, then he starts crossing the road again and gets knocked over by a police car, then he gets it a third time as the gangster car comes doubling back. Bubba and I could have had a conversation, but we didn't. I sliced right to the inside of Bubba and cut back and went down the sidelines. I think Rick Volk jumped at me, but he missed me, and Lenny Lyles chased me into the end zone. I have to say it myself, I made a helluva run.

People always ask me how I run with the ball, and I can't tell them. It's all pure instinct. You have to have the speed and quickness of course, especially the quickness at hitting the holes. Speed isn't as important as quickness. Any back who's playing professional football has speed; that's immaterial to me. I consider football a game of five- and ten-yard sprints, because you very seldom break a fifty-, sixty-, or seventy-yard run. The hole's there and you hit it, and you've got to be quick enough to see it to hit it and get out, get that five, that ten yards. When you see the hole and you know you can't get to it, it's time to give it up. Quickness is the main asset for a running back. A lot of backs don't have it. They're fine backs, but they still don't have it.

And with quickness you need a change of pace and leg action and head fakes and all that stuff. My teammate Brian Piccolo once said, "The thing that makes Gale different is the way he's able to put a move on somebody and not lose a step. He'll give a guy a little fake and he's full speed. I give a guy a move like that and it takes me fifteen yards to get in stride."

I suppose that's part of it, but I really don't know what kind of moves I put on people. I certainly don't plan ahead. If I did that, I'd be finished as a runner. It all has to come naturally. I remember I was once asked about one long run I made in college. I said very seriously, "It was an inside-outside-inside fake, followed by an outside-inside-outside fake." And maybe it was.

In high school I had a close friend, Vern Breakfield (he still is one of my best friends). We played in the same backfield together and did everything together. Break was the extrovert and I was the introvert of the act. He liked to dance and go out with girls and jive a lot, and I always hung back and listened to the music.

One time Break taught me a dance called the Run-Around. It's where you put one foot forward, chop your step, put another foot forward, sway from side to side— a kind of give-and-go swing. Well, I never used it on the dance floor, but one day we were playing West Side High and I was on defense and I intercepted a pass. I took the ball away from this guy and put one step forward, chopped my step, put another step forward, swayed from side to side—and stepped out sixty yards for the touchdown.

I came back to the sidelines so happy. "Did you see me do it, Break, did you see me do it?"

"Yeah, I saw it." Break muttered, "My God almighty, the Run-Around." He was so mad. "Man, here I teach you this stuff to do on the dancing floor and I get you to a party and you won't even do it. You get to the game, do it, and go sixty yards for a touchdown."

The thing was I didn't know what I was doing out

there—I was just doing it. I do things without thinking about them, and in 1968, up to my injury, I seemed to be doing things better than ever.

We lost to Detroit again, then we beat Philadelphia, Minnesota, and Green Bay. And I got 143 yards against the Vikings (the game in which Bobby Joe Green tore up his knee) and 205 against the Packers, which was my first 200-yard day in the National Football League.

It seems that I've always had pretty good days against Minnesota and Green Bay. Henry Jordan, who was an outstanding defensive tackle for the Packers, once said he'd always thought I was Polish. I moved so fast, he said, he never got a good look at me. I do have good averages against both the Vikings and Packers. It may be because neither team blitzes much. When they don't blitz you know you can get your guards out around the ends and you can trap men. And once you get past the front four you have just the linebacker, and I've always felt I could beat any man one-on-one and seventy-five per cent of the time I could beat then one-on-two.

That Packer game was a peculiar one. It started off bad for us. I ran the first play and made about five yards. The second play I ran for about twenty, but it was called back for holding. On the third play we dropped back for a pass and that was incomplete. Then they gave it to me on an end run and I went about twenty-five yards and still we had to punt. We had them 3–0 at the half and finally beat them 13–10.

Most of my yardage was accumulated on short runs —ten, five, eight yards; mostly off-tackle and quick openers. I think they were keying on my end sweeps a lot. Ray Nitschke, the Packers' fine middle linebacker, always did key on me. And every time I started to the right or to the left he'd come barreling over. He'd pursue along the line and I'd cut right behind him; when he started to swerve inside or come in at an angle, to try and cut me off, I'd cut behind him against the flow.

I did have one long run, sixty-three yards. It was a regular off-tackle play. Tom Brown, their cornerback, grabbed me at the line, but somehow I got away from him. I made a cutback, coming back against the grain, against the flow. Doug Hart came by and got me by the leg and I shook him off. But they hemmed me in finally on the five-yard line.

With about four or five minutes to go, someone on the side lines told me I had 189 yards and said I should try for 200. I thought I was through for the day, but I went back in. I broke one for about fifteen and that took me over 200. I ended up carrying the ball twenty-four times, the most I had ever carried in a game before.

That turned out to be quite a big day for runners, because Leroy Kelly got 174 yards. But I was still ahead of him; I had 824 yards for the season and he had 721. Of course he ended up as league rushing champion with 1239 yards. Missing those last five games, I finished fifth in the league. But they still thought enough of me to name me to the National Football League All-Pro team for the fourth straight year, and when I heard about that, shortly after the season ended, my spirits were lifted quite a bit.

Another big lift came on December 18, when Dr. Fox removed my cast.

I had carried the big cast around for four weeks and it bothered me a lot. It had loosened and there was wobbling on the leg. I could pick up the cast and move it up and down and it was rubbing my incision. So he took that one off and put on a small one of about five pounds. I was able to put my pants over it and I got around much better. Then, on December 18, I got that one off.

Immediately, I was gung-ho. "Just watch me bend the knee," I told Dr. Fox.

He said, "Oh, no you won't."

I said, "Oh, yes I will."

I tried, all right, but I could barely move it, there was just a little play on it. Actually, it took about two weeks before I could straighten it out, and even then I overdid it, trying to get the leg to bend, to break down the adhesions.

One day Dr. Fox examined the leg and said, "You've been working it too hard, Gale." When you operate on

a knee there is a certain amount of bleeding and these
areas become little bands of fibrous tissues, and adhesions form that have to be stretched; but they have to
be stretched out gradually instead of torn. If you tear
them it causes more hemorrhaging and that means more
pain and swelling and fluid. The idea is to stretch the
adhesions gradually to avoid the complications. And I
overdid it, I went too fast too soon. Dr. Fox compared
it to having someone's finger stuck in your eye and
having the eye tear. Same way with the joint. It begins
to tear and fluid accumulates in the joint.

He explained all this to me, then he pulled out a
three-inch needle and drained about a cup of fluid from
the knee.

My cast served a good purpose, as it turned out. A
high-school player, Gary Steger of Roselle, Illinois,
Lake Park High, had been paralyzed in a game and a
foundation had been started for him. So they took my
cast and auctioned it off and George Gillet, who is
president of the Harlem Globetrotters, bought it for
$3500. I never have had the courage to ask him what he
did with it, whether it's hanging on a wall in his home.

But even with the cast off I was still in a mean mood,
still snarling at Linda and upset with everyone who kept
asking me about the knee. I had good occasion to feel
bad about the way I treated Linda. We were invited
down to Miami to see the Orange Bowl game—my alma
mater, Kansas, was playing Penn State—and we took
Gale Lynne with us. Linda was three months pregnant
at the time. On the night of December 31, New Year's
Eve, we had to rush her to the hospital. She suffered a
miscarriage.

People were very nice. They asked me how Linda
was and I told them she was fine. Which she was; the
next night she went to the Orange Bowl game with me.
And then they asked me how my knee was. And I told
them it was fine, too. But I would have rather they
asked about Linda. I would have been just as happy if
nobody mentioned the knee at all. I didn't want to hear
about it; it was almost as if I had a block about it. As

I said, I had never been hurt before in my life. I was still wondering why this had happened to me and trying to reconcile myself to it. And, I suppose, in the back of my mind was some doubt. Would it get better? Would it be O.K. for the 1969 season? I felt all along that it would be O.K., but the doubt lingered in my mind. It was always there.

One night early in the spring we had some friends over for dinner. Among them were two of my teammates, George Seals and Frank Cornish. After dinner I got out the projector to show the Bears' 1969 highlight film. This was my first time seeing the film, too.

I enjoyed watching it until they came to a one-minute sequence—my injury. In the darkness George Seals, trying to be funny, hollered, "Get up! Get up!" And a chill, almost like an electric shock, went through my body. I don't know why, but I actually got the shakes. After the guests had left I told my wife that I would never look at the film as long as I lived.

That night I couldn't sleep at all. I just thought about it all night long, and I got up the next morning thinking about it.

A couple of days later I had to show the highlight film to a civic organization. When it came to the point of my injury, I picked up and left the room. I really never did want to see that again. Much later, about the time the fellows were joking about my "marlin," I was able to say to myself, The hell with it, and stay and watch myself popped and falling to the ground with three ligaments in my knee ripped apart. But it did take me a while before I reached that point, and even today I do not for one moment enjoy reminiscing about what is still one of the worst moments of my life.

3

The Loneliness of Being
by Yourself

I dedicate this chapter to my friend Tommy Dare, who, with his father, runs a Chinese restaurant in Chicago (possibly because they *are* Chinese). Since my days with the Chicago Bears, Tommy and I have shared the tortures of the damned, both enrolled in a gym club at the Lawson YMCA run by a not-to-be-believed little trick named Dick Woit.

Woit is the only man I know who *reversed* the Charles Atlas training method. He turned from a 175-pound professional football player into a 145-pound Hitler.

Dick played running back and end for the Detroit Lions in 1954 and 1955. His career ended abruptly in a 1955 game against the New York Giants when he took a comeback pass from Bobby Layne and was hit with a forearm by defensive back Em Tunnell. The forearm caught Dick in the back of the head. He was in a coma for twenty days and they ended up putting a plate in his head.

Dick came back home to Chicago as a health nut (he eats maybe three meals a *week*—nuts and fruit and half-cups of black coffee the rest of the time). He also came back with ideas about physical fitness that he put into practice at this Dearborn Club in the Lawson Y. Now there is a list a mile long waiting to get into Woit's class, just panting for the chance to endure all the most creative tortures Woit's tough little Polish mind has been able to dream up.

I had heard about him my rookie year in Chicago. Right after the 1965 season I went to him. "I'd like to start working out with you," I said.

He looked at me and sneered. Flat out he said, "I don't think you can make it."

"Well," I said, "let's try it."

There were times that year I thought he was right. I know a lot of Chicago Bear football players and athletes from other teams who enrolled in Woit's classes and then quit. They couldn't stand either the pace or Woit's insults—I don't know which is worse myself. It was tough and it *is* tough, but I enjoyed it from the first.

Woit's theory seems simple enough: "Physical condition," he says, "is your recuperation power after you've had physical exertion." It's how he puts that theory in practice that hurts.

We go thirty minutes a day, six days a week. We start off doing situps, with knees flexed. We do up to fifty of these, followed by a five-second rest. Then it's leg lifts. We lie prone and lift our heels inches off the floor and hold them that way for sixty seconds. Five seconds' rest, then a second sixty-second leg lift, then forty situps, five seconds' rest, four more minutes of leg lifts, then thirty rapid situps. All this to warm us up.

Now we're ready to lift weights—bench-pressing fifty, one hundred, one hundred ten pounds over our heads, up to twenty-five times at a clip. We alternate the weights with chin-to-mat pushups, legs elevated on a bench, of course. But, remember, we've got five seconds to rest in between.

Finally, we run down the fire escape to the parking lot in the back of the Y and Woit throws us passes while we run eighty-yard dashes full speed—anywhere from ten to twenty a session, depending on the mood he's in. And the hairy part of all of this is that Woit does everything we do—everything. He has tendonitis in his throwing arm, for instance. And sometimes it hurts him to throw four hundred passes at a time. So what does he do? He shoots himself in the arm with Novocain and hollers, "O.K., let's go." A man like that commands respect.

I've invited friends to work out with me, and their reactions have been something to see. The spring I was trying to work my knee back into shape I had Willie

Davis of the Green Bay Packers over for a workout.
Willie ended up outside heaving over a Volkswagen—
if you can believe the sight since Willie is bigger than
that car. His body was steaming. A few weeks later my
younger brother, Ronnie, who was about to start his
rookie year with the San Diego Chargers, came in for
a visit. I phoned Woit.

"I'm bringing my brother Ronnie in—kill him."

Dick Woit shook hands with Ronnie and was all
innocence. He said, "You're a big boy, just do what the
other guys do." He put Ronnie next to an older man
with a paunch and gray hair and all, and Ronnie
couldn't beat him or anybody—in anything. I thought
he was going to die. When I took him home that afternoon he had trouble getting out of the car. "I can't lift
up my arms," he said.

"Come on, Ronnie," I said, "don't embarrass me."
He went right to bed. The next day I practically had to
carry him to the airport. He wasn't right for two weeks.

It was almost as tough for me my first year with Woit.
I think the worst part of it was all the insults. Woit loves
to taunt people, loves to needle the men who willingly
pay a small fortune for the privilege of being stomped
on by him. "Hey, you black buffalo," he'll yell at me,
"you're cheating." We have rich Italian spaghetti kings
and Woit calls them "Woppos," and worse. Jewish
businessmen get the "Jew" treatment, and Tommy Dare,
the only Chinese member of the club, is Woit's house
"Jap": "Don't ever come around on December seventh,
you slanty-eyed Jap."

That first year I got the treatment good from Woit,
and everyone else. "Think he's as good as Livingston?"
they'd holler, a reference to my then running mate,
Andy Livingston. Woit would yell out loud, his words
dripping with sarcasm, "Look at the comet, look at the
big Kansas comet, will you?" And Tommy Dare, who
had been in the class for a couple of years, picked right
up: "Look at Mrs. Sayers go."

Once you got used to Woit's nature—and understood
that he was being mean and vicious just to keep us

going, and maybe keep himself going, too—and once you were able to lift up to his level, you discovered that he was doing so much good for you. I know I would come to training camp every season in better condition than anyone on the squad. I'd tell people, "I hate to come here because it gets me out of shape."

And in January 1969 I needed Dick Woit more than ever.

Before I started in at the Y, I had begun to work out at home. I took a weighted shoe with me on our Florida trip, plus a suitcase full of forty-pound weights. The Bears were nice enough to let me borrow their knee machine. It's a benchlike device. You sit on it, put the weights on a spindle that is attached to a padded bar, and lift your legs off the ground—lift up easy and hold. I started with fifty lifts, in sets of ten, lifting against the pull of five pounds of weight. Eventually, I got up to sixty pounds, but it wasn't so much the weight that counted but the repetition, keeping it going. In those days I would go down early in the morning and lift and do it again at night. And every day I visited the hospital and put the leg in the big whirlpool, trying to get it to bend all the way.

The first thing Dick Woit said to me when I went over to the Y on January 6 was, "Now, Gale, a child crawls before he walks." He started me slow because I couldn't bend my knee all that well yet. I jogged around the building. After a workout, I'd go down to the swimming pool and take a paddle board and kick my legs in the pool, kick up and down in the pool, for about four or five laps.

Then he started me working on a couple of torture machines of his own, specially designed for knee victims. One is a device with a padded shoulder yoke. A chain hangs down from the yoke and hooks on to two hundred pounds of steel. You place your shoulders under the yoke and raise the weights by coming up off your toes. The other is a platform with weights. You lie on your back and push up and raise the weights to the full extension of your leg. I started doing that with the weights at one hundred pounds. I'd do it as far as I

could go and then push it back up again, and this
helped bend the knee more.

As usual, Woit knew just what he was trying to do.
He had this watchword about the knee: "Violence
injured it, surgery corrected it, the cast atrophied it,
and exercise is strengthening it." Amen.

It felt good going to the Y, and I looked forward to
it more than ever in 1969. Because at least I was with
people there. As the weeks and months went by and
my workouts increased, I found the loneliness to be
the worst thing of all. Once I got out of the hospital bed
and started walking, I don't think I had any fear of
not being able to come back. Oh, I did have doubts,
constant doubts, but the doubts were there because I
wasn't able to prove myself. The doubts would stay in
my mind until I got into a football game and ran with
the ball. The doubts were there, too, because I was
dealing with the unknown. I was trying to face up to the
first injury of my life. Also, I had heard and read about
all the football players who never came back from knee
injuries, or came back at only fifty per cent of what
they had been. I had seen this happen to my own teammates. So there was nothing I could really do to shake
the doubts. And yet, with all the doubts, I still knew,
deep in my heart, that I would be able to come back
within a year, and I welcomed the challenge. My feeling has always been that I can control my body, I can
control my destiny.

But I knew that in order to come back, and come
back one hundred per cent, I had to do certain exercises
to get my knee back together. I had to work at it. Dr.
Fox told me that for every day the knee was not exer-
cised, for whatever reason, it takes at least six days of
exercise to catch up. He pounded into my skull the fact
that the operation had been a success. He had repaired
the ligaments and reinforced them so that they would
be as good as, if not better than, ever. But he also told
me that the ligaments contribute only twenty per cent
to the stabilizing force of the knee. The muscles contribute *eighty* per cent. "So, if you've got perfect liga-

ments, Gale," he said, "and you've got muscles developed to only fifty per cent of their strength, you are losing a tremendous amount of stabilizing force. After the operation, it's all up to the motivation of the individual—how hard he works, how much desire he has to restore the knee to its former capacity."

That was all right with me, that was fine. It is part of my character to drive myself. I enjoy working hard. A lot of people don't enjoy sweating. When I work out, I enjoy perspiring. So it wasn't the work that bothered me, and I didn't mind the pain, either, as long as I understood why it was paining. In a way, it was like hell week when you joined a fraternity. It's bad while you're doing it, but once you get over it, it seems like it was nothing.

It wasn't the work or the pain at all, only the loneliness . . . the loneliness of getting up and doing my exercises, of running in the park by myself, of not being able to do what other people are doing at the time . . . the loneliness of being by myself.

It's so easy, when you're off by yourself, to say, The hell with it. How many football players with knee injuries, I wonder, said, The hell with it, and didn't do the work they should have done and didn't come back because of that, because they weren't willing to pay the price? And I can understand them. That bothered me, too. It was so easy to say, I can slack up here and catch up tomorrow. But it doesn't work that way. You've got to keep doing it.

And I kept doing it to the point that it became an obsession with me. Sometimes I would get up at four in the morning and go down to the basement and work on the machine and then go upstairs and lie in bed and get up again at five-thirty or six and lift the weights again. I'd lift them before I went to work at Paine, Webber. From work I would go to the Y. When I got home in the evening I would lift the weights again. Then I'd sit around during the evening and go back down before I went to bed.

In the other years it wouldn't bother me to miss a day here and there from the Y. But in 1969 I went on

Monday, Tuesday, Wednesday, Thursday, Friday, and
Saturday. The Y came before everything. If I had something to do that day, it was canceled. If I had to be out
of town and missed a day, I'd take two workouts the
next six days in a row. Everything stopped when I went
to the Y. I would kill myself to get there. One day I
got over to the Y a little late and Tommy Dare said,
"Where you been?"

"With some idiots, some dudes."

"Oh? What idiots, what dudes?"

"The governor and the mayor." I was kidding, naturally, but there were some politicians at this luncheon
I attended, and I just walked out of the luncheon because I had to be at the gym.

No reflection on the governor or the mayor, or any
politician within earshot. I tend to talk that way about
people. I'll never forget the first time Linda met Tommy.
My first season at the Y I was kind of scared of people.
I never said a thing to Dick Woit. It took me a while
before I dared call him a white s.o.b. after he had called
me a black buffalo. And I talked to Tommy maybe five
times. But that's the way I am around people. It takes
time for me to warm up to them. Not only that, but I
can't remember names. I'm hell on names. Well, one
day Tommy drove over to my house. "Hey, Gale, what's
shakin', baby?" he said.

And I didn't remember his name. But I had him
drive with me to the airport to pick up Linda. She and
Gale Lynne were coming in from Omaha. Lind got off
the plane, and I wanted to introduce Tommy but I didn't
know his name. Finally, he said, "Hi, I'm Tommy Dare."

Later, when he had gone, Linda asked, "Who is he?"

"I don't know," I said, "some idiot, some dude. Don't
ask me."

He got back at me later. Taking off on Superman
he'd say, "Meet Super Soul Man, Clark Dark." Actually, that was better than what comedian Phil Foster
tried. He called my home one day and said, "May I
speak to Mr. Crime?" But the nickname I like best was
pinned on me by Ed McCaskey: "Black Magic." Today,

most of my teammates call me Magic, and I like that.

Anyway, Tommy and I got to be good friends. We began to do things together. He taught me some choice Chinese words, like *lawfine,* which means white, and *hakooey,* which means black. We'd be walking down the street and a big fat black girl would go by and Tommy would say, under his breath, "Look at the *hakooey.* I thought Linda was at home, Gale."

I got even with him one day when I went up to his father, who is a fine man and from the old school. "Mr. Dare," I said, "what is wrong with your son?"

He said, "Why?"

"He keeps calling me *hakooey.*" Mr. Dare turned all colors.

Another time we were playing softball against some *lawfine* girls, the Bunnies from the Playboy Club. All of the other guys were hitting these little bitty balls and Tommy and I were trying to knock 'em out of the park. I told him, "We got to play to win—kill 'em."

Once I was rounding base and one of those girls grabbed me by the shirt tail and I just dragged her around. "We got to play to win," Tommy said approvingly.

And Tommy and I did have a little competition in the gym. He is a good athlete, and we always tried to beat each other in pushups, running, and playing one-on-one in basketball afterward.

Tommy's big kick in life was making "All Calvin Park." Calvin Park High School is a small school and Tommy was a big star there. One day, for my birthday, he gave me a picture showing him when he was sixteen years old playing basketball. He signed it, "To Gale Sayers, from your No. 1 admirer. Best wishes, Tommy Dare, All Calvin Park." My cleaning lady saw this picture and she said, "Mr. Sayers, who is this gentleman? I've seen him with you before."

I said, "Oh, didn't you know he was a famous athlete?"

"He is?" She was impressed. "Well, so many important people come here and I just forget to ask you who they all are."

I said, "Yes, he's very important. The next time he

comes over, you have to be sure to ask him for his autograph."

I always tell Tommy that there are only two things I want when I die. I want to be reincarnated Chinese, and I want to be All Calvin Park, because that's the only award I've missed.

Tommy kind of enjoyed going up against me in 1969 because, at the beginning of my recuperative period at least, he was whipping me in everything. He always did have pretty good speed, but he could never beat me in a race. But now he was beating me. One day in that period he put his son on the phone. The boy said, "Mr. Sayers, don't feel bad. Maybe someday you'll be able to beat my daddy running."

When we first started running together that year he'd beat me by three strides. Another week would go by and he'd beat me by a stride. Then maybe another week would pass and he'd just nip me at the tape. After that, he knew that any day he was through. By late spring I was beating him again, and beginning to feel stronger all the time.

Gradually, I tried to increase my distance running and my speed. At home I went out to the park near us and jogged, doing two, three, four miles at a time. In the early days my leg didn't feel too good when I ran. It was still tight on the thigh. I began to feel apprehensive, and more so when, in February, Dr. Fox went off to Europe for three weeks. Now I couldn't wake him up at three in the morning to ask him about my latest ache. In this period I was calling him all the time. I might wake up at night in pain and I'd call him for an explanation. And he always told me exactly what was happening. And he never got mad at me for calling him at night. "Gale, you call me any time of the day or night that you feel something is wrong." And I did.

But with him away, I began brooding worse than ever, thinking about my knee and the season coming up, wondering if it would be better, if it would really come around. I still felt it would, but there was always that little doubt in my mind. And the doubt increased with

Dr. Fox gone, because I had come to depend on his assurances. It's true that I had thrown away my crutches early, but all along I was using him for a crutch.

He came back, finally, in late February and examined me and said that the knee looked fine. I said, "I want you to come out and watch me run." I was eager to take this test before the doctor; to me it was like a final examination.

On February 27 I went over to his house in Winnetka. I had my football shoes with me. We went out to a soccer field near his house. It was very muddy, but that didn't bother Dr. Fox. He said, "O.K., now we're going to put you through all your paces." And he had me run every conceivable pattern that I would be called upon to run in a game. I made like I was going off-tackle, I took off around end, I went out for passes, looking over my left shoulder and my right shoulder, at full speed. I made all the cuts, all the moves. He clocked my speed and it was the same as it had been before the operation. I found I could do everything I wanted to. And when I was finished he said, "Gale, if there was a game this Sunday, you'd be able to play."

This really made me happy. I knew all the time that my knee was coming along fine, but I needed that little reassurance. And overnight my whole attitude changed, at least that's what Linda felt. She said I had become a human being again.

I think I got most of my confidence back when I started playing basketball in the early spring. At first I would play by myself, dribble around, shoot the ball around. Then I would get in the games with Tommy at the Y. In April I went back home to Omaha and tested my knee again under very tough conditions—playing basketball one-on-one with my friend, Vern Breakfield.

I really needed the workout because I had missed a couple of days at the Lawson Y, which was like losing a year off my life. At that time, anyway. But I knew Break would give me a workout. He's like me. If he can kill you he'll kill you. He hates to lose. We've played together a lot of times in recent years. When he comes to visit me we get in the back yard and play maybe eight hours at a time, and we play like we're enemies. He elbows me, I elbow him back. He jumps all over me, I jump over him. We fall over each other's shoulders trying to block shots, we fall all over the cement. The wives hear the commotion, come out, and Linda hollers, "Be careful, Gale." And Break's wife hollers, "Be careful, Vernon."

And that's the way I wanted it in April. No favors. "You ready to do some running?" Break asked me. And I said yes.

Basketball is a helluva test for the knee. It may be the most difficult sport to play if you have a knee injury because you're always cutting. Lots of times in football you're running straight ahead, but in basketball you stop and go and twist and turn and jump. And I think Break went out there thinking he would be taking advantage of me. Which he doesn't have to do, because he is as quick as I am and it is hard for me to move and hold him. He can give me the hip and take it back like I give the average guy the hip and take it back. And he knows my moves.

So we went to the Y and we were the only two guys there and we loosened up playing 21. Then we played one-on-one. We played one-on-one half court and we ran for about two hours. And it was something else. At one point in the game Break thought he had injured me. He faked a shot, then turned around, and I turned around and blocked him out. Then he turned around again and shot and missed and went up for the rebound and came right down on my knee and I fell to the ground.

"Oh my God, what have I done?" he moaned. "Are you all right?"

I got up and said, "Take the ball out—you got it, don'tcha?" So he went back and took it out. Then he pulled a quickie on me, maybe to see if I could cut it. He gave me the hip one way, went the other way and went up with the ball. I went up with him and blocked the shot, knocked the ball up in the air.

"That's when I knew you were going to be all right,"

Break said after we were finished. "Shoo, the way you handled that, I knew you were ready." People came to Break later and asked, "How's Gale's knee?" He said, "Oh, man, the cat's ready. If he gets a chance to go he's ready."

And that's the way I felt. When I started working with Woit and Tommy at the Y back in January I weighed 186. When I finished my workouts in June I was 209, and it was all muscle. I remember when I went down to Acapulco for a hotel promotion. (Before I went, I had to ask Tommy where Acapulco was. He said, "It's in Mexico." I said, "Where's Mexico?" He said, "Where you been all your life?" I said, "Well, heck, I wasn't a history major.")

I had my shirt off all the time down there, and one morning someone came over, looked at my arms, now size seventeen, and said, "Are you Mr. Cassius Clay?"

I have to admit I liked the look of my muscles. Linda's girl friends commented, "Gee, you got some big arms." I went to a football writers' dinner in New York in April and Bob Vogel of the Baltimore Colts was on the dais. He walked by and said, "Damn, Gale, you look like you gained twenty pounds."

Around that time someone asked Linda how I was getting along, whether my knee was rounding into shape. She laughed. "Well, I don't know about the knee, but his arms keep getting bigger. He just comes home, looks at his arms in the mirror, and goes to sleep."

That was true. And I was sleeping better, too, waiting for mid-July, when I would report with the rookies at the Bears' training camp. That's the day I had been aiming for all along. I couldn't wait.

4

I Am Third

I did look in the mirror a lot in those days—every day, in fact. And not just at the arms. I'd look in the mirror, and what did I see? Why . . . a handsome black man.

No, I don't know what I saw. Every time you look at yourself in the mirror you see something different there, don't you? Sometimes I don't like what I see. Sometimes I hate myself because I have been lazy, because I have put things off, because I have been mean to Linda and my family. Sometimes, though, after I have had a helluva game I look in the mirror and say, "You're a bitch." And sometimes after a hard game and I come home tired I might look in the mirror and ask myself, Did I play my best? Did I do all I could to help the team? And many times I have said no. Coming to the mirror after a game in which I gained thirteen yards, or twenty-four yards, I say no. But on a Tuesday, after looking at the films, I might look in the mirror and have a different attitude because I have discovered there was nothing there and there was nothing I could do about it.

After our third exhibition game in 1969, I looked in the mirror and was upset by what I saw. We beat the Green Bay Packers, but I came out of that game with my knee hurting. And I remember that staring back at me was a face full of uncertainty, anxiety, and doubt. And my question to myself was, Will I really be the same player I was before the injury?

That night, coming back from Milwaukee, it was a terrible drive. Gale had fumbled two or three times and his knee was sore and he had had a bad game. He was trying to make small talk but he couldn't. When we got

*home he just didn't have anything to say. That night he
was up pacing the floor because his knee was in pain,
but I didn't know if the pain was in his knee or in his
mind. He was really afraid at that point: was he going
to be the same player he was? I think that was when he
had the worst doubts. Not before then. I don't think
he ever really doubted it before then. Like he would be
disgusted at different points, wondering whether it was
coming as fast as it should be. But he never feared it
until, I think, that point. He was really afraid then, and
he didn't want to say anything to anybody. That was
the worst I have ever seen him in my whole life.*

*When he left for camp the next day I just couldn't do
anything but cry. I said, Golly, if that's what he has to
go through, I wish he wouldn't because it's not really
worth it. He was brooding and he kept rubbing his knee.
He called Dr. Fox two or three times that Sunday, and
Dr. Fox said there was nothing wrong, it was something
he was going to have to live with, that he would have
to understand that. He didn't, he wouldn't listen to him.*

*My mother was with us at the time. She knew some-
thing was wrong with Gale, and after he left I went
upstairs and I started crying. I had just had it. I said,
"I just have to let it out." Mother came upstairs and she
started bawling, too. She just felt so sorry for him. He
was going through a lot of personal agony and that was
the worst time, that particular time.*

I felt great when I first reported to camp. The Chicago Bears train in a cow town called Rensselaer, Indi-
ana. It is about seventy-five miles south of Chicago.
Just as you enter the town you see a sign pointing the
other way to MOROCCO 17 MILES. Then you hit
Memory Gardens. But there is nothing exotic about
Rensselaer: it is all cemeteries, granite works, and farm-
land. The town has a main street and a movie house that
has one showing at night, at seven-thirty, naturally, so
the football players can't go. Our training headquarters
is located at St. Joseph's College, a liberal-arts school
with an excellent reputation. The football fields are

bordered on one side by a cornfield and on the other by Rensselaer Ready Mix Concrete. After you have spent a few weeks in Rensselaer you begin to feel like concrete, and you can't wait to get back to Chicago again and see that skyline, which suddenly becomes the most beautiful sight in the world. But Rensselaer is the right place to get ready for the long football season.

And I was eager to get started. I am always anxious to start a new football season, which is why I keep reporting with the rookies each year. But in 1969 I had three extra incentives. First, I felt good; I was in the best physical condition of my life. Second, I had just signed a three-year contract which, I like to think, made me the highest-paid player in professional football. Third, the pro-football Hall of Fame had just picked an All-Time Pro Football team as part of its fiftieth anniversary celebration, and I made first-string running back along with Jim Brown. I felt that was quite an honor, especially since I had played only three and a half years of professional football. To be picked over Red Grange, Hugh McElhenny, George McAfee, people like that. It means something.

As for my contract signing, I had to do some negotiating with Mr. Halas, but I expected that. He doesn't pull any punches with you. He's not a subtle man. He just tells you exactly how it is and he'll fight you tooth and nail for every dollar. But he's not a cheap man, either. I know some players feel they're underpaid, but the only way I can judge George Halas is on the basis of what's he's done for me, and I can't knock him—no way. In each of the four years on my original contract he gave me a sizable bonus. I would have to call him a generous man.

And I respect him very much. It always amazed me that a seventy-four-year-old man would be out coaching in the wind and rain and bitter cold, taking abuse from the press and from the fans and staying with it. He didn't have to do it, but he did it because he loved the game. And he would be out there every day. He wouldn't miss a day. It just seemed like I could run all day for that man. Ever since I first met him, our relationship has been more like that of a father and a son. I respect him as a coach and I respect him as a man and I think he knows I would do anything he says.

Of course that didn't eliminate the need for a discussion about my new contract. The first time I went in to see him in the spring he said, "Have you thought about what you want, Gale?"

I said, "Yes."

"What do you think you'd like to receive?"

"I want five hundred thousand dollars for three years."

He grunted. "Impossible, there's no way I can do this. It's not feasible for me to give you so much money."

"O.K.," I said. "I'll talk to you later." I didn't expect him to give me what I asked right off, but I went back to him in three days.

"Coach," I said, "I don't want to play games with you and I know you don't want to play games with me, but I do think I'm worth a hundred thousand dollars a year."

He said, "I'd like to give you that, but we'll have to talk about it." We talked some more and then that meeting broke up. In the next meeting we were pretty well set on the contract, until Mr. Halas called his son in. George Halas, Jr., whom everybody calls Muggs, didn't seem quite as eager to pay me a lot of money. In fact, he said, "Consider yourself lucky. If my father didn't like you as much as he does, you wouldn't be getting that much."

I got up and walked out of the room.

I was mad. Muggs and I had always gotten along O.K., though I always dealt directly with his father. Sometimes, when you're tired and irritable, you say a lot of things you don't mean. But it did upset me to hear him pop off that way to me. I didn't see Mr. Halas for about two weeks. I knew he was getting ready to go to England for a second operation on his hip and I had heard that he was a little upset because we hadn't settled the thing, so I went back to see him.

This time we were alone. Muggs wasn't there. Mr. Halas said, "Gale, let's settle it now."

I said, "Fine, I want to settle it." And I signed the three-year contract I wanted. And I was very happy about it, and I think Mr. Halas left for England happy, too.

I left home at six-thirty on Monday morning, July 14. A couple of days earlier I had given the press a lengthy statement on the condition of my knee. I told them I wanted to devote all my energies to the demands of training camp and hoped they would not burden me with time-consuming questions about my physical condition. I didn't want to hear any more how's-your-knee business. Unknown to me, Dr. Fox had said the same thing to the coaching staff. He told me later, "Here's what I said to them, Gale [Dr. Fox sometimes talks to people as though he's lecturing a class of medical students]: I said, 'I don't want anybody to treat Gale Sayers as if he had an injury. I don't want anybody to mention his injury. I don't want anybody to be concerned about his injury. I don't want him to be given special privileges because he had an injury. His knee is better than it ever was, and I don't want anybody to emphasize the negative. I want everybody to emphasize the positive. I want him to come to camp and be treated as any other player would, as if nothing had happened.' "

And that's the way it was. That first morning we were in shorts, and I put on my helmet and my football shoes, and there was nothing like it. I felt like a million dollars.

I remember we went through some running plays. They had some rookie backs who had been in camp a few days and they weren't nearly as quick as I was, so the rookie linemen weren't ready for me. When I got in there I kept running over my pulling guard. And Jim Ringo, the offensive line coach, looked up and said, "Well, he's running over people already." And he told the linemen, "Look, we put this honcho in"—pointing to me—"and you've got to be on your horse. You can't be loafing like you were all week."

Then, that afternoon, we went out in pads, and I went out in pads, too. Coach Jim Dooley asked me, "Do you want the same practice?"

I said, "Yeah, that's what I'm here for." But I really wasn't too keen on it. I always tend to be apprehensive about those early practice sessions, because you're with rookies and they can make mistakes and somebody in practice could break your neck. I think I kind of felt my way in that particular scrimmage. I can remember reminding the rookie linemen, "Don't miss your damn block . . . don't get the running backs killed."

I carried the ball five or six times, all inside plays. I got five yards once, six another time. I ran into traffic on one play and Willie Holman, our 255-pound defensive lineman, came around and blindsided me. He got me just below the knee and there was a pileup. But I got up easy.

When it was over I asked Ed McCaskey, who had been standing on the side lines, "How'd I look?"

He took a puff on his cigar. "You're all right," he said and turned away. I'll say they weren't making a fuss over me.

Those early days in camp were really enjoyable. I'd get up at six every morning (I've always been an early riser). I'd eat breakfast and go back to my room and read a while. I never read much before, only some magazines, but Ed McCaskey gave me a couple of books at the beginning of camp. I started reading. And I found I enjoyed it. I read *Siege*. I read *Soul on Ice*, though I had trouble with that one—you need a dictionary beside you; that's a heavy book. And I read *The Autobiography of Malcolm X* in three days. I liked that very much. Here was a man who was a dope addict for so many years and he got off it. Here was a man who changed his feelings completely; at the end he felt that people of all colors could live together. Here was a man who believed he could do anything he wanted. I admire a man like that. So I did a lot of reading, when-

ever I had the time. I found there is something that
keeps you going into books, you don't want to put them
down.

At eight o'clock I would go down to the basement
of our dorm, where our training rooms were set up. I
would take a whirlpool bath for ten minutes to loosen
the knee, then go into the weight room and lift sixty
pounds on the knee, a set of fifty lifts. Then I'd go back
up and read some more until the morning meeting.
Until the exhibition season started, we had two-a-day
practice sessions, mornings and afternoons, with meetings mornings and night. After the night meeting, I'd
go down and lift some more. Ed Rozy, our trainer, who
has been with the Bears a zillion years, always kept
encouraging me. "You're ninety per cent now, Gale.
Keep it up."

I said, "I'm a hundred per cent now."

Rozy always told the guys recovering from knee
surgery that it was like a diet. "If you follow the diet,"
he'd say, "and then go down to your friendly tavern for
four or five beers or a malted milk, forget it." He meant
for us to follow that diet of steady exercise, and I had
been doing that right along.

During that period I read an interview Rozy gave a
writer. He said, "The big thing to overcome is the
mental attitude, the subconscious feeling—is it or isn't
it? See, Gale's got to believe it, it's got to be proven to
him, he's got to prove it to himself."

Well, I'd felt that way all along, but it seemed that
after the veterans reported to camp I wasn't getting
much chance to prove anything to anybody. They were
using Mike Hull, a second-year man, veteran Ralph
Kurek, and a rookie, Ross Montgomery. And I said to
myself, They're babying me, I know they're babying me.
And it bothered me because I have to get my timing
down. With the other running backs in there, the timing
is different. The guards can be a little slower. But with
me in there, they've got to go full speed. I'm much
quicker, so they have to set up their blocks fast. When
I'm in there, I'm running up their backs.

On the Saturday before our first exhibition game of the season, against the Washington Redskins, I played about a third of a scrimmage. I felt good. I felt I had my moves and I had my speed. I didn't break away at all, but I felt it was all there. I took some shots, too. One time I went up the middle and someone grabbed me by the legs and Dick Butkus came along and rammed me in the chest. And you haven't lived until you've been rammed by Dick Butkus. No one hits like Butkus. He doesn't hit you low. He hits you in the chest and sort of rakes you over. When he first hits you he jars you. Then, a second or two later, here comes his body—his knees, his feet, his arms. It's like that Slinky toy: the first half of the spring comes down a step, followed by the second half. Butkus puts his whole soul into tackling people.

There's no one I respect more in pro football than Dick Butkus. The man is a pleasure to watch. When I'm on the sidelines and I see him hit someone it makes me wonder. He has so much size and when he spreads his arms it's like he's got a twenty-five-foot wingspread. I like to watch him work over the center when the other team is in punt formation. The center is afraid to snap the ball because he knows he's going to take a shot from Butkus. And he's afraid he'll get his neck broken. Butkus has hit me harder in scrimmages than I've ever been hit in a game.

And he hit me a good one in that scrimmage, but I got up and I felt fine and I was really looking forward to starting against the Redskins. Then, on the Monday morning before the game, Coach Dooley came up to me.

"Gale," he said, "we're not going to start you against Washington."

Well, I was damn mad. It's like Ed Rozy had said. I was waiting to prove myself. I had been going through hell all these months in anticipation of that first exhibition game, my first opportunity to show people that I'm ready. I wanted to prove it to the players and to myself. I wanted to prove it right away and get it over with. And now I wasn't starting.

"Look," Dooley explained, "we've got an inexperienced line. Two of our regulars are out. The kids make a mistake—boom."

We finally compromised. He agreed that I could run back kickoffs and punts against the Redskins.

We flew into Washington late in the afternoon on Friday, August 1, and we took a bus to our motel.

When Henny Young burst into the room I was lying on my bed in my undershorts, resting and trying to ignore that five-inch scar that runs along the inside of my right leg, thighbone to kneebone.

"You got a tan!" Henny exclaimed. "Where's you get that tan? You been sittin' in the sun?" I laughed. Sure, I'd been sitting in the sun, for almost a month, and maybe I was a deeper brown than usual. Henny Young is Buddy Young's son. Buddy Young works for the NFL and once ran with a football as well as anyone ever did. It was Buddy who got me to sign with the Bears, and we became very close. He's another one who's like a father to me. Seldom a day goes by that we don't talk to each other on the telephone. I get hurt when I don't hear from Buddy. Henny Young and I became good friends when we went to stockbroker's school together in New York in 1968. Henny works for Paine, Webber in their Washington office.

"Let's go eat," I said to Henny. We went into the dining room and sat with Ed McCaskey. Ed smokes cigars all the time and sometimes he comes on like a tall, educated W. C. Fields. He is always carrying on. A pretty blonde waitress was serving our steak and she heard someone mention that McCaskey had eleven children. "You've got eleven kids?" she said, as if she couldn't believe it.

Ed said, "Don't let that deter you, my dear, if you find that I'm fascinating." A little while later, when she was clearing the table, McCaskey said to her, "Make up your mind—are you interested in Sayers or me?"

Well, I was only interested in getting back to my room and resting. And getting that game over. A first exhibition game ordinarily doesn't mean much, although you can't go into it with that attitude. Do that and you have a short season. Every game is important and you always like to start off with a win after all that training. And, anyway, I hate to lose. Also, I knew that Vince Lombardi was going to be up. He had just taken over the Redskins and he was going to have his team up.

But beyond that was the personal challenge. This was the first test in public since the injury. This was not an exhibition game to me.

Sitting by my locker deep inside Robert F. Kennedy Stadium forty-five minutes before the game, I never felt so tense. Normally I put on my "game face" the Friday before a game, and it reaches a climax in that period just before I go out on the field. I call it my game face, but Linda says it's when I turn evil.

I was never aware of it in college because the Kansas team always spent the night before the game together in Topeka. The first time I noticed it was when we were in San Francisco for the East-West Shrine game. We were riding up to San Francisco on the bus and we were laughing and talking and having a good time. And I was leaning over across the aisle talking to Craig Morton and his wife. And all of a sudden I looked at Gale and I said, "What's the matter?" And he said, "Do you realize that I have to play a game in two hours and you're up there laughing like you're crazy?" And that was the first time I had ever been with him before a game. And I just couldn't believe it. I said, Oh God, is this what I'm in for?

My rookie year with the Bears I used to vomit before every game. I considered for a long time going to a hypnotist. I suppose if I knew one in Chicago I would have tried him. Then I got the idea, Well I can't be hypnotized, I'm not the type to be hypnotized. But I had to do something because I was going out on the field tired and beat. I decided I had to stop vomiting. And, somehow, I did. But the nervous tension was always there. And now it felt worse than ever.

I sat there like I was in a trance. I was wearing my white game pants with the orange piping down the side. I had my cleats on, but I was still in my T shirt. I felt for the gold medallion dangling around my neck. It seemed so heavy at that moment, but it was comforting to have it there. The medallion is the size of a half-dollar and on it is an inscription: *I Am Third*.

In college my track coach was Bill Easton, who had compiled an outstanding record at Kansas. Easton's track teams won like eleven out of eighteen indoor Big Eight meets, twelve out of seventeen outdoor meets, and at least two national championships. And it was Bill Easton who taught me about work. He was a helluva man and an important influence on me. He taught me that nothing can substitute for work. And in my sophomore and junior years (I didn't run track as a senior) he worked the hell out of me. And I did things I never thought I could do.

I remember once we were in a triangular meet. I was in the hurdles and broad jump and that day Easton said, "Why don't you run the 330-intermediate, too, just to keep in shape and get your wind up and everything?" So I ran it and, I tell you, I liked to die. I finished third —which is last really, but third sounds better. People were laughing at me. The first five hurdles I was ahead, then six got that big, and seven got *that* big, and I tried to go under the last two because I was real tired. I was so tired, and I struggled across the finish line and Easton came up to me and said, "Way to go, at least you finished the race." The one point I got finishing that race enabled us to beat out the third-place team by a point.

The first time I went into Coach Easton's office, when I was a sophomore, I saw the sign, like a placard, on his desk: I AM THIRD. Just a little thing on his desk. And for two years I wondered what it meant. So finally I asked him.

He said, "The Lord is first, my friends are second, and I am third."

When I was in my second year with the Bears I decided I wanted to wear something meaningful around my neck, like a religious medal. I'd been thinking about that saying all along and I decided to get that medallion. And I have worn it ever since.

Now I don't consider myself a very religious person. I don't think you have to go to church every Sunday to be a religious person. But I do think about God, and I try to say my prayers every night. And I thought this saying made sense. *The Lord is first, my friends are second, and I am third.* It held a lot of meaning for me. And, if you think about it, it is a good philosophy of life. I try to live by it. Sometimes it's hard. I don't live by it all the time, I know, but keeping that saying close to me helps bring me back, keeps me from straying too far from that philosophy.

And now before a game that meant so much to me, I did draw some comfort from *I Am Third*.

In the past, in those forty-five minutes of torture before a game, all kinds of thoughts ran through my mind. Before the knee injury, I thought about how I never had suffered an injury, and I was hoping I would never get hurt, that I could make it through the game. Now it was the knee, all the thinking was about the knee . . . how it happened . . . could it happen again . . . how would it hold up. This is the mental torture of football. Some people call it butterflies. And once you go out and get hit it's over with. But those forty-five minutes before you get hit form the mental torture of the game, and I think this is going to happen to me before a game as long as I play this game.

The players know I like to stay by myself, that I like to be alone with my thoughts. But this time, as I sat there, deep into myself, my head bowed, my eyes closed, Bennie McRae, one of our veteran defensive backs, came over. He was concerned about me. He leaned over and whispered, "Are you ready, man?"

I just nodded. I didn't feel like talking. "Are you all

right?" he repeated. "You're gonna be all right." He put a hand on my shoulder. "Hang loose," he said, and I nodded again and he drifted away.

My mind was full of things. I thought of my old teammate, Andy Livingston, who had such trouble coming back from a knee operation. I thought of two current teammates, George Seals and Doug Kriewa, who had had operations right after me and still weren't right. But I also thought about the old Bear halfback, Willie Galimore, who had survived two knee operations and come back fine; and of Tommy Mason, who had six knee operations and continued to play. And I cursed out all those who had had their knees cut and didn't come back. "They didn't work at it," I cried out to myself. "I worked at it." And I said, "I consider this my game. A damn injury like that is not going to keep me out of it."

Just then our backfield coach, Ed Cody, came over and he said, "About a minute, Gale."

I finally roused myself. I stood up, slipped on my white jersey with the big navy-blue numeral, 40, picked up my helmet, and went out of the room.

I had almost forgotten what fifty thousand people sound like. I heard this funny noise as I was coming through the runway leading up to the field. It sounded like a piece of heavy machinery sucking out air. But when I got through the runway and hit the dugout I finally realized what it was—it was the roar of the crowd.

It was a very hot and humid night, very close. The clouds seemed to be getting darker and darker and it looked like we might get some rain.

I went trotting up and down the field, exchanging passes with Ronnie Bull. Then I got into a passing drill. I went downfield and took a short pass and almost smacked into Vince Lombardi. He shook my hands and said, "I'm very glad to see that you've overcome your injury." I remember having bumped into Vince in Pete Rozelle's office in the spring. He had said to me then, "How do you feel, son? I hope to see you out there this fall." And I had said, "You'll see me on August second." I was pretty cocky at the time. But I wasn't feeling so cocky now, especially knowing that I wouldn't be doing much except running back kicks.

We finished the drill and went back to the dressing room to put on our pads, and when we came back onto the field it was raining. It was really coming down, a hard, slanting rain with thunder and lightning and a rising wind. The field, especially the skin part of the Washington Senators' infield, was already filling up with puddles.

We had won the toss, so we would receive. I stood back on the five, with Ross Montgomery in front of me. I captain the kick and kickoff return teams, so I tell the other deep back where to go. The idea is for me to cover three-quarters of the field, to make sure that I get the football.

Just as the kicker put his foot into the ball, I told Montgomery to deploy right. The ball came out of the night and rain and into my arms at the six, and I started straight up the middle. One man broke through the wedge and challenged me. I gave the guy an inside move, a head-and-shoulder fake, and he was out of it and I cut in and back outside, toward the sidelines.

I was in full stride now. The ground was still firm and the footing was fine and I went down the sidelines. Around the Redskin forty, two defensive backs came up at an angle and lunged at me. I pushed one away with my left arm. The other one threw himself at me. He jostled me a moment, but I kept my feet and re-gained control and ran right into the end zone.

A ninety-four-yard run, I thought. But they said I had stepped out of bounds on the Redskin twenty-five. I don't think I stepped out at all, but the side-line markers had been wiped out by the rain.

And that was the game for me. The rest of it was ridiculous. The rain came down heavy and the field was a mess, unplayable. I got to move the ball one more time, when Dick Butkus lateraled a kickoff back to me. I just put my head down and bucked into a moving mass of mud. Later, our coaches had to throw out the game films because you couldn't see anything, you couldn't see a damn thing. The whole game was nothing, a wipeout, except maybe for that run. But what did that prove? Nothing. It was an anticlimax.

The Redskins won the game 13–7, and that was an anticlimax too. The next morning I went down to breakfast at seven-fifteen. I ordered some ham and eggs, but I couldn't eat them. It always takes me a day, a day and a half to unwind after a game.

The Washington papers were nice to me. One story started out: "It took the sellout crowd of 45,988 at RFK Stadium last night only a matter of seconds to see for themselves that Gale Sayers is as good as ever. . . ."

Another paper said: "Gale Sayers returned to action after knee surgery that kept him out of the last five games of the '68 season and made a sensational debut with a sixty-nine-yard kickoff return of the opening kickoff. . . ."

Well, it was a beginning, a modest beginning. But otherwise that game proved nothing. It was no test.

I started the next week against Miami and got maybe ten yards the first half. I didn't do a thing. I missed assignments, I fumbled, I just wasn't with it. And it was the same thing in our third game against Green Bay. Only there was this difference: I got hit fielding a punt and I fell back on the leg and felt something pop in my knee.

The knee hurt the rest of the night and the next day when I drove back to camp. Dr. Fox had explained that when my leg was in the cast it was lying straight out. And I still had maybe five-hundredths of an inch to go before the knee would bend perfectly. The popping noise when I caught the punt, the doctor said, probably did it. I broke adhesions in there and the knee came loose and now it bent all the way. Just as it should. He said there was absolutely nothing wrong with the knee and no way I could hurt it.

I hoped he was right. But with the knee bothering me

and my state of mind the way it was, I thought back to a conversation I had had earlier with Sid Luckman, our sometime quarterback coach (Luckman works with the quarterbacks when he has the time). Before the exhibition game in Miami, I went down a day early with Luckman for a testimonial for Jim Dooley, a local hero. And Sid and I talked about different things. He was telling me that in my first four years I had probably done as much as Jim Brown had in his first four years, maybe more. "But," Sincere Sid said, "it's what you do the *next* four years that counts if you want to go down as an all-time great running back."

Sure, I thought to myself. Provided things go well. Provided there's blocking on the line. Provided my knee holds up. Provided I don't get another injury. Sure. And I decided I'd be satisfied if I could just go out there and do my job. That's all I ever wanted to do. Records and recognition are fine, but only if they're proof that I'm doing my job. My achievements in football normally do not impress me. So what if I gain 200 yards in one game, or score six touchdowns in another? I figure that's my job, I'm getting paid to do that kind of thing. All I have ever wanted, and all I wanted now as I tried to get ready for a football season, was to be able to do my job.

5

A Season of Strange, Crazy Things

In 1969 the Bears won only one game, and lost thirteen —the worst record in the team's history. That tells only part of the story. It was one of the weirdest, craziest, most unbelievable seasons any sports team could have. Because nothing worked for us. Because everything we did went to the dogs. Because every man connected with the team was touched by a kind of fate that struck like an epidemic.

Back in July, a Miss June Low, whose business it is to read horoscopes for the Detroit *Free Press,* was given the birthdays and birthdates of the four coaches in our Central Division. She had something good to offer three of them, but for Jim Dooley she wrote: "If I were him I wouldn't leave the house. Flukey things will keep happening to him."

Or maybe I should have taken seriously the horror-scope I received from a guy. He wrote: "The reason you got hurt was because you let your hair grow." Well, it was true I used to cut it off for football, and in 1968 I decided I would wear it a little long. But I got to think my knee injury would have happened even if I had a head like a billiard ball.

I think we all should have been tipped off to the kind of a year the Chicago Bears were going to have by several key indicators. Like what happened one day in rookie camp. One of the Bears' high draft choices was a big defensive end from Stanford. He was supposed to be a very good football player. Well, he reported to camp with long hair, wearing leather pants and no shoes. He was there a couple of days, then told Coach

Dooley that he didn't need that kind of life. "I want to be a hippie," he said. And he walked out of camp. Last I heard the guy was working as a mailman out West.

During the season Miss Frances Osborn, a lovely and kind woman who had been George Halas's secretary for about thirty years, jumped out of a twenty-sixth story window. She had had a stroke about six months before and it had affected her speech. She was always a very strong woman, and maybe she just couldn't stand having the handicap of a speech defect. So she took her life.

In November my roommate, Brian Piccolo, was operated on for a malignant tumor in his chest. That desolated us all.

And Ronnie Bull tore up his knee. And one of our quarterbacks, Virgil Carter, was fined $1000 for sounding off in public. And our prize rookie offensive tackle, Rufus Mayes, ended up in the hospital with a bleeding ulcer—at age twenty-one.

The things that were happening down on the field would give anyone an ulcer.

We lost our opener to Green Bay 17–0 and penalties killed us in that game. Then we lost to St. Louis 20–17, and there's no way that should have happened. We outgained them three-to-one, but they scored what was the winning touchdown on a play that you won't see happen in a hundred years.

Coming out of the huddle early in the game, I wasn't sure of the call. I hollered to quarterback Jack Concannon to hold it. So Jack got ready to call time out. But we were going on a quick count; the snap was on the first word, "set." As soon as Mike Pyle heard Jack holler "Time," he snapped the ball. It hit Jack's leg and shot straight up in the air, and their linebacker, Larry Stallings, fielded it and ran it in for sixty-two yards. And none of us chased him because we thought time had been called.

The next week we had the Giants 24–21 until the last minute, when there was a mixup on the coverage of their halfback, Joe Morrison. He was permitted to draw clear and catch a touchdown pass.

In the Los Angeles game they beat us 9–7. We held them without a touchdown, and any time you hold a team without a touchdown—especially a team like the Rams—you should win. They were winning 7–6 when Jack Snow caught a pass, went to the Bears' thirty-nine, and fumbled. And one of our men kicked the loose ball by mistake. They got the ball back on the penalty. Plus an automatic first down and fifteen yards. That set up the third field goal.

We were losing to Detroit 13–7, but in the fourth quarter we were on our way to a score when Jack Concannon rolled out and fumbled the ball on their six-yard line.

We had Cleveland 21–20 with two and a half minutes to go. They punted to us and one of our men dropped the ball. Cleveland recovered and went on to score the winning field goal.

We had Baltimore beaten in a game we had dedicated to Brian Piccolo and wanted to win so badly for Pick. And they caught us at the end.

We lost two games to Minnesota, 31–0 and 31–14, and both could have turned around. In the first game they were ahead of us only 7–0 when we blocked a field goal at midfield. But instead of it being our ball at midfield, the ball went right back into Fred Cox's arms and he ran it for the first down at about our twenty-eight. And they scored right away.

Our second game against the Vikings was even weirder, a succession of nutty happenings:

(1) We set up their first score when one of our players ran into their punter.

(2) With the score 7–7, we kicked off, and the ball was kicked around in the end zone before a Viking fell on it. It should have been a safety. But they didn't rule it a safety. They gave them a fifteen-yard penalty and we had to kick over again. With a safety, the score would have been 9–7, and they would have had to punt to us. The next day it came out in the papers that the officials had made a mistake. They quoted Commissioner Rozelle to that effect.

(3) Fred Cox missed a fifty-two-yard field goal, but we had twelve players on the field. The five-yard penalty enabled him to kick the field goal.

(4) The same player who dropped the punt in the Cleveland game did it again against Minnesota. They recovered on our thirteen and went in to score.

First it was 7–7, and we hardly get our hands on the ball again before it's 24–7.

All those freak plays, all those weird things. Every time, it seemed, we had something weird like that go against us, and it was just not to be. A whole season of strange, crazy things.

Not the least of which, I suppose, was the way they buried me, the way they wrote me off after the fifth game of the season.

All you had to do was read the Chicago newspapers after the Minnesota and Detroit games, our fourth and fifth of the season. I had gained fifteen yards in thirteen carries against Minnesota and twelve yards in nine carries against Detroit. Before then, I had gained seventy-six yards against St. Louis and eighty-one yards against New York. If you gain eighty yards a game throughout the whole season, that's one thousand yards right there. But they didn't remember those games, they remembered the Minnesota and Detroit games. And the thing that discouraged me was the Chicago writers' saying I wasn't running like before the knee injury.

I didn't bother reading the papers at the time because I knew what they were writing about me. Someone always managed to come along and say, "Hey, did you see this article that guy wrote about you. Isn't that silly?" Or, "Did you see what that commentator had to say on television about you?" So I knew and George Halas knew I knew and he called me into his office a couple of days after the Detroit game.

He had some of the articles on his desk. One headline read: LET'S FACE IT, GALE SAYERS IS NOT THE GALE SAYERS OF OLD. Another one: BEAR FACT: SAYERS IS NOT PERFORMING AS A "GALE FORCE." Another:

BENCHED! IT'S NO FUN JUST SITTING THERE, SAYS FALLEN STAR GALE SAYERS.

"Articles like this don't mean a thing," Mr. Halas said. "I wouldn't get upset about them. Just go out and run like you've been running, and things will finally break for you."

Well, that's what I was trying to do. In the Minnesota game there were no holes, there was nothing there. But after the game, a Chicago writer really put it to me. "There is something missing," he wrote. "There is the smallest amount of hesitation that prevents him from taking full advantage of an opening." The writer mentioned that I was caught, after a fifty-two-yard runback of a kickoff, at the Minnesota forty-one when I stopped to make a move on a defender at the sidelines. What happened was that I was running and the sidelines caught up with me when I got pushed out of bounds. The sidelines is the greatest tackler in the world. You just can't get away from the sidelines. I was aiming back across the field and the defender was coming and I was trying to jockey for position. He had the angle on me and there was no way in my life I could have beaten him.

But I really caught hell after the Detroit game. It was 7–7 at the half and Jim Dooley came over and said he was going to bring in our rookie back, Ross Montgomery. "I want to pound Detroit a little bit, Gale," Coach said. By that I guess he meant that he would have Ross run a little up the middle; Ross weighs 220. Of course I had been running up the middle for four years and I couldn't quite figure out why he wanted to put a rookie in there. The pounding didn't work all that well—Detroit led 13–7 when I went back in late in the fourth quarter. And, still, everyone said it was a benching, that I had been benched. I would just call it a kind of change of game plan. I would call it that mostly because I don't like to use the word "benching" in connection with myself, since I had never before in my life been benched.

After the game, a local writer came over to me and

asked, "Do you feel all right?" All I said was that it takes more than one man to win a ball game.

It seemed as if I was back where I was as a rookie. When I first came up I was very shy. And I used one-word answers with reporters. That's all I answered, one word. I'm running and feeling O.K., I'd say to them, and then forget it. Really, I was too shy and scared to say anything else. And they wrote that I was a dummy. Well, I started reverting back to that, mostly because I was hurt at what they were writing about me.

I try to hide my emotions but I can't always. If I'm mad at something I just have to let it out. I'm a pretty open guy. And by now I couldn't understand some of the writers. I didn't see how they could print what they did one day and come back the next and look you in the face. Most of them think I'm supposed to put a cape on my back and fly over everyone—Clark Dark. But they know that football is played by an eleven-man team. The plain and simple fact was that we weren't playing good football as a team, and football is a team game, and anybody who thinks that it isn't a team game is out of his mind.

But is was so easy for them to put two and two together. My statistics were lousy. After five games, I had run for 220 yards in sixty-eight attempts, for a 3.4 average. And that put me sixteenth among National Football League runners, way down the line. And remembering that I had gained 205 yards in one game the year before, naturally everyone wanted to know what was up. And they immediately pointed to my knee. One guy summarized it this way: "The conclusion has been reached by many that the twenty-six-year-old runner is not his old self. It is felt that last year's knee surgery has robbed Sayers of some of his old acceleration and speed."

They were just jumping to easy conclusions. What these people didn't remember was that I have had terrible games before, terrible games. But nobody paid any attention to them. I've had games when I carried fifteen times and gained maybe thirty yards and we lost the game. One game in 1967 I carried the ball twelve times for *two* yards. But they didn't say a damn thing about it. Because I'd come up with a good game the next week or the week after; the people would overlook the bad things and see only the good things. But in 1969 all I had to do was have a bad day—and I did have a few—and, Oh, it's his knee, the guy will never make it.

And I got to wondering myself. All the time I tried to put on that everything was fine and everything was going to be cool and all that, but I was concerned about it. It began to bother me. Maybe, I said, you can't come back. And I went to people for advice. The first person I talked to, of course, was Dr. Fox. Or maybe I was the last one to talk to him; it seemed that everyone had gone to him asking about me—George Halas, some of the other coaches, and the newspapermen. And Dr. Fox related one conversation he had with a writer.

"Now, listen, doc," the writer said, "you don't think Gale is the same as he was?"

Dr. Fox said, "Goddamn it, get off my back. Why don't you give this kid a chance to prove himself to himself? I told you he was going to be as good as ever."

"Don't give me that bull, doc. Nobody's ever as good after that type of an injury."

Doc Fox blew up. "Well," he said, "you wait and see —you're going to eat those words."

He told me all that, I guess, to loosen me up, and then he hit me right between the eyes. He delivered one of Dr. Theodore Fox's one-hundred-dollar gold-plated lectures.

"I want you to listen very carefully to me, Gale. Your God-given talent is what you can do instinctively, by reflex. What you're doing now subconsciously is holding back. You're trying to think yourself into doing what you should be doing instinctively. In other words, if you have to stop and think, it changes your timing. The reflex action which you could do so gracefully and so well—you can't do that any more, not if you're going to stop and think. Because you can't send the message down to your legs quickly enough to make them do what you have to do. You've just got to stop thinking how you're going to dodge this guy, just go out and do your thing. When you can go out and do your thing without stopping to think, you're going to be running the way you did before."

I didn't really believe him. I'm still not sure he was right. But maybe he was, because other people whose judgments I trust were saying almost the same thing. Brian Piccolo, for instance. He knew I was concerned because I wasn't off to a good start, he could tell it was bothering me. I hated to bring up the subject—I still don't like to talk about the knee—but Pick would ease into it. He'd say something like, "You know, Gale, you know what I think you're doing wrong—you're getting out of the wrong side of the bed." Then he'd tell me, "Geez, you must get it from a hundred guys—you're doing this wrong, you're not lifting your knee up, you're not holding the ball this way, you're not planting your right foot firmly. Nuts to them." But, finally, he did say he thought I was just a little hesitant at the hole or approaching the hole. He said, "I think the only reason you're that way is that you're so anxious to break a long run and prove to everybody you can still do it that you're being a little hesitant. It used to be that you'd run in there and pop out of a lot of things and break a long run. Just pop in there and not think about it."

I got mad at him. "Pick," I said, "the only hesitation I can see in the films is there's no hole there."

And he'd laugh it off. "You give me the lip like that and I'm calling the Mafia and tell them to get ready to do the other knee."

Buddy Young was another one who gave it to me. The day after the Giant game in New York we were having lunch at Gallagher's restaurant. Buddy didn't waste any time.

"Sayers," he said, "you blew it yesterday."

I said, "What do you mean?"

"You walked on and off in that game when you wanted to. You just don't want it any more."

I was mad as hell. "You don't think I'm hurting?"

"No, you're not hurting. You're looking for Dr. Fox

and he ain't gonna be on that football field. It's illegal
to have twelve men on that field."

I had heard enough. I just gave him a look and left
the restaurant.

At that point I didn't know what to say or what to
think. I'd look at the films of those early games and I
couldn't see any holes. Say if it was a four-hole play
and it's not there. I'm looking down the line or looking
back for another hole. That was the only hesitation I
could see. I'd be a fool trying to run over an Alex
Karras or an Alan Page in the four-hole. And if I was
hesitating, as Pick had suggested, it was not because of
the knee. At least that's what I thought.

Pick also felt that I was too tight before a game. He
told me to try and relax a bit. "The looser you are the
better you do," he said.

The day before our sixth game, against Los Angeles,
Linda and I were talking about my season. I asked her
how many yards I had and how many I had to average
the rest of the year to gain 1000 yards for the season.
She said it figured to about eighty-seven yards a game.

"Well, I'm gonna do it," I said. "I'll have a good
game tomorrow. I don't like to say to people that they're
wrong, but they are wrong. I'm going to have a good
game tomorrow."

We went into that game knowing we'd have to run
against Los Angeles because of that big front four's pass
rush. We knew we probably couldn't pass against
Deacon Jones, Merlin Olsen, and company; our linemen probably wouldn't be able to give the quarterback
enough time. So we went out with the thought that we'd
run against them.

We ran all right, and still lost the game 9–7. But it
was an outstanding team effort. Our offensive line jelled
for the first time, our rookie, Rufus Mayes, played a
helluva game against Deacon, and I found some holes.
I ran for 109 yards in fifteen carries and scored my first
touchdown of the season, and they told me later that
the only other guy ever to gain 100 yards against a
George Allen Ram team was Ken Willard. And then

someone asked me if I had proven my point, that I wasn't finished.

"I didn't prove a thing," I said. "We had to win and we didn't, and that's all that matters."

And we kept losing. I averaged over 100 yards a game in the next five games but we lost them all, except Pittsburgh. I got 116 yards against Minnesota, and Jim Marshall was quoted afterward as saying that "I was cutting quick and sharp, right through those little cracks in the line." The point is the cracks were there now. Jim Ringo had come in as offensive line coach in 1969 and brought in a completely different system of blocking and our line wasn't used to it and it took time for them to adjust. I think this is one reason why they weren't getting the holes open in the early games.

In the Cleveland game I carried twenty times for 126 yards to take over the leadership in rushing in the National Football League. And I went on to gain 1000 yards and lead the league in rushing for the second time in my career. And I had to wonder: I lead the league in yardage on a team that hasn't won anything. It's not even worth it. It's like batting your head against a brick wall. You know you are working for your personal gain, and still you want to be on a winning team.

What went wrong with the Chicago Bears in 1969? It was a combination of things. Bad luck was part of it, certainly, and it held to the very end. Pittsburgh and the Bears had tied with the worst records in professional football and they held a coin flip at the Super Bowl to decide who would draft first. Ed McCaskey called heads and, naturally, it came up tails. "Ed McCaskey," someone hollered, "you're a bum." And another one yelled, "That's one-and-fourteen."

But luck was only part of it in 1969. There was a breakdown of discipline by some players. There was a breakdown of communications between the players and the coaching staff, and between the players and management. And there was a definite lack of desire on the part of some players. Even though there was a communications gap, if you like to win, if you have pride, nothing should interfere with that. I think on the Bears in 1969 we had maybe ten players who had the pride, who gave one hundred per cent all year long. The rest were just biding their time, waiting for the season to end so they could get out.

It's easy when you're having such a bad season to cry dissension, blame the coach, blame the management. When things go bad everything goes bad. I think Jim Dooley is a sound fundamental coach. I think every game we played in 1969 we had the right game plan, a solid game plan, a game plan that should have won us the game. But there was a breakdown here, a breakdown there that lost the game for us. The only thing I can fault Dooley for is that he might have let the discipline get a little out of hand. The coaches were a little lax in sticking to the rules, in enforcing them. Like you had some fellows coming in late to practice or to a meeting with some jive excuse and getting away with it.

I really think this leadership and coaching stuff is overrated. If the ballplayer doesn't have it, the coach can't do anything for him on the field. He can give you a game plan, but if you don't have enough pride you're going to get your butt beat every play, and that's not the coach's fault. And in 1969 we had a lot of players that just didn't give a damn about playing. They just wanted to collect their salaries every Tuesday.

But I think you can learn a lot from a losing season, especially the kind of losing season we had in 1969. You can learn things that have to benefit you the next year. When you're winning, you know, everyone looks good—even a third-string player. If everything is working right for you the dissension is subdued; even if there are some grumblings they're covered over. But when you're losing you're naked; this is when the players who will play for you stand out. This is when you see a Dick Butkus giving his all on every play even if it's a 1–13 season. And this is when you see the other type of player just going through the motions, saying to himself, We can't win anything now, so the hell with it.

And 1970, because of all of what went before, would,

I hope, be a year of redemption. The players would come back with different attitudes. The coaches would come into training camp with a set of rules and regulations that they would stick to, and they would enforce them. And there would, I hope, be more communication between player and coach and player and management. And then we could redeem ourselves. I don't count it very redeeming to have won three games in 1970 instead of one. I wouldn't consider it a better year even if we got to 7–7. That wouldn't be enough for me. The only way to forget about a 1–13 year is to go out and win nine or ten games the next year.

So the only satisfaction I got from the 1969 season was silencing the doubters and proving to myself that a knee victim can come back in one year; that if you work hard enough, if you're willing to endure the pain, if you're willing to sacrifice yourself, you can make it back right away.

I think that down through the years a lot of players have been brainwashed about knee injuries. They heard that it took two or three years to come back and they said to themselves, O.K., I'll baby my way through the first season, filling the knee back in, and the second season I'm going to try to play. I can see where it would be easy to do that. Because in the first season you are testing your knee, you are learning how to run on your knee again and letting your ligaments work for you again. And there is a lot of pain involved in it.

The fact is there is pain all the time. The scar tissue still has to be torn down, adhesions have to be torn down. When it gets cold the knee hurts you, you feel like you're walking on an ice pick. It is painful when you turn a certain way on the adhesions. I know now that as long as I play ball I will have some pain in the knee. My knee will react to weather changes and I will get little aches and pains here and there that I won't get on my good knee. I know I am going to have to live with these things.

And in 1969 I played in more pain than I ever had

before. I figure I got nineteen shots during the season, a combination of cortisone, which is an anti-inflammatory agent designed to speed up healing, and Novocain, which is supposed to deaden pain. The worst thing, as far as I was concerned, was the shots themselves. I am the worst shot-taker on the team. There's no way I can ever get used to that big needle, jabbing up and in and back to the left and to the right and down and over. And I always cry out. I mean, I give a good yell when he's jabbing that thing to the spot.

At the start of the season I had pain from fatty pads on my knees. My fat pads—the filler between the ligaments and the bones—are exceptionally large; I've got big knees and they're very hollow and they're filled with fat pads. And I pinch them a lot of times when I straighten out my leg. They just pinch between the joints. So I got a couple of shots in the fat pads.

For the New York and St. Louis games I had charley horses in the leg and I got shots for those. Then, through midseason, I didn't get any shots. In the Atlanta game I started to get shots in my knee. And I got three shots in the Baltimore game, three shots in Cleveland, and one in San Francisco. I think it was a combination of a bone bruise on the knee and something to do with the capsule over the knee, which figured in my operation. Every time I bent or straightened my leg there was a pull and it was painful. And it seemed like every time on every play I was getting hit on the thing. And if I hadn't taken those shots I couldn't have run on my leg because it hurt that much.

But I never once had the knee wrapped, or put a piece of tape on the knee, not before practice or games. A lot of the fellows commented that they had never seen anyone come off a knee operation and not have the knee wrapped. I think my teammates understood by the end of the season that I was fine, that I had come back, that there was nothing wrong with me.

But I'm not kidding myself. I expect that for the rest of my career I will hear people say, "He doesn't have that great speed any more," or, "He's not running as

good as he did in the past." Heck, people got on me in
'69 for not breaking one longer than twenty-eight yards
from scrimmage.

I don't think my knee had anything to do with that.
There were only twelve rushers in the NFL *and* AFL
who knocked off a run of fifty or more yards from
scrimmage. I just think it's because the defense is
tougher than ever, and improving all the time. You can
do only certain things on offense. You can't jazz up an
end sweep to out-fox the defense. An end sweep is an
end sweep. An off-tackle play is an off-tackle play. But
the defensive line has so many tricks and red dogs that
it's really very confusing to the offensive lineman trying
to make the blocks. And the fellows on defense are
getting bigger, stronger, faster. The pursuit is so tough
that it's almost impossible to run sweeps; they cut them
right off. So we're all going to have to run up the middle
more than we ever had. Which is O.K. with me because
I like running inside the tackles the best.

Jim Brown used to say football is a game of five- and
ten-yard sprints. And he was right. Still, seventy-five
per cent of touchdown runs are off-tackle plays and
quick bursts up the middle, and I'd rather run inside
than run laterally, where you get tired easier and where
the pursuit is so great.

Buddy Young claims my injury couldn't have happened at a better time. (Incidentally, I didn't stay mad
at him long after he gave me that dig in New York. One
thing about me: I may get angry quickly, but it passes
just as quickly.) I found that hard to believe—any time
you get a knee injury is the wrong time. But his reason-
ing did make sense. He said it happened just at the time
that the game was changing. The dimensions of the field
had become much smaller and more compact because
of the defense, the size and speed of the defensive
players. "There ain't gonna be many guys who will
break fifty any more," he said, "until the offense does
something to catch up."

That meant, he said, that I would have to run inside
more and I would have to carry the ball more. Buddy

explained, "You're just finding out you're as tough as you know you are. Before the injury you weren't always sure how tough you were."

"Say that again?" I asked.

"The injury had made you a complete runner. You had a fantastic three years, but you didn't believe you could run inside and you didn't believe you could carry the ball twenty-five, thirty times a game. Now you know you can. You know, baby," he said, "you got a mean streak in you. And if you're going to carry the ball thirty times you need to have a mean streak in you."

I did carry the ball more in 1969—236 times—than I ever had in a season before. I used to average sixteen or seventeen carries a game. In the past, as Buddy said, I didn't feel I was capable of carrying the ball twenty-five or thirty times a game. I thought I would get too tired. But now I know that I can. Maybe it's because I'm older, and stronger, and wiser. Or maybe it's because of my new knee.

When I got back to Chicago from the Pro Bowl game in Los Angeles, where I was voted Most Valuable Player on offense, Dr. Fox said he had something to show me. It was a photo taken at the game. It showed me in traffic, planting my right foot to the ground, my leg almost parallel with the ground, maybe ten inches off the ground, about to make a cut on Larry Wilson. I did get by him and went eighteen yards before being stopped.

"Look at that," Dr. Fox said proudly, "look at that. You're putting eight hundred to a thousand pounds of pressure on it. Look at how it's holding up."

I looked at the picture and grinned. There was nothing I had to say.

6

Pick

Brian Piccolo and I began rooming together in 1967 and we became close friends. It's easy to make a big deal out of the fact that he was white and I'm black and to wonder how we got along. But there was nothing to it, although I admit at first we did feel each other out. I had never had a close relationship with a white person before, except maybe George Halas, and Pick had never really known a black person. I remember him telling me that he wondered at first, "Are they really different? Do they sleep in chandeliers, or what?"

The best thing about our relationship as it developed was that we could kid each other all the time about race, do our thing in perfect ease. It was a way, I guess, of easing into each man's world. It helped take the strangeness out of it.

Like, before that 1969 exhibition game in Washington, a writer came into our room to interview me, and Pick really laid it on.

"How do you get along?" the writer asked.

Pick said, "We're O.K. as long as he doesn't use the bathroom."

"What do you fellows talk about?"

"Mostly race relations," I said.

"Nothing but the normal racist stuff," he said.

"If you had your choice," the writer went on, ignoring all the digs, "who would you want as your roommate?"

I was very tactful. "If you're asking me what white Italian fullback from Wake Forest, I'd say Pick."

Piccolo was born in Massachusetts and raised in Fort Lauderdale, Florida—by way of He-Hung-High, Mississippi, I always said. At Wake Forest he was the

campus honcho. He made All-America running back.
He led the country in rushing and scoring in his senior
year, but he wasn't drafted. They claimed he didn't
have too much size or too much speed, but the Bears
took him as a free agent. Like all free agents, he was a
long shot to make it in the pros. But he hung in there
with determination and guts and he turned out to be a
helluva football player.

How good was he? Well, he was always proudest of
the fact that one year he graded higher than I did. At
the end of the season the coaches review all the game
films and grade each player. And in 1968 Pick graded
about 98 and I graded like 74. "If I do something,"
Pick said, "I do it. If I'm told to block the linebacker,
I do it. I'm a ballplayer's ballplayer. They got to go
with me."

I first met Pick at the All-America game in Buffalo,
New York, after my senior year. There were four of us
in that game who were going on to the Bears' camp—
Dick Butkus, Jimmy Jones, Pick, and myself. And
Butkus and I never said a thing to any of the others, or
to each other. "You were so bad then," Pick once said
to me. "You were a real hotshot."

The thing is I was very shy then. I'm not outgoing,
anyway. I don't try to push myself on people. And I
was really quiet. I was always listening—I still am a
very good listener, which I think is a good trait—but
I was no talker. While the other Bear rookies socialized
among themselves, said, "Hey, how you doing? We'll
see you in training camp," Butkus and I didn't have one
word to say to anyone, including ourselves. Piccolo
claims we both changed amazingly over the years, and
I guess that's true.

Anyway, I did give Pick a glancing hello that first
time in Buffalo and that was it. We were on different
teams in the All-America game and he didn't play
because he had a pulled hamstring. Every year we have
a ten-day rookie camp at Soldier's Field, and he wasn't
in there because of the pull. The hamstring really ruined
his rookie season.

The next year, 1966, we got a little closer. We lockered next to each other, his number being 41 and mine 40. ("I had Dick Gordon on my left," he once said, "Sayers on my right. I felt like an Oreo cookie.") And we got to know each other a little better. We became friendlier and friendlier.

I had to get friendly with him because he was my backup man and I needed him. When I was tired I depended on him for a blow. He always said, "I have the distinction of never being put into a game by a coach." We always worked it between ourselves. Mr. Halas was head coach then and he never liked to take me out of a game. But there were times when I just ran and ran and ran and I was completely whipped. And Piccolo knew it, but he would have to engage in a lengthy charade before they'd take me out.

First Pick would ask me, "Gale, are you tired, do you want a blow?" If I said yes, he'd go to Ed Cody, our backfield coach, and say, "Gale's tired, he wants to take a blow." And then Ed would come back to me and say, "Gale, are you tired?" Just to make sure, you know. Then, if I said yes, Ed would go to Mr. Halas and the old man would turn to Piccolo and say, "Pick, come here, Gale's tired. I think maybe you ought to go in for him." That was always kind of interesting, except it was a little tough for Piccolo to get into the games. By the time that ritual was finished the game would be over.

But after a while the coaches just let us do it by ourselves. And Pick got on to my ways and could tell when I wanted to take a blow. All I had to do was look over to the bench and he would see. He would know by the way I was standing in the huddle, by the way I hung my head. If I made a long run, starting at one side of the field and ending on the other, he'd know to come in for a play. And he was always around the side lines ready to come in.

There were times, of course, when this didn't work to Pick's advantage. Once, against Minnesota, I had just finished running what we call a "sucker play." On a sucker play the guard doesn't block the defensive tackle. He tries to pull the tackle the opposite way, making the tackle think he's leading a sweep or something. He takes the tackle with him and the runner shoots through the hole. And I shot through for forty yards. Naturally, I was tired and Pick went in.

In the huddle our quarterback, Jack Concannon, called, "Same play," and Pick's jaw hit the ground. After a tackle has been had on a sucker play—which you never call more than once a game—you know the tackle wants to kill somebody. He just wants to sucker somebody himself. And Piccolo got his good. He came out of the game and his nose was bleeding and his eyes were watery and he was muttering something about being the biggest sucker of all.

But the worst moment for Pick came in a game against Detroit in 1967. We had played the first game with the Lions at Wrigley Field and beat them 14–3. Afterward their linebacker, Wayne Walker, came out with this comment: "Every time the Bears play us they nickel-and-dime us to death. This time we're gonna get 'em."

So we went to Detroit about three weeks later and they tried very hard to get us. It was a pretty physical game—a tough game. It was one of the most physical, most vicious games I've been in since I've played pro ball. They were punching and gouging and twisting legs in there and getting away with a lot of stuff the referee couldn't see.

In the fourth quarter we had a fourteen-point lead and I decided to get out. I really wasn't that tired, but I said to myself, We're ahead, our defense is playing good ball, enough to hold them, I'll take a blow. With eight minutes to play, we punted and I came off and said to Pick, "Finish it up."

That puzzled him because it was not like me to leave a game with eight minutes still left. The puzzle was solved right away the first time he carried the ball. He hit into the line and someone started twisting his ankle and another guy started punching him in the guts and

Alex Karras was hollering at our center, Mike Pyle, "When the season's over I'm coming to Chicago and I'm gonna kill you." And Pick came back and said, "This is one of the great favors you have done for me over the years, Gale."

And, in the summer of 1967, we began rooming together. In Birmingham, Alabama.

I was in the room when Pick came in. "What are you doing here?" he said.

I said, "We're in together."

He was a little surprised, but I had known about it. They had asked me if I had any objections to rooming with Brian. I said no, none at all. I had been rooming with a fellow who got cut, and I think Pick was rooming with a quarterback, Larry Rakestraw, and they decided maybe they ought to room guys together by position. But I think Bennie McRae, one of our co-captains, also suggested that they start some integrated rooming, to get a little better understanding with the guys. And Pick and I were the first on the Bears.

But it really didn't make any difference. I think they tend to make too much out of it. Friends like to room with friends, and it has nothing to do with segregation or anything like that.

You can bet we didn't have dinner together in Birmingham that weekend. We joked a lot about it, but we went our separate ways. I don't know if we ate dinner with one another but a couple of times that first year. It was always that when we got into a place I'd call the guys that I normally went out with and he'd call the guys that he normally went out with and we'd split. It was just that he had his friends and I had mine. I think we were both a little unsure about the whole thing at first. And I guess I was a little distant that first year. I think once people get to know me I'm easy to get along with. Pick always knew that on the day of a game I liked to be left alone—just let me be—and this is what he did. But by the end of that first year we had both loosened up quite a bit.

I think he actually helped open me up because he was

such a happy-go-lucky guy. He always had a joke or
two in him. One day he read me this letter he had just
received from a guy in Chicago who actually signed his
name. It went: "I read where you stay together with
Sayers. I am a white man! Most of the people I know
don't want anything to do with them. I just don't understand you. Most Italians I have met say that they stink
—and they really do!" And Pick couldn't resist his own
P.S.: "Well," he said, "that's true, of course, you can't
get away from that."

He was always getting in a dig about something. Like
we'd be having breakfast in the coffee shop and a
waitress would say to me, "Can I ask you your name?"
And before I could answer, Pick would mumble, "They
all look alike."

When Pick heard that Vince Lombardi had taken
over in Washington, he said he thought he would like
to play a little bit for Lombardi before his career was
over.

"I can arrange that," I said.

"Would you?" he said. "I'm tired of playing in your
shadow. I want to be a legend in my own time."

But he never was that much in my shadow. He meant
a lot to the Chicago Bears. One game in 1967 he got
the game ball for his performance against Minnesota.
He had a way of playing a good game when I was
having a good game. When I was going well, I'd be
making a lot of long runs and so I'd be taking a blow
more often and maybe my playing time would be a
little less. And Pick would come in and play a helluva
game. You'd have to say he was an opportunist. The
day I tore up my knee against San Francisco Pick came
in and ran for eighty-seven yards on eighteen carries,
and caught four passes for fifty-four yards.

And he did a beautiful job the rest of the year.
Against New Orleans he rushed twenty-one times for
112 yards. He ended up rushing for 450 yards, a 3.8
average. He had a favorite line then: "I won't get you
sixty [meaning sixty yards in one run], but I'll get you
ten sixes." Every time I saw him that year and into 1969

he'd look at me and say, "I won't get you sixty, but I'll get you ten sixes." And he'd burst out laughing.

He was really a comfort to me during the 1969 exhibition season and into the regular season, especially those early games when the writers had written me off. He was one of the few guys who seemed to have confidence in me, who built up my morale. He would read what they were saying about me and he'd say, "Don't worry about them. You're running fine. The holes aren't there, you know, just keep your chin up." Which I was trying to do, but it wasn't always easy.

And he knew I was tight in those early days, wondering if I had lost something, and he did his damnedest to loosen me up. One time in camp a writer asked about my knee. "There's one big difference in Gale now," Pick said, standing right beside me. "He runs all right until the knee starts to wobble."

The trouble was that a lot of writers began to believe that. We have one local writer who is always sneaking around, trying to pick up conversation among the players. He wants to know everything and he always edges in trying to hear what doesn't concern him. So one day after practice we saw him coming. I put my back to him and Pick made believe he didn't know he was there, and he started in.

"It really feels that bad, huh, kid?" he said.

I said, "Yeah. I don't know if I can make it."

"Well, don't worry about it. Hell, I filled in for you last year. I'll do the job. The team will get along O.K., Gale. We can do it."

"Well, I hope so, but I'm just not so sure. Damn knee. I may have to hang it up after the season."

"Well, what the hell," Pick said. "It's your fifth year. You've got your pension in."

That writer stole away, not sure that he had heard right and wondering, probably, Was it a put on, or should I write it?

It's ironic the way things happen. Because of my injury and my mental state afterward, I got to know Pick even better and became closer to him than almost

anybody else on the team. And then when he became
ill, it seemed that our friendship deepened and we got to
understand each other even better. And that's when I
found out what a beautiful person he really was.

In July, when we report to camp, we all have to take
complete physicals. And of course Brian had one and
he had a chest X ray and nothing showed. Brian didn't
smoke, didn't drink much, and he always took good
care of himself. And when Ronnie Bull tore up his knee
in the Detroit game, Piccolo was switched to fullback
and played alongside me and was doing a helluva job.

But just about this time he began to develop a cough.
It wasn't much at first. He wouldn't cough much at
night, but he'd get up in the morning and start to cough,
maybe four or five times, then stop for a while, then
start again. Later he was coughing at night. He would
excuse himself every few minutes—because, I guess, he
thought he was disturbing me.

We went up to Minnesota on November 2, and the
cough got a little worse. It was kind of cool and damp,
and he figured maybe he was catching cold, so he got a
prescription from one of the team doctors and started
taking cough medicine. Then we played in Pittsburgh,
and he still had the cough. And in the Atlanta game it
really got bad.

It was warm down there, and he coughed so bad that
he almost lost his breath a few times. Dick Gordon was
sitting on the bench next to him. Brian was hacking
something awful, and Gordon just couldn't believe it.
He looked at Pick and said, "How the hell are you
playing?" But he played the whole game and played
well and he scored a touchdown.

And at this time he could still joke about it. He would
get this coughing jag and then say to Ralph Kurek,
another of our running backs and a good friend of
Pick's, "I think I'm having a coronary."

Kurek, who's nuts, said, "Try this heart massage. I
use it all the time when my heart stops."

Pick got back at Kurek by spraying his roll-on deodorant with a sticky substance, "Firm Grip." Every day he'd load it up with "Firm Grip" and Ralph never caught on to it. Pick swore that Kurek never raised his arms once he put that stuff on.

The Tuesday after the Atlanta game Pick decided he'd better see Doctor L. L. Braun, our medical doctor. Maybe he just needed a stronger cough syrup or something. So he went to the doctor's office at Illinois Masonic hospital and Doctor Braun wasn't in. Louis Kolb took Pick upstairs for a chest X ray.

He threw the X ray up on the light, and Piccolo, no medical man, nevertheless knew when an X ray wasn't right. He saw a big spot on his left lung, a clear area where all the rest was dark. He said, "Hey, doctor, what's this?"

Dr. Kolb said, "I don't mean to be an alarmist, but it's something that shouldn't be there. But we'll have Dr. Braun come down and look at it and we'll see what we can figure out. Don't worry about it, it could be a swollen gland or something."

Piccolo told me he waited an hour or so, because Dr. Braun was busy, and while he waited, he said, he sat there looking at that X ray and just wondering about a lot of things.

Finally, Dr. Braun came around, took a look, and told Pick he wouldn't be playing the game Sunday against the Baltimore Colts. He thought Brian had better stay in the hospital for some tests.

And he did. The chest specialist came in and looked down Pick's throat with a tube and he couldn't see anything. So they made an incision in his chest. And that's when they discovered it was a tumor. And it was malignant.

The doctor told Pick that he apparently had had a tumor there all his life, lying there benign, and for some reason it just decided to take off.

The first time I heard about the seriousness of Brian's illness was Friday night, when Coach Halas called me at home. He said, "Brian's very sick. He's got a malignant tumor in his chest that's got to come out. We're sending him to New York to the best hospital in the country for this type of tumor."

I was stunned. I was absolutely stunned, and shocked. I just didn't know what to say, or think. After practice Saturday, I went over to the hospital to see him. He was in a fantastic mood. "I'm ready to play, man," he said. "It's just a little cough, you know." He was disappointed that he couldn't play. His wife, Joy, was with him and she was in good spirits, too. I really didn't know what to say to him. We kidded around a bit and then I left.

That night, the night before the Baltimore game, Mr. Halas called me again. He said, "Gale, I think maybe you ought to say something to the team before we go out tomorrow, try to dedicate the game to Brian. You're Pick's roommate. I think it would be appropriate."

And I said I would. The more I thought about it, the more I liked the idea. Because I think a lot of the fellows didn't realize just how sick Brian was. There had been no announcements in the papers, and the Bears wanted to make no announcements until Brian got to New York and was operated on.

I had never in my life talked to a team. I don't consider myself a leader. All the leading I do is by example, by the way I go out and play the game. And I didn't know how it would go. I was a little nervous, but that didn't matter. I wanted to get something across to the guys, that was all.

Sunday morning I went to church, which I seldom do during the football season. I went mainly to pray for Brian.

Before we went out for our pregame warmup, I told Jim Dooley I wanted to say something to the team about Brian. He said it was O.K. So after the warmup and just as we were getting ready to go back on the field, Dooley told the team, "Gale has something to say to you."

I just told them that we have a tradition after a winning game to give a game ball to the outstanding player of that game. I said, "As you all know, Brian Piccolo is very, very sick. If you don't know it, you should know it. He's very, very sick and he might not ever play football again. And I think each of us should dedicate ourselves to try to give our maximum efforts to win this ball game and give the game ball to Pick. We can all sign it and take it up to him. . . ."

About this time I was getting pretty choked up, and they probably didn't even understand the last part of what I was saying, because I had started to cry.

As we went on the field, they started playing "The Star-Spangled Banner" and I couldn't help crying then. We were going to kick off, so I went to the bench and just leaned over with my head down, sobbing. Jim Ringo came over to me and said, "Gale, I've been in football for twenty years and never heard anything like that before." And Abe Gibron came over and said it was a great thing to do.

And then I went over to Ross Montgomery, who was my backup man now, and I told Ross that although he was a fine football player he might as well not suit up because I wasn't coming out of this game. I was going to play this game for Brian.

And we went out and we played ball and we should have won the damn game. We had them by a touchdown with six minutes to go and John Unitas came in and drove them eighty yards. Then, as we were getting into field-goal range, they intercepted a pass and they got the field goal and we lost the game. But most of the players had given their all, I knew that.

After the game, Linda and I went to the hospital to see Brian. He was leaving the next morning for New York, and a bunch of the players came by. Mike Pyle was there with his wife, Ronnie Bull and his wife, Jack Concannon and his wife, Ed McCaskey was there, Jim Ringo, and Ralph Kurek and his wife. McCaskey ordered a bunch of pizzas and a few beers and stuff and everybody sat around.

Linda and I stayed for two hours. At one point, Pick, Concannon, Kurek, and myself went upstairs to see this little girl who had dived into a shallow swimming pool and broken her neck. She was about thirteen and was paralyzed from the neck down. She had kind of become the darling of the Bears, because every time a player came to see Dr. Fox he would send him up to see this girl. Mainly because of the girl, Brian said, he wasn't as concerned about his own troubles. The next morning, the day he left for New York, he went into the girl's room to give her a signed photograph of himself. She was asleep and he left it. Some weeks later we heard that the girl had passed away.

We talked a lot that Sunday. We clowned a little bit, but it was sort of a serious mood, considering Pick's normal disposition. But he was in fine spirits. Listening to him, I found it hard to believe that here he had played football so long without getting knocked out by an injury and, all of a sudden, this terrible thing had struck him down. It was a tough thing to believe that this kind of thing could happen to him. But he was such a strong person. He just said, "It's a tumor and it's got to come out, and it's got to come out now." And he was loose about it because that was his way. He's always been loose about things. His attitude was, What's the use of getting solemn and serious? It doesn't change things. He said he felt he was fortunate in that respect because he knew a lot of people who just couldn't look at things that way. He said he was resigned to anything that happened to him. He felt, he said, that all our lives are plotted out in advance and nothing we do can change things. His only concern, he said, was for his wife and his three small daughters.

What he was really doing, I think, was carrying through the I Am Third philosophy of life. Really carrying it through. And yet it was a very positive attitude. And I think you have to be that way. I wasn't really impressed by Brian's courage because I knew Brian. I knew he was a very courageous person, and I expected that of him.

Pick flew into New York Monday and they operated on him on Friday. Dr. Edward Beattie, who is a famous specialist on such tumors, performed the operation. He told Brian beforehand that he might have to quit playing

football for a couple of years. Pick knew that would
be the end for him. Because if he laid out two years he
would be trying to make a comeback at twenty-eight.
So he told the doctor, "Well, listen, don't worry about
it. We won't talk about it now. We'll wait and see."

Dr. Beattie also told Pick the tumor figured to be
the size of a baseball. When they got it out—after a
four-and-a-half-hour operation—it was closer to a
grapefruit.

We had a Saturday game in San Francisco, and right
after the game I flew back to Chicago, then into New
York for an appearance. Sunday morning I went in to
see Pick.

Same old Piccolo. He had watched the San Francisco
game—it was on national television—and he gave me
hell for not fielding a punt that went on to roll seventy
yards. He said, "I kept yelling, 'Gale, pick it up, pick
it up.' " Well, I caught hell from Abe Gibron for not
picking it up, too.

Considering everything he had gone through, he
looked well and he was in his usual good spirits. The
room was full of flowers. "I don't have any oxygen for
myself," he said to me. And he had gotten thousands of
cards and letters. Then he showed off a personally autographed picture and album he had received from Frank
Sinatra. He flipped over Sinatra.

And, naturally, he showed me his scar. It made my
knee look like nothing. It was a wicked one, coming
almost from his throat down to two inches above his
navel, with another scar from the middle of his sternum
to just under his armpit.

Brian's attitude after the operation was so phenom-
enal it made me feel all the worse about how I had
acted just after my knee surgery. The day after I was
operated on Pick and Bobby Joe Green came to see me.
Bobby Joe was still on crutches from his knee surgery
and he had a struggle to get to my room. And I just lay
there and said nothing. Pick tried to make small talk,
but it was like talking to a wall. Pick was so mad. He
told me later, "Gale, I really felt like saying to you,

'you're a miserable S.O.B. and I won't come and see you again. Just lay in there and be miserable and feel sorry for yourself.' "

It was true. The first day or two I was terrible. Pick would say something that would normally get a chuckle, and it was like I was deaf. I lay there like stone.

And here was Brian Piccolo, after probably the most critical moment in his whole life, in fine spirits, cool and hopeful and so positive about things. He really helped lift *your* spirits.

He spent fifteen days in the hospital in New York. Pete Rozelle visited him on Thanksgiving Day and brought an autographed book about professional football, *The First Fifty Years.* And he watched part of the Viking-Ram game with Pick. I expected that from a man like Rozelle. He's a straight, down-to-earth guy. A helluva man.

When Pick got back home he naturally took it easy for a while. The doctor said he could go outdoors and do anything he wanted as soon as he felt up to it. And he did make one of our last practice sessions, before the Detroit game, our next-to-the-last of the season. And the guys were all glad to see him.

We talked on the phone a lot and Linda and I visited him a few times, and he seemed to be making terrific progress. He had gotten his weight back up to 188 and was getting ready to play a little golf and start working out a little in the gym.

When I got back from the Pro Bowl game in Los Angeles I called him. I had been named MVP on offense in that game, and Piccolo said, "I missed the first half. I was at a meeting at the country club. But somebody there had been watching it and was saying what a great game Sayers was having. So when I got home I turned on the TV. As soon as it goes on, the nigger fumbles. That's when I turned you off. I didn't watch another play. Typical nigger play."

I couldn't stop laughing on the phone. "You're terrible," I said, "you're so bad. You haven't changed at all. You're as big a racist as you've ever been."

Shortly after, he went out to play in the Astrojet golf tournament in Phoenix, in which they pair a pro-baseball player and a pro-football player from the same city. Pick was paired with Ernie Banks of the Chicago Cubs. "Wouldn't you know?" he said. "You can't get away from them."

When he came back from the golf tournament he called me to tell me about it. He also said that he had to go back to New York for more tests. He had discovered a lump on his chest.

That night we played basketball together. The Bears had a team, if that's what you want to call it, and Pick was player-coach. He played pretty well, too, and he was a very tough coach. He pulled me out of the game for taking those eighty-foot shots. Well, I'm a guard. When you're a guard you can't get under the basket and you have to take the long shot. I was pretty bad, though, I admit it.

He was in good spirits, as usual, he was the same old Pick, playing down his little lump, which turned out to be a big swelling under his chest.

He went to New York, and they put him on medicine for a while. I came in and spent some time with him. His wife, Joy, was staying with him, and we took in movies, went to a couple of New York Knick basketball games, and ate pizza, which was Pick's favorite food.

They hoped that the medicine would reduce the tumor, but finally they decided he had to be operated on. He was operated on once, and a few weeks later he underwent his third operation.

Ed McCaskey and I flew into New York to see him before his second operation. He was coughing quite a bit and all the medication and stuff had weakened him physically. But mentally he was as strong as ever. I thought to myself, If anybody can lick it, it's got to be Pick. He can do it.

It happened that I have the same blood as Pick—B

positive—so I gave a pint. A couple of days later, just before he was to undergo his second operation, he was telling friends about how Gale Sayers had given him blood.

"I don't know what it is," he said, "but lately I've gotten an awful craving for chitlins."

As much as they cut into this man, as much as he was inflicted with terrible pain and discomfort, as much as he suffered because of this wicked disease that struck him like a thunderbolt flashing out of a clear sky . . . as much as he was faced with all these tortures, his spirit would not be destroyed. That was the beautiful nature of Brian Piccolo.

There was the time, just before he went into the hospital again, that he sat down at home and wrote a letter to Freddy Steinmark of the University of Texas. Steinmark had played on Texas's 1969 national-championship football team. Just after the season they discovered that Steinmark had bone cancer. They amputated his leg. And Pick sat down and wrote him a letter. I asked him what he said to the boy.

"I told him that I, more than any other football player, understood a few things that must have gone through his mind. Because I had gone through the same thing. I told him never to lose courage and to remember that there was always hope."

At the end of May I came into New York to attend the Professional Football Writers annual dinner and receive the George S. Halas award as the most courageous player in pro football. I had wanted Brian to attend with me if he was strong enough, but the day I arrived in New York was the day Brian and Joy left the hospital to go back home. He had finished a series of cobalt treatments and the doctors said he could spend a few weeks at home, then return to the hospital for more treatment.

One reason I wanted Brian with me at the banquet was that I intended to give him the trophy right there. But at least I was able to tell the audience something about Brian Piccolo.

"He has the heart of a giant," I said, "and that rare form of courage that allows him to kid himself and his opponent, cancer. He has the mental attitude that makes me proud to have a friend who spells out the word courage twenty-four hours a day of his life."

I concluded by saying, "You flatter me by giving me this award but I tell you here and now that I accept it for Brian Piccolo. Brian Piccolo is the man of courage who should receive the George S. Halas award. It is mine tonight, it is Brian Piccolo's tomorrow. . . . I love Brian Piccolo and I'd like all of you to love him, too. Tonight, when you hit your knees, please ask God to love him. . . ."

The next day I flew back to Chicago and called Pick on the phone. He had read about the speech in the paper and the first thing he said to me was, "Magic, you're too much. If you were here now I'd kiss you."

I said, "Yeah, well I'm glad I'm not there."

The next day Linda and I did go to see him. He was wearing shorts and sitting on the couch and he looked very small. But his spirits were as high as ever. Virgil Carter and his wife dropped by and we talked football and I cracked a couple of jokes, which was a big upset. "Gale, what is this?" Pick said. "I'm supposed to be the joker around here."

We left feeling better about him because he kept us in a lighthearted mood. He cheered *us* up. I'm glad of that last memory of Pick, since I was not to see him again.

He and Joy went to Atlanta to see their little girls, who had been staying with Joy's mother. He got very sick down there and they immediately flew back to New York.

Joy told us later that he had suffered a great deal the last week of his life. She said that up to then they both still had hope, but that last week, coming back to New York, they knew the end was near. And Brian faced up to it and started talking about it. "You know I love you, Joy," he said to his wife, "and I hope I have been a good father to the girls." And he told Joy things he would like for his girls. And when Joy would start to cry Pick would cheer her up the only way he knew how—by ridiculing his own condition. "Joy, can you believe this?" he'd say. "Can you believe this, Joy? Nobody would ever believe this."

I wanted to come in to New York to see him but at that time my parents were involved in an automobile accident. My mother got off light with some broken ribs but my father suffered a fractured skull and was in a coma, and I flew to Omaha to see them. And when I got back to Chicago I had a temperature of 104 and they put me in the hospital with a strep throat.

Tuesday morning, June 16, at six-thirty, Linda called me at the hospital to tell me that Brian had passed away a few hours earlier. A few minutes later I got another call from Ed McCaskey, who had been in New York with Joy and Brian until the end. I couldn't talk. I wasn't able to say a word to anyone the rest of that day.

I was discharged from the hospital that afternoon. When I came home I found that my trophy had arrived from New York. I sat down and wrote Brian's name on a piece of paper and pasted it over mine on the trophy. The next morning I went to the wake with the trophy and gave it to Joy and told her I wanted it buried with Pick. Joy said no, she wanted to keep it because it meant so much to her.

The funeral was held that Friday, a clean lovely morning in Chicago, and I went through it like a sleepwalker. I was one of the pallbearers along with Dick Butkus, Ralph Kurek, Ed O'Bradovich, Mike Pyle, and Randy Jackson. I think the only thing I remember about that funeral service was one line recited from the scripture: "The virtuous man, though he dies before his time, will find rest."

It was at the cemetery, as the priest was delivering his final words, that I broke down. He referred to the trophy and to our friendship and it was too much for me. I couldn't control myself. I just started to cry.

As soon as the service was ended, Joy came over to

me and put her arms around me and we embraced and I told her how sorry I was. "Don't be sorry, Gale," she said. "I'm happy now because I know Brian is happy, and I don't have to watch him suffer any more. He's through suffering now."

She comforted me. I thought to myself, if she can really be that composed, Brian must have really given her something. And I thought, Well, he gave us all something, all of us who were privileged to know him. And that helped compose me.

Part Two

7

Santa Claus, Go Straight to the Ghet-to

He thinks of the days when he was in the Toe, his days in the Toe. That's his expression. He asks if I've ever been to the Toe. We asked him one day, "Where's the Toe?" "The ghet-to, you idiot." He had all my kids singing it—"Santa Claus, go straight to the ghet-to." All the guys at work were singing it. He called me up. Guess what those lawfine stockbrokers are doing—singing, "Santa Claus, go straight to the ghet-to." I said, "Oh my God."

—TOMMY DARE

The first time I ever talked to Linda on the telephone was right after Christmas of my senior year in high school. We had just started dating and she asked me what I got for Christmas. I told her I got a record player, all these suits and shirts and clothes—just a list of things. Then, every time we went out, I wore the same pair of pants and the same shirt. So one time she asked me, "Where are all those clothes that you got for Christmas? Why don't you wear something different?" It was embarrassing at the time, but it's been a standing joke between us since then. The fact is I didn't get anything for Christmas. That year my father earned $2300 for polishing cars in Omaha.

When I was fourteen years old my father, Roger Winfield Sayers, was called the best car polisher around Omaha. He's still remembered as one of the best car polishers in the city. There's a real art to it. I once talked to this fellow at the local Pontiac agency. He said, "If you can find a good car polisher, you've got something." You've got this buffer that weighs about ten pounds, and you have to hit it just right on the car. You apply the paste wax and buff it all over. If you hold the buffer too tight to the car, it'll take the paint right off. There's a real skill to it.

All the major dealers knew about my father, because he had this reputation for his car polishing. He moved around a lot. Maybe he made $55 a week at one place, so he'd quit to go to a place where he could make $60. Then he'd move to another place for another $5 a week. And until an auto accident in 1970 forced him into retirement, he was making $75 a week working five and a half days.

I look at his life and it still shakes me—because, I think, it could have been so different.

When I started speaking before kids at slum schools in Chicago I would use my father's experience as an example. I put it to them this way: "An older man that I know could have been a lawyer. He had an uncle who offered to send him to college and on to law school, but this man dropped out of high school when he was in the tenth grade. So instead of being a lawyer and wearing nice clothes and working pleasant hours, this man works as a car polisher in a used-car lot."

Then I'd give them the punch line. "The man I'm talking about is my father. He works long hours and comes home tired every night, for $75 a week. He's been working that way for thirty-three years."

And, really, it didn't have to be that way. My father was born in a sod house on a farm near the town of Nicodemus in western Kansas. He is about five-feet-seven—short, as men go, but very muscular. Working the buffer all his life, he developed real large arms. He was the kind of man you always thought you could whip but you never really wanted to try to.

His family goes way back to one of the first settlers in Kansas. He had two uncles who were the first Negro lawyers in western Kansas. My great uncle, W. L. Sayers, was the state's first Negro county lawyer, practicing out of Hill City in Graham County. I once read an article that at one time he owned more land in the state of Kansas than any other individual. He was certainly quite well-to-do and he gave my father a chance to be a lawyer. He said, "You stay in school, Roger, and I'll send you on to law school."

But my father had other things on his mind than school. He was athletically inclined. He played semipro baseball. He broad jumped. He said he once did about nineteen feet, which was very good in his time, I guess. He was built for speed, like my brother Roger, short as he is. Roger is all legs. Dad has long legs. He was also a piano player and he played a while with those traveling bands and orchestras. He didn't want to go to law school. Like, I guess, all young kids, he wanted to get out, get a job, make some money, and buy a car. And this was a decision he probably has some regrets about today.

My memories of my first seven years, living in Wichita, are hazy. I know my mother, Bernice Ross, came from Gilmer, Texas, and her family moved to Wichita when she was young. I don't know how my mother and father met, but they married and settled down in Wichita. The years in Wichita were probably the happiest my mother and father spent together. We owned our own house. It was really nice with a little back yard. And there was a little house in the back of our house, which we could use if we wanted. And they were happy years because we didn't want for anything. We had money to buy things we wanted, and I really don't remember them drinking that much in Wichita. And I can't remember my mother and father arguing or fighting at all.

My brother Roger came along in April 1942. My mother was hoping that her second child would be a girl and she had a name all picked out—Gale. So when I turned up, on May 30, 1943, Memorial Day in the middle of World War II (they had parades for me all over the country that day) my mother must have been disappointed. She took one look at me and said, "Since I don't have a boy's name picked out, we'll call him

Gale, anyway." I've got one baby picture of me and, damn, I do look like a girl. I even had a ribbon in my hair. I was a chubby baby, so I must have been well fed.

My father had a good income in those days. He didn't have to go into the service because he had an essential job as a mechanic for Goodyear Tire and Rubber Company. He also had his own little brake service in our back yard. I remember once when I was five or six I was playing in the garage and I broke one of my father's brake shoes. I didn't tell him about it, but he found out anyway and whipped me pretty good.

He was really a strict father in those early years. I got whippings all the time for doing things wrong, only I always thought the whippings were without cause. My mother used to whip me all the time, too, for sucking my thumb. She tried everything to stop it—tape, pepper, salt. Finally, one day I broke it. I don't know when, I just stopped doing it.

The one other thing that stands out in my mind about those Wichita days was the time my brother Roger backed into a gas burner we had in the middle of the living room. He had no clothes on and he was fooling around and he leaned back against the heater and got a bad burn on his right hip.

In 1950 we left Wichita for Speed, Kansas, and that was the beginning of my parents' downfall.

Speed is a small town in northwestern Kansas, not far from the Nebraska border. It's adjacent to Graham County, where the Sayers clan had settled down. It's five miles outside of Phillipsburg, which is where we went to school. My grandfather had a big wheat farm in Speed, about 360 acres with maybe 200 or so acres of wheat. He leased or rented out some of it for other farmers to use for grazing. My grandfather was seventy years old at the time and his wife—my father's stepmother—was an invalid. I don't know what her problem was, but she was a cripple, confined to a wheelchair and crutches for the most part.

My grandfather had taken sick and he wrote my father asking him to come out and take over the farm while grandaddy was sick. Because of the attachment they had, my father agreed to it. So he just sold everything and went out there. I know my mother wasn't happy about it; she didn't want to move. She wanted to stay in Wichita because all her relatives were there. I imagine her drinking started in Speed and my father's in Omaha, when things began to get worse for us.

None of us boys liked Speed too much. Ronnie had come along in 1948, and I don't remember him too well as a child because he was five years behind me. In Speed, he was, of course, just a baby. But Win and I were tight in those days—Roger's middle name is Winfield and we all called him Win. Heck, we were only thirteen months apart. Also, we were the only blacks in the community and the only blacks in the school. So we stuck together.

We went to one of those two-room schoolhouses where they had the first, second, third, fourth, fifth, and sixth grades in one room and the seventh and eighth in another room. The school system was terrible.

But we did have some good times in Speed. I remember when my father bought us a couple of BB guns for Christmas one year. We'd go off shooting all the time. One time we were messing around by some barbed wire and I dropped my gun and it rolled down the hill and I started off after it. I slipped on some rocks and hit the barbed wire fence on my way down and I tore a big hole in my back. I still have the three- or four-inch scar in my back.

Another thing I remember is the time a fellow came to visit. His name was Randolph and he weighed 290, 300 pounds. One morning my mother cooked a big breakfast and I decided to outeat Randolph. We were having pancakes and I don't remember how many I ate, probably twenty or twenty-five pancakes. I staggered away from the table sick as a dog. Randolph was still there, eating. He could really eat, I tell you.

Other than that, all I remember about Speed was the big rains coming, and putting up fences, and killing snakes, and going to the outhouse.

We stayed there sixteen months. My grandfather died and then relations between my parents and his wife kind of deteriorated. She was from Louisville, Kentucky, and her family was all there and she got the feeling that she was being shafted by my father, or something. This is what I remember of it. And it just came to the point where it was best for one side to move—call it quits, settle the thing as rapidly as possible. And that's what was done.

I don't really remember why we decided to move to Omaha. I know my mother was bitterly against it. She wanted to go back to Wichita, where her family was. I think the primary reason my father decided not to go back to Wichita was that he was a little embarrassed that things hadn't worked out the way he had planned. Pride had a lot to do with his not moving back to Wichita.

He had a brother, Guy Sayers, living in Omaha. They corresponded. Guy Sayers had his own home and he said, "Why don't you come to Omaha?" He offered to put us up until we found suitable housing. So rather than go back to Wichita, we packed up and moved to Omaha. I imagine if he went back to Wichita he still would have made it. I don't know about me: I might not have played football. Wichita at that time didn't have a midget program. Omaha did. Win and I got involved right away, so that helped a great deal. It was a break for us when we moved to Omaha, but it was the worst thing that could have happened to my mother and father. It was totally downhill from then on.

Omaha today has a black population of about fifty-five thousand out of a total population of four hundred thousand. When we moved to Omaha in 1951, when I was eight years old, there were about forty thousand Negroes. And they all seemed concentrated around 24th Street, which is the main artery of the ghetto. It's about a two-and-a-half-mile stretch, from 24th and Ames to 24th and Cummings, and this is where most of the guys hung around. The street is full of pool halls and bars, and on Friday night or Saturday night, when the people who worked in the packing houses got their checks, they went right down to 24th Street and drank half of it up. Most of the black people in Omaha worked in the meat-packing plants—Cudahy, Swift, Armour—and the wages weren't bad. That was the best money around besides construction work.

But my Uncle Guy worked for an automobile dealer as a car polisher and he managed to get my father a job polishing cars. And that was the start of it.

Guy Sayers and his wife had a small, two-bedroom house. That meant that some of the Sayers from Speed slept on the floor, at least the older boys did. We stayed with Guy Sayers for about two months and then moved into the 30th Street projects, which had just opened up. And that was the start of the rat race that saw us moving nine times in maybe eight years, and always, it seemed, going from bad to worse. And as things got worse, my father kept saying, "Well if things don't work out this year we'll wait until next year and we'll try something." But it gets to a point where age and desire catch up to you. And you find yourself in a trap. This is what happened. The pressures increased on my mother and father, and they started drinking to try to get away from the pressures, and the trap just sprung tight on them.

We stayed on 30th Street two years. You know, in the projects if you start making more money they start raising your rent. I think my father may have been making $55 a week and was raised maybe to $65 a week, and so they raised the rent. We wanted to get out of the projects anyway, so we moved to a house on Pinckney Street. We stayed there for about a year, then we moved to 27th and Grant, then to 18th Street, then to Spencer, then back to Pinckney, to a house over a bar, then to Ohio, then from Ohio to Miami and from Miami to 30th Street, where my parents are living now. So you can see we were a bunch of gypsies. Each house got worse. At the end it seemed we were just trying to find a place, you know, that we could live in.

I remember the arguments and drinking heating up on Pinckney Street. One time in this period they both went to jail. They had been drinking and got into an argument and a fight. They stayed overnight, and the next day things were the same as they always were.

On 27th and Grant, I remember, we used to be hungry a lot. Lucky we still had our BB guns, because we had heard that you could get sparrows and catbirds. So we would go out and shoot the birds and feather them and cook them, just fry them. A catbird was a little bit like a blackbird but with a speckled chest. He didn't taste bad, either. When you're hungry, they all taste good.

My mother did her best to make ends meet. We used to eat chicken feet a lot, just the feet. You could buy them in the store, a hundred for fifty cents. My mother used to fry them or stew them.

Hell, there just wasn't enough money for food. My father was earning $65 or $75 a week and he had to pay $75 a month for rent, and lots of money went to whisky. They liked to play cards, too. They would always have a poker game at our house every Friday and Saturday night. It wasn't a big poker game, nickel and dimes, but it could add up, especially when you had no money to begin with. If you lost $10 you lost your meal money for the week.

But the worst time was on 18th Street, when I was a freshman in high school. I remember going for weeks at a time without coal for the furnace in the dead of winter. We had two bedrooms. My parents slept in one, my brothers slept in the other, and I slept off the dining room, if you want to call it that. I had a little bunk bed in a hall near the kitchen. We'd put on the oven to keep warm and I'd wake up each morning with those gas headaches.

That was the roughest time because my mother left home just when it was at its worst. She went to Denver to stay with her sister and she was gone a month or so. She would just get depressed. It wasn't because she didn't love us or love our father. You know, women get depressed sometimes. I think she felt there had to be something better, someplace else, and she just took off.

She took off four times in all those years, but she always came back. And my father reacted gently. He'd

say, "Momma's gone and we got to do the best we can."
He never did talk much, but sometimes he would open
up a little bit more. "You know," he'd say, "maybe it's
my fault, maybe I drove your mother off." He would
say that and he'd add, "We got to stick together now,
because maybe if we stick together she'll come back."

And, as I say, she always did come back. The weirdest thing was that they seemed to communicate better
when they were separated than when they were together. Because as soon as she came back they'd start
fussing and fighting again. It seemed like they never
could live in harmony—like you can't live with them,
but can't live without them, either.

But through it all we got along together—Roger and
Ronnie and myself. We took care of ourselves so we
never did feel we were neglected. We knew what was
going on, but I guess we just felt it was something we
had to put up with. We knew many of our friends who
were in the same boat, so we just took it as a way of
life. We would try to tell them stop drinking, but I
guess when you're down, drinking is one way to relieve
your problem. And they never got mean to us. They
would just argue back and forth with themselves.

Maybe it was having all boys that hurt. I remember
when Win and his wife, Madelyn, had their second child.
It was a girl, and Mom was so happy. She said at the
time, "I wish I had a girl around instead of three hard-
headed boys."

Of the three, I was the most hard-headed. I was the
black sheep of the family. Mom loved Roger because
he always studied. I never did. I was always out playing
ball or messing around someplace. They always told me
I would never make it, I would never be like my older
brother. They were just goading me to try harder.

And Ronnie was a favorite because he was the
youngest and he developed a heart murmur. I remember one Christmas in the projects Ronnie and I were
throwing a hassock back and forth. Anyway, I threw it
at him and he hit a plug and the thing sparked up and
burned all the skin on the back of his hand. I ran down-

stairs and we took him to the hospital, but they wrapped it up and that was it. I was scared, scared for him and scared I would get a whipping. But my mother and father were just as scared and they never did bother to whip me.

Maybe I was the black sheep because I was the most independent of the boys. I always seemed to be out on my own. I was moodier than the others, too, and yet unemotional. I put bad things out of my mind. And my mother was very emotional, very sensitive. So she kind of identified more with Roger and with my little brother, Ronnie.

No matter what my parents have done to their lives, I understand them and I still love them dearly. They are living together today and it is much better with them. They were in a terrible car accident in the spring of 1970 and my father ended up in a coma; he got a fractured skull. My mother just broke some ribs. Now she has to take care of my father, and that has brought them together closer than ever.

But at the time I went through this period of growing up—my parents drinking, not enough food in the house, cockroaches over things, no heat in the winter—my parents were at each other all the time. Still, it seemed that all my friends were going through the same thing. Hell, I didn't even realize we lived in the ghetto until I moved away from the ghetto. Now when I go back home I say, Is this where I lived? But at the time I didn't feel deprived because, when you get right down to it, everyone living in the Toe is deprived.

And I know now that I learned something from that experience, something I probably couldn't have picked up outside the ghetto. I learned that if you want to make it bad enough, no matter how bad it is you can make it.

8

Going for the Pookie-Burger

I was twelve years old when I pasted my first award in my first scrapbook—marble champion of Room 15, seventh grade, Howard Kennedy School. But I wasn't confining myself to marbles in those days.

I have said that things grew worse for my parents and better for us when we moved to Omaha in 1951. This was because there were so many opportunities to compete in sports in Omaha. Our grade school was just like high school. We played in city school leagues and we took city titles in baseball, football, and basketball. Right from the start, when I was eight years old, I ran track, played basketball and some baseball. I played center field, but I didn't particularly like it. After every baseball game we played, we had a track meet. So we didn't concentrate too much on baseball because we knew we were going to win the track meet.

I remember one meet I was wearing my football shoes—you weren't allowed to run in spikes—and the shoes were too big for me, they kept sliding on me. So I started off in the shoes and kicked them off before we hit the curve—I always ran better on curves than straightaways—and I caught this guy running barefoot. And I won the race. They wanted to disqualify me for running barefoot, but what could they say when we told them that my shoes had just slipped off?

But football was always my favorite sport. In grade school we played "flag" football. Each back and pass receiver wore two flags or bandannas, dangling from a belt around each side of his waist. Instead of tackling the ball carrier, you had to yank the flag from the belt. We won the city flag-football title in the fifth, sixth,

95

seventh, eighth grade—all the way up—and I can't remember our team ever losing a game. We had a bunch of guys who went on to become all-city or all-state in high school.

Don't think we neglected tackle football in those days. We were always out in the street or in the local park playing tackle. Kuntz Park, in the middle of the Toe, was where we played mostly. It was a typical ghetto park. The field had holes in it, there was very little grass, and it was full of cockleburrs. They'd stick to your clothes and they'd stick to your body—they'd break off, but always a little-bitty thorn would stick in. And all the kids in the neighborhood would go down there and play ball.

But usually after supper, when we had pickup games, we didn't feel like going to the park, so we played in an alley adjoining our street. It was about 100 yards long, and at the end of the alley was a big stone wall which surrounded two houses. If you made it to that wall it was a touchdown. I hit that wall a few times, but we didn't care how hard the wall was. We just cared about scoring. We took our lumps and bumps in that alley, but we didn't think anything about it.

Then there was another empty lot right next to the projects where we had pickup games every afternoon. We played until it got dark, and we had a unique rule: No matter what the score was, when it began to get dark we'd always start a new game—whoever makes the next touchdown wins. A team could be twenty points ahead, it wouldn't matter. Whoever makes the next touchdown wins. Then we would quit.

I remember one time we were playing under this sudden-death rule and a kid named Jimmy Wright had the ball. His father ran in the Olympics with Jesse Owens and this Wright kid was pretty quick. He broke around end for a long run and I went over to tackle him. Well, I didn't tackle him. His foot caught me in the mouth and put about a four-inch gash inside of my jawbone. Vern Breakfield, who was playing with me, came over and said, "Come on, I'll take you home, you're bleeding kind of bad."

I said, "No, I'll wait till the game's over with." The next play they threw a pass and I intercepted it and ran it back about sixty yards for a touchdown. And that satisfied me. I wouldn't have been satisfied otherwise. We would have played there all night with me bleeding until we won. I got home and the cut had turned green inside and they put a little iodine or something on it and that was it.

I'm not sure where I got that drive and desire to play football. I know I had it from the moment I moved to Omaha. I think the sense of competition gave me the drive, always wanting to be the best. And since I was always competing against the best—whether it was my brother Win or my best friend, Break—I always had to strive as hard as I could to be best.

I remember one game I played in high school against Benson High. Break had scored two touchdowns and three extra points and I hadn't scored any yet. I was leading the city in scoring at the time and I just couldn't stand back and see Break make all the touchdowns. But midway in the game I fell and a guy took a swing at me (I don't know what he was mad at, because they beat us that day). He broke my eyetooth, knocked it out clear to the gum. They wanted to send me to the hospital right away, but I said, "Uh-uh, I'm not going anywhere." I wound up with two touchdowns and two extra points in the game.

I think the competition with my brother Win was a factor, too, in pumping up my own desire. When we first moved to Omaha, Win and I were pretty tight. We had a newspaper route together for a couple of years and he used to hand his clothes down to me. Until, in my sophomore year in high school, I became bigger than he was. Then I handed *my* clothes down to him. Or we shared them. One time I had a plaid summer blazer and I bought a couple of pairs of pants to go with it. Whenever Win had to go out somewhere he put on a pair of the pants and the blazer and I just wore the pants. If I had to go out, I wore the blazer and the other pair of pants. That was the one sports jacket between the two of us, and we had a few fights about who was going to wear it on a certain day.

We did chores at home together, too, as kids. We always had to do the dishes at night before we went out to play. He'd wash and I'd wipe, or vice versa. And when Mom wasn't home he'd do the cooking for the family. He was, and is today, a helluva cook.

And he was a helluva athlete. Of course we played sports together, and Win was always the star of the teams. In flag football I played end until the seventh grade and he was the wingback. In those years Win was still bigger than I was, too. And he always had the speed. In 1962 he beat Bob Hayes in the 100-yard dash; I believe he was the only man ever to beat Hayes in college in that event.

But the big kick between Win and me was not flag football but midget-league tackle football. The weight limit in midget football was 110 pounds and we never had any trouble making that. And there was no minimum weight. You just needed the heart and desire.

The first coach to make an impression on me was the coach of my grade-school team, Robert Rose. He had been a Negro quarterback from Omaha University. He was a great coach. He coached us in everything—basketball, track, football—and I respected him quite a great deal. He taught me a little bit about attitude. I remember one time he kicked me off the basketball team. I was horsing around at the beginning of practice. And he said, "Go home."

"I don't want to go home."

"Well, get off the court even if you don't want to go home."

So I went out and got my clothes on and sat on the sidelines and watched them practice. The next day I was running around the track that bordered the basketball courts and he saw me and he said, "Don't get too tired, we have to play tonight." So he let me back on the team. It was probably because I had stayed to watch practice.

Rose had come from Boys Town and he knew about the problem of growing up and the stepping stones of life. He helped us so much because he was always behind us trying to make us do better. I remember once when Break let a guy get behind him in a football game. Not only that, but Break was jacking around when he should have been playing ball. So Rose took a paddle and whipped Break all the way home. Break said when he got home his mother whipped him, too.

Rose developed an excellent football team at Howard Kennedy Grade School the years I played. My first year, when I was in the seventh grade, I didn't start. Win did. We went along the entire season and I was running second-string and then our other halfback got hurt and I started the last couple of games. We won the state championship that year and Win was the star. He scored about twenty touchdowns.

"All right, Win," I told him after the season, "I'm gonna score more than you next year."

He came right back, "No way in the world you're gonna top me."

Well, the next year we won the state championship again. I scored twenty-five or twenty-seven touchdowns. We beat Boys Town for the title 39–0, and I scored five in that game. But Win was out of it by then; he was a freshman in high school.

And it was the same kind of thing when we got to high school, each trying to outdo the other. The competitiveness was always there and I think it helped both of us, but it also helped separate us a bit. As we grew older, we found we had different interests, anyway. Win was a student and I wasn't. And the fact that we felt we had to compete against each other kind of eliminated some of the closeness that might ordinarily have developed. Also, he had his friends and I had mine.

Break and I go all the way back to the third grade at Howard Kennedy. He lived about seven blocks from us. He came from a real poor family. His father died when he was ten and there was a brother and twin sisters who had to find their way just like us.

We found we had a lot in common. We grew up together and played ball together and hung around the corners together and went to each other's houses and sat around and listened to the record player.

We both loved music. I would spend all hours of the day and night listening to music. In those days it was Chuck Berry, the Platters, Little Richard—I knew all the words to all the rock-n'-roll songs that ever came out in those days. When Tommy Dare and I are driving together he's always quizzing me. A song comes over the radio, he says, "What is it, Gale?" And I know them all. I could have been an A student in high school if I spent the time on studies that I did listening to music.

Break taught me all the dancing I know how to do. He had his arm around me quite a bit in those days. He introduced me to a few girls, too. Because, you know, he had all the girls and he'd dance with them. He was outgoing and I was quiet then, very shy. We went to parties together, and he would dance, but I would just listen to the music. And I didn't think about anything else in those days—just sports and music.

Ardell (Charlie) Gunn was another friend of mine then, though not as close as Break. Gunn was more of a loner. He liked to be by himself. And he smoked and drank a little bit and Break and I didn't. And Gunn was always getting into trouble. In grade school he kept getting kicked off the football team. In high school, just before his senior year, he was in jail for three months for a little mischief. He's straightened out since then, and last I heard he was running a couple of motels down South.

There were lots of other kids our age in those days in real trouble. The Toe breeded trouble. I guess each generation is different. The older generation, they would drink wine. The younger generation, they were popping pills. But Break and Gunn and myself were always the type that played ball till late at night. Other kids might be out doing different things—fighting, robbing, getting hung up on drugs—and we would be practicing and playing till ten, eleven at night.

We were on the same basketball team in grade school. Break was a guard, Gunn and I played forward. We had a fast break that nobody could beat. We were on the same 880-relay team, too. Why the night before a meet we'd be out under the street lights at eleven o'clock passing a baton. That must have been a sight—three idiot black kids running up and down the street in the glare of the street lights or car lights, passing the stick back and forth.

And we had run in the same backfield together since the sixth grade. Break was the fullback, and Gunn and I were the halfbacks. And we decided we would all go to the same high school together.

At that time the blacks in the ghetto had their choice of two schools, Tech or Central High. Both were located in downtown Omaha and they didn't have any neighborhood boundaries. The black kids had their choice of the two high schools and we got recruited from both schools. Tech was kind of a trade school. It was predominantly black because academic requirements weren't as high. It was noted for athletics—basketball and particularly football. Bob Boozer, who became a fine pro-basketball player, went to Tech. Central High School at the time, I think, was only nine per cent black. It was primarily an academic school. Most of the kids who went to Central were rich Jewish kids, other well-to-do whites, and some academically inclined blacks. And there was a push to get more blacks in the school.

I was inclined toward Central because that's where my brother was going, but Break thought he might go to Tech. The coach at Tech had talked to Break and was convinced that Break would go to Tech. Break was a little bigger than Gunn or myself in those days, and Tech seemed more interested in him than us.

Central's football and track coach, Frank Smagacz, came down to see us several times. "If you want to go

to college," he'd say, "you ought to come to our high
school." And to me he'd add, "Your brother mentioned
that you're doing a great job, and we've got a great
football team." Stuff like that. I was convinced.

One day I told Smagacz, "Well, all three of us are
coming here." Break and Gunn went along with me.

I don't think any of us were sorry about our choice.
Smagacz (pronounced Smah-gahz) turned out to be a
fine coach and a wonderful guy. He was the father of
thirteen children, so he should have known something
about handling kids—and he did. He could make you
run faster than you ever had, jump longer than you ever
had, put out more than you ever had. And he was easygoing. Everybody loved him and had a lot of respect
for him. We all imitated the way he talked. Like he
said, "Oh, you guys, you can do better than that."
And whenever the guys did something, we would always say, "Oh, you guys, you can do better than that."

He wasn't just a coach to us, he was a friend. One
time I was having trouble in an English class (I always
had trouble with English) and I wrote this anonymous
note to the coach: "A word of advice: If you want Gale
Sayers to play next year, you better talk to his English
teacher for he's having trouble in English." I signed it:
"A friend of the team." I stuck it in Coach Smagacz's
desk and he found it. I guess he talked to the English
teacher, because things got better right away.

It's hard to imagine Central High School doing anything in sports, because the facilities were nil, at least
in my day. The school is housed in a dirty old graystone
building that served Nebraska as its capitol until the
reconstruction days after the Civil War. It's located
between an art museum and the Jewish Community
Center, and there's no land. We didn't have a decent
football field, gym, or running track. We had a fenced-
in playground (fenced to keep out the kids from Central Grade School across the street) and the track was
one-tenth of a mile. We could never set up more than

three hurdles in a row and the distance runners had to take to the streets.

We had a little dirt track, seventy-five by forty, and that's where we practiced football and track. We practiced on the dirt, and when we went out on a grassy field we used to catch leg cramps all the time—because of the switch from practicing on a hard field to the soft grass. We played most of our games at Benson High's field and a few at Creighton University. During the football season we would practice at six-thirty in the morning, which I enjoyed because I am an early riser. We would run, do belly flops in the dirt, then go to the park about two miles from the school and run around it, run around twice, back and forth. And if you stopped and complained that you were tired, Coach would say you weren't in shape, and you'd run again.

Break, Gunn, and I formed three-quarters of the freshman team backfield, and we won the intercity league championship with five wins and a tie. It was the first time that Central had won a freshman football championship in twenty-three years. At that time, Charlie was five-six and 138 pounds; Break was the big man at five-nine, 155; and I was still a 110-pounder. But something happened between my freshman and sophomore years. That summer I had a job pushing a lawn mower. Some fellow had a big lawn and I worked very hard pushing that mower; it was not a power mower. The guy paid me by the hour and I pushed it up and down the fields all summer long. When I reported to Smagacz that fall I had gained fifty pounds and grown about three inches and had the biggest arms and legs. Break saw me and said, "Oh, look at that giant."

It may have looked good for football, but when I tried sprinting I couldn't turn it on. Coach was planning to use me as a quarter man in track, but I didn't do too well. "You've had a relapse," Coach said. "How come, what's the trouble? You looked like you were going to be the fastest man we ever had here."

I said, "Coach, it's that I've grown too much, too fast. My speed just didn't keep up with me."

And that was the case well into my sophomore season. I didn't have my speed and good quickness. I had played middle linebacker as well as halfback on our freshman team, and I started for the varsity as a middle linebacker. My friends called me Horse in those days, because I played linebacker and I didn't use too much agility as a running back. I just ran over people. So they called me Horse, even after I got wiser and started using some moves.

That came later in my sophomore season, when I finally seemed to absorb all that growth, when I matured; also, when I got a chance to play offense. But my brother was the big gun that fall of 1958. Roger won the intercity scoring championship with sixty-eight points and polled more votes than anyone for the all-city team.

Break and I were running second-team offense until late in the year. I got my chance when a halfback named Willis McCanns got hurt. Break moved in for a couple of games when Roger hurt himself. Win and I did play together in a few games. I remember one against Thomas Jefferson. We beat them 26–0, and Win and I split the scoring. I gained 130 yards in seven carries and had two touchdowns. Win had touchdown runs of twenty-seven and seven yards. He was tremendous all year. We beat Lincoln 33–20, and Win had touchdown runs of seventy-nine and fifty-nine yards.

He probably would have been even better in his senior year, but he decided not to go out for football. At the time he was doing really well in track. As a sophomore, he had won the state class A titles in the 100 and 220. His junior year he ran the 100 in 9.7 and the 220 in something like 21.5. And it seemed like every college in the country was after him. So Mom kind of talked him out of football. He had stopped growing (he only weighed about 150 and stood five-eight) and Mom thought he was too small for football. Mom had a lot more influence on Win than she had on me—well, she cared about him more. Win liked track better than football, anyway. So he didn't play football his senior year, and he never did run track because he pulled a muscle at the beginning of the season, and that blew the whole thing. His scholarship offers went from one hundred to one—Omaha University. He was great at Omaha, running the 100 in 9.2 and the 220 at 20.5 (he made the United States team that competed against Russia), but with luck he could have gone so much farther.

Luck plays a role in every person's life, but I think luck is an even bigger factor in the career of an athlete. Like I didn't suffer one injury in high school and I don't know what you would call that but luck. It enabled me to go out in my junior and senior years and lead the city in scoring both years (which made it three years in a row that a Sayers had won the city scoring title). And why was I born faster than most kids? And where did my moves come from? They were just there, from the time I started playing football.

Luck and God-given ability are the big factors, I think. No coach I have ever been under has taught me anything about running with a football. I mean—nothing. Every coach I've had has been a good coach. But as far as teaching me how to run, no. Because it's always been there. I always had the knack of visualizing two or three steps ahead; that's why I cut these guys to death. A coach can't tell you any of this. He can't even tell you how to hold the ball, how to switch from hand to hand—that just comes to good football players. Take Mike Hull, who played with the Bears. You could throw his left hand away, cut it off, because he never put the ball in his left hand. He just felt more relaxed running the ball with his right hand. The coaches would tell him, All right, move the ball, but he couldn't because it didn't feel comfortable to him.

I think Frank Smagacz did teach me something about running the hurdles and broad jump. And he helped me in football by making me a hurdler, because hurdling improved me as a runner. I think it helped my knee action and the spring to go with my speed.

I went out for the hurdles almost by accident in my junior year at Central. One day I was in the gym and I saw the high hurdles out there on the floor and I said to myself, I'll run 'em. Everyone else who was running the hurdles for Central was taking five steps between hurdles. I went out there and took three steps between. Coach saw me, and that's when I started running the hurdles.

In my junior year I finished fourth in the state in the high hurdles. I did pretty well in the lows and broad jump too. In my senior year I won just about everything. Except there was this one guy I had trouble beating in the jump, and it was between him and me when we met in the state outdoor meet at Lincoln—the biggest track meet of the year.

I won a gold medal in the low hurdles at that meet and another gold for running on the winning 880 team (Break led off for us and I ran third). But the broad jump was the big competition. Bobby Williams of Lincoln was the cat I had to beat. He ran the 100 in 9.5 and he was an outstanding jumper. Later he became a defensive back in pro football, playing for the St. Louis Cardinals and Detroit Lions. In 1969 he led the National Football League in kickoff returns. Nebraska boys amounted to something in football, I tell you.

Williams had been my chief competitor all season long. I would jump 22 feet, he would be right on my tail. I met him and beat him in an intercity meet, with a jump of 23–11½, but then he beat me in a district meet.

His first jump of the day in the big state meet held under the University of Nebraska stadium he hit 22–11. That broke the state record by a quarter of an inch. My first jump was only a half inch less. On my third try I stretched out to 23–3 to take the lead. But then he hit 23–3¾ on his sixth try. I did 23–2¾ on the same round. And with one jump left, I had to try to beat that 23–3¾ mark. And I knew I was in trouble.

I called Break over. "I got to win, man," I said. "I got to beat this cat." Among other things, we had a possible state championship on the line.

Break said, "Yeah, this is it. All we've done through the years we got to put out of our minds because this is it."

I said, "Get Smagacz."

Coach came right over and said, "What's wrong?"

"Coach," I said, "I want to jump farther than I think I can jump."

"How far?"

"Maybe 23–6, something like that."

"All right." So he went into the pit and he laid a handkerchief beside the figure. And when I went back to the runway, with my back to him, Smagacz kicked the handkerchief forward about a foot. I found out about that later.

We didn't have much time because they were yelling, "Sayers up! Sayers up!" But before I got set to jump he looked over the pit. Smagacz was always thinking of something, he had a very good mind. He said, "Gale, let's try something."

I said, "What?"

He had noticed that the runway slanted in relation to the jump pit. My jumps had all come off a straight run up to now. He said, "I think that maybe that dog-gone bend might be having some kind of psychological effect on you. Go over the side and count back your steps and let's see you hit the board."

He changed my angle of approach for the last jump. He had me move to the side of my earlier starting points, and I didn't like that idea too much. It's like a baseball player changing his stance with two strikes on him. But I knew I was going to do it his way. I had to do it his way.

"You ready now?" he asked me.

"I'll settle this," I said.

I knew it was beautiful when I took off. I hit that board perfectly, I got good height, I started kicking and springing forward, and I landed smack on the towel.

They measured the tape and one guy hollered, "Holy cow, 24 feet, 11 and ¾ inches."

Well, everybody ran up there, and this one fellow said, "Wait a minute, let's remeasure that."

So they remeasured it and that's what it was: 24 feet, 11¾ inches. That was nine inches better than the best high-school jump in the country that year. It was four and a half inches better than the Big Eight's winning broad jump that year. And it is still, I believe, the state high-school record in Nebraska.

I was glad to have won the broad jump because it helped us win the state championship, but after the meet, that was it. There was nothing angelical about it. I enjoy winning. I just don't show emotion winning. I just get a good feeling inside, a satisfied feeling.

But there was one moment in high school that I did almost let my emotions come through. That was in the annual Shrine High School All-Star football game, held in July 1961 at the University of Nebraska. For me, it was almost a grudge game.

I had had a big year in football. As a junior, I had scored sixty-eight points to lead the intercity. As a senior, I scored 108 points, breaking the intercity scoring record, and our team went undefeated. One of the reasons I enjoyed scoring so many touchdowns was that it kept me from going hungry in what was a difficult year at home.

There was a drive-in in Omaha that featured what they called a Pookie-Burger, which was a big double-decker hamburger. Every time you scored a touchdown they would give you a certificate for one Pookie-Burger. In three different games my senior year I scored three touchdowns. Each time I went down to the place and ate three of those huge double-decker things. Nothing to it. And after that they had another nickname for me—Pookie.

My last three Pookies probably tasted the best. They came in my last game for Central, after I had scored three against West Side, a game that was enjoyable in many ways.

For one thing, Coach Smagacz says the touchdown of mine he got the biggest kick from came in that game—because he had to wait for the movies to see it. In the second quarter they had fourth down and I was backing up the line and they went for it. They threw a little screen pass over to the right. Coach told a reporter (I have the story in my scrapbook): "I saw it was going to fall incomplete. I turned to the offensive team and ordered them into the game. They started laughing and shaking their heads, said I didn't need 'em. I turned to see that Sayers had got the ball out of the kid's hands and ran for the touchdown."

My last touchdown in that game, the one that gave me the city scoring record, was most fitting because it was a collaboration with my best friends. First I took a double reverse from Break, and then Charlie Gunn delivered the key block, letting me slip through for fifty yards and a score.

Scoring like that was fun, of course, but the football game I enjoyed playing in the most was one I didn't score in, against Creighton Prep. We were both unbeaten at the time and they were favored—all the writers had picked them—and it ended in a scoreless tie. I didn't do that much on offense. I carried the ball about twenty-five times and got only about eighty yards. But I had a really good day on defense. I was playing outside linebacker, and I made a lot of tackles. And we should have beat them. Gunn ran eighty yards for a touchdown, but they called it back. I threw an option pass to our quarterback. He was behind everyone and the ball was his, and he dropped it. So we could have won the game 14-0, but it wasn't meant for us.

It was a big year for Central. We took the city title in football, the state in track, in golf, in swimming. We took it in almost all sports. The thing I was very proud of too was that we had only about fifty black guys in the school out of maybe fifteen hundred. And we had seven black starters on the football team (Break made all-city that year, too), four on the basketball team, and all the sprinters were black.

Up to that time I had never thought much about being black. But I wasn't thinking much about anything in those days. And I had never encountered any racial discrimination, for the simple reason that I always stayed with my own people. I lived in the Toe, my whole life revolved around the Toe. I had very few white associations. At the end of my senior year I got my first recognition of what being a black man could mean.

The Omaha *World Herald* always picked the high-school Athlete of the Year in the state. And that year I had set the city scoring record in football, I had made the All-America high-school team, and the All-Midwest team (Butkus was on that team, too). Plus, I had won three gold medals in track in the state meet and set a state broad-jump record. And I wasn't picked as Athlete of the Year. The newspaper picked this kid from Broken Bow, Nebraska. His name was Kent McCloughan and he went on to become a really good defensive back for the Oakland Raiders. McCloughan was a running back for Broken Bow and he scored more points than I did that year, but they were a Class B school and we were Class A. He also won two gold medals in track in the state meet—he tied Bobby Williams in the 100 and he won the 220. And he got the big buildup. They called him the Custer County Comet.

He was a good athlete, I'm not questioning that. But I was from a larger city and I think I had the better record against tougher competition. And the only reason I could figure that he was named Athlete of the Year and I wasn't was that he was white and I was black.

I felt a little bad about the whole thing, and that was one reason why I looked forward to the annual Shrine game.

In that one they pick the best senior players in the state and divide them between North and South. And this kid McCloughan was running for the North and I was running for the South.

Well, we beat them 32–0. We killed them. Kent McCloughan didn't do much the first half. In the third period, playing defense, I caught McCloughan at the sidelines and pinned him and kind of slammed him to the ground. He pulled something on that play and stayed out the rest of the game.

I played the whole game—offense and middle line-backer on defense. I scored four touchdowns. I caught two touchdown passes of fifty-one and twenty-six yards. I ran forty-three yards and twenty-seven for the other two. They were good runs, too; I mean, I was really worked up. On the forty-three-yarder I slipped two tacklers, stepped out of the arms of two others, and coasted the last thirty yards. On the twenty-seven-yarder I ran around left end and was almost stopped three times but managed to shake loose, cut back against the grain, and make it in.

I carried the ball six times from scrimmage for ninety-five yards. And they voted me the game's outstanding player.

So that made me feel a lot better about not being named Nebraska high-school Athlete of the Year. That and having my brother, Win, come into the dressing room so happy for me and telling reporters, "I never saw anyone run like that." And having my mother and father there to see me play, even though they weren't living together at the time. And, most of all, having the girl I had just become engaged to watching me, and maybe understanding now why I liked to keep a little scrapbook.

9

Linda

Evening.

Linda, the wife, is sitting on the sofa in the living room with a newspaper at her side. She is wearing a green blouse and brown slacks. She has just fed everyone and now wants to reminisce.

Gale Lynne, the daughter, is kneeling on the green rug, in front of a chair. A picture book is open on the chair and she is looking through it, but also maybe listening to the conversation. She is not yet four, but she hears everything.

Gale, the husband, wearing a white T shirt and dark-gray slacks, is sitting back on a chair, his hands clasped behind his head, trying to remember how he and Linda ever got involved with each other.

LINDA: Didn't you fall in love with me?

GALE *(pausing, and then smiling at the directness of the question):* I don't know. I don't know. Really, now seriously, I was pushed. I was. I was pushed. I don't regret it, but I was pushed. I think one of the reasons was that you wanted to get away from your parents, because you were having a hard time at home.

LINDA: That's true. I really didn't enjoy my home life at the time. But my mother didn't want me to get married. And didn't think we would. She thought, Well, Gale won't want to get married, he's going to be a college boy and everything. . . .

GALE: She hates me.

LINDA: She does not! *(Now calmer)* But do you remember the time we were together and I asked you, "Would you ever consider marrying me?"

GALE: No.

LINDA: You do, too! I asked you then because I didn't think you were serious about me. It was the first time we were ever alone together. You were always with Break. We never went anywhere by ourselves. You and Break would always be off giggling somewhere and, I used to think, talking about me. So the first time we were ever alone together I asked you if you would marry me.

GALE *(in disbelief):* And what did I say, Linda?

LINDA: You said no, you wouldn't marry anybody.

GALE: I didn't plan on getting married. I was pushed into it.

LINDA *(voice rising):* I never brought up the subject again—you did.

GALE: Oh, no!

LINDA: The only time you asked me. I remember. When Tech won the state basketball tournament. I was supposed to be going down there. I skipped school and you skipped school and we stayed over at your house all day long.

GALE *(frowning):* And I asked you that?

LINDA: That one time you said, "Are you serious about getting married?" I said, "I guess so," and you gave me an engagement ring.

GALE *(in a softer tone):* Really, I don't regret it.

LINDA: If I had the choice of marrying you at nineteen, I'd probably do it over again.

GALE *(laughing):* I doubt it.

LINDA: I think we were drawn to each other because we both wanted to get away from our home life. I was seeking something that wasn't in my home. You were, too.

GALE: That could be it, Linda.

LINDA: Really, who knows what love is at eighteen, nineteen? I think that's what it was, because we really were so dependent on each other. With each other we had something. It was like . . . People would ask me, Well, why did you want to get married? And I would say, Well, why not? What else is there for me to do? I'm not really losing anything. I'll never be worse off than I am. I'll finish four years of school and be a schoolteacher in Omaha the rest of my life. I really didn't see any great things I could have done with my life without you. I mean, you had talked about the possibility of becoming a professional football player. I didn't think you were that good—because, at that time, I had never seen you play football.

GALE (biting off the words): You missed something, sister.

Linda hates to admit it, but she called me up first. That's how I met her. She was going with a fellow on the track team, and they weren't getting along. And I was going with another girl, too.

Linda actually was my second girl friend. My brother's wife's sister, Joan Adams, was my first. I was a senior in high school at the time and I didn't think about girls—nothing. Just sports and music. I met Joan through Win and I went with her during the football season of my senior year. It ended after the football season.

I had met Linda once before she called me and I had seen her several times, but it was just Hello, how are you doing, and looking off somewhere else. That was it. One night I wanted to take Joan to a basketball game, but her mother wouldn't let her go. So Break said, "Why don't you take Linda?" So I took her.

She was on crutches at the time. She had gotten out of a car in the middle of the street and another car came along and hit the car door and smashed against Linda's leg. Her leg was broken in three places and she was in a cast from her toe to the top of her thigh. She was pretty conspicuous, and, naturally, one of Joan's friends saw me at the basketball game with Linda and told Joan and that was it. Finished. It was silly. We shouldn't have broken up over it, but we did. Funny thing, I liked Joan very much. She's married now, married to a fellow I know, and they live in Omaha. So I took Linda just because Joan couldn't go. And we started dating. She was still going with a fellow on the track team, but they were on the verge of breaking up.

My brother-in-law had a record shop and I worked for him after school and Saturdays. That's when I first met Gale. He came in there and I saw him around a couple of times. I was a sports fan, and I think I dated Frank because he played basketball and track and I used to love track at the time. I went to Tech, which was pretty close in distance to Central but had two different types of people. Like Gale's high school was predominantly Jewish and middle-class white and my high school was predominantly Negro and lower-class white. I remember when Tech and Central met in track. I didn't think Gale was that great. I used to think his brother was like the great one in the family. I used to go to see Win run. Besides, Gale never noticed me that much. He was like aloof, just floating off somewhere. He really never noticed anything.

One day I was reading about Gale in the newspapers and I just called him on the phone. Our first date we went over to a friend's house, Dennis Rose. I thought Gale was going to take me out somewhere. He took me to his buddy's house. He had to carry me in—I had a ten-pound cast on my leg and was wearing a really heavy fur coat. He carried me across the hall. Dennis and Gale played ping-pong all night. And the next time we went to the basketball game.

Linda's former boy friend wasn't too happy about my taking her out. His name was Frank Jones. He was about six-three, but slender. I was sitting on Linda's porch one day. Right down the street from her house is a recreation center in a grade school. Frank was playing basketball at the center and he came down the street and saw me, and he wanted to start a fight right then. But I wouldn't fight. Why should I fight? Over what? Linda really wasn't my girl.

About a week later Frank was on the telephone.

"Gale," he said, "are you supposed to be going with Linda?"

I said, "No, I'm still going with Joan Adams." Well, I wasn't going with Joan any more, but I wasn't serious about Linda either, and Frank was really serious about her. Linda refused to see me until I broke up with Joan. That took about two weeks.

Then we started going out a little more and getting a little more serious. I would see her at the record shop and take her home after work and take her to school every morning. I had a little '49 Chevy then. I had worked the summer before polishing cars with my father. He taught me how to run the buffer. I'd get $15 a car and do maybe three a night. So I bought this little car, and we had a good time in it—until I wrecked it.

One time I was driving along and I was thinking about a girl (it wasn't Linda). I was daydreaming and I ran right into a truck. Break came by and saw the fenders all torn up. Then I got it fixed and I let my brother borrow it. He was going with this girl, and he let her drive it and she wrecked it. She tore the radiator out of the car. I threw it away then.

But it got us around that late winter of 1961 when Linda was still on crutches. We went to church together in the car, too. It was a little house church, the Church of Christ, with maybe twenty people in the congregation. The music was good, the singing was good. And one Sunday Frank and his friends drove by in the car and told us what they were going to do to us. So I got mad.

When I got out of the church I called Break and we went and got Linda's brother-in-law. His name is Albert Allen and he owns a night club in town now. His nickname was Little Caesar. He was wild in those days. And we went up to Frank Jones' house and we had a showdown.

But I didn't fight Jones. I fought his partner, because his partner did all the shouting and wanted to do all the whipping.

I stepped up and said, "I don't like the idea of this. I don't like the idea of your calling my girl those names.

If I ever hear that again, me and you are going to do something about it. I'm gonna get to your chest."

"Well," the guy said, "why don't you get to my chest now. No use to getting to my chest later. Why don't you do it now, because I don't think you can do it."

We went at it pretty good, with Little Caesar on one side and Break on the other, to keep the peace. I don't think I'd fought since I was six months old, but I always had quick hands and I punched him out. And that was the end of it. Frank never did bother us again and we never bore a grudge against each other.

When we started dating I just couldn't get used to Gale. Maybe that was the attraction, because he was the strangest person I had ever met. He never talked to me. He would call me up every evening. He would say, What are you doing? Well, I'm coming over. He would get in his car and drive over, stay two minutes, and leave.

I couldn't figure him out. I really couldn't. That's why I used to ask him things all the time, because I didn't think he had any kind of intentions for me at all. He didn't because he was young, but I couldn't figure out how he thought about anything. Sometimes I still can't figure out how he feels about things.

I know I liked Linda, but I didn't think I wanted to be tied down, like some teen-agers. We started dating in January. Around March I went off to Notre Dame to look at the campus, and I discovered I missed her. That's when we started getting serious.

Another indication: Break would come over and say, "Let's do something," and I'd say, "No, man, I got to do this with Linda."

In May we decided to get engaged. And the reaction of both our families was something else.

I remember it was a scorching hot day when we talked to my mother. It was right before she went away and she was lying in bed.

"I got something to tell you," I said.

I couldn't bring it out. I was hemming and hawing. Finally, she said, "What, is she pregnant?"

"Oh, God," Linda said.

I said, "No, she's not pregnant. We just want to get married."

She seemed relieved. "Oh, is that all?" Just like that. She kind of sighed. "I don't care. If that's what you want to do, go ahead."

As for Linda's mother, she stopped speaking to Linda. She said they weren't going to stop her but they wouldn't speak to her. And they disowned me. They felt it was the most ridiculous thing Linda could ever do, because I didn't have anything to offer her. The only one who didn't disown me was her oldest sister, Pat. She had gotten married when she was sixteen. But the rest of them, they hated my guts. They were mean to Linda, too. They didn't speak to her for almost a year.

It's true that my mother resented our marriage at the very beginning. Who wants her nineteen-year-old daughter to get married? Especially to somebody who doesn't have anything, a boy who has never said two words to her when he came to the house? I could understand it.

My mother was thirty-eight when I was born, and because of that we had no kind of communication. She was completely out of touch as to how to reach me.

My mother was one of eleven children and she came from Oklahoma City. She had a hard life because her mother died when she was young and left four children under her for my mother to care for.

My father came from Jackson, Mississippi. He got to the third grade and that was all his schooling. But he was the kind of man who didn't need schooling. He could expound on every subject in the world. He was in World War I and he said it was one of the most wonderful things that ever happened to him because he was able to get to Europe. All he talked about was how life was really good in France and Italy.

He used to read the encyclopedia and the newspaper from front to back. He knew everything that was going on. Like every day he would lecture to us. I'd say, Oh, God, who wants to hear all this baloney? I didn't appreciate him when he was living.

He was thirty-one when he married Mom. She was twenty. And he was forty-nine when I was born. Father said he enjoyed the first years of married life because they didn't have any children. The children started coming during the Depression, and he had a hard life.

He worked as a janitor. There were times when he held four different jobs. Like he would leave at four o'clock in the morning, work until twelve, come home till three, and go out and work till nine. He worked all the time. We were poor, but we were never as bad off as Gale's family. My father gambled when he was young, he would throw away money. But by the time I came along all that was past him.

I was the last of five children. I had two sisters and two brothers, and they were all extremely smart. The sister next to me—we're twenty-one months apart—is the Einstein of the family. She got a degree in sociology, was married several years ago, and went on to graduate school on a $7000 fellowship.

She was always studying and I was always playing. I was kind of rebellious in my early years. I resented the fact that my teachers used to compare me unfavorably to my sisters. I wanted to go out and do things and have fun.

My father died when I was a freshman in high school, and that changed everything for me. After his death, I began to realize what a waste this was, and from then on I studied hard and I got straight A's through high school. I could have had a scholarship to college. My mother and sisters thought it was ridiculous to give all this up. They couldn't understand why I wanted to get married and have a bunch of babies. My family was always that way, really deeply concerned about what happened to me, that I become a nice person. Because that was my mother's life. Because she never had any outside interests—just being married and being a mother

*and maintaining a home. When you come from a family
like that you really have a lot of pressure on you.*

*But I really felt a lot for Gale, and I just didn't want
to give him up.*

I think the real reason we got together was out of
mutual need. Linda is the kind of person who likes to
be needed, to be depended on. She was the youngest
child in her family and there was never anybody that
ever needed her. She wasn't important to anyone. She
became important to me. All my life up to then I had
shut out things—I was living only for the present. I
don't think I ever thought seriously of anything. Whatever came, came. Fine. That was it.

When I got close with Linda my thinking began to
change. I probably wouldn't have gone to college if it
hadn't been for Linda. Or passed enough subjects to
have been able to go. Almost from the beginning she
gave a sense of purpose to my life.

*I think one of the things that made me fall in love
with Gale was his dependency on me. He just like depended on me totally. Now that he has so many diversi-
fied activities he doesn't depend on me that much. But
he still depends on my judgment and other things quite
a bit, and that makes for a good marriage.*

*I'm the kind of person who likes to have people
depend on me. It gives me a reason for being. I don't
want to be domineering, but I do enjoy the feeling that
he depends on me, somewhat at least, because what else
is a woman's life?*

About that time we had a toy shepherd, name of
Penny. We always had dogs when we were growing up,
but this was the longest we had ever kept a dog. She
was the smartest, nicest dog we ever had.

That summer after my senior year Penny developed
some kind of liver trouble. The dog was really in pain
and we took her to the vet and he said he couldn't do
anything for her.

It was a Sunday, at a time when my mother was gone from our house. The pain was so severe that Penny couldn't walk. All she could do was lie down and whine. It was agony to watch her and be around her. We couldn't get hold of the Humane Society to come out and pick her up and put her away, and she was going through misery. So my brother and I decided that the best thing for her was for us to put her out of her misery. We talked about it and decided she had to be killed.

It must have been about three in the morning when we decided this. Penny was whining and we knew she was suffering so much.

"I'm going to get a knife," I told Win.

He said, "I'll hold her still and you cut her throat real quick."

At the last moment, Win couldn't do it, he chickened out. So I did it myself. I kept stabbing her and stabbing her, and finally, just before she died, she wagged her tail—kind of like she was relieved to be out of all this pain. It was something that really hurt me, I tell you.

We wrapped her up, took her out to the car, found a nice place, and buried her. And I must have cried for three or four hours after that.

The next morning I went over to Linda's and told her about it and she started crying, too. We got through it together.

Just before I left for college I bought her an engagement ring—one of those two-for-$49 jobs. And we decided we would be married the June following my freshman year.

10

I Say Yes to Seventeen Colleges

One day in my senior year we were going to have a big history test—you know, 150 questions, multiple choice, A, B, C, D. Since I never took books home, I was in a little trouble. But I knew this fellow sitting in back of me and he was very smart. I said, "Look, I haven't studied a lick. So you can do me a favor. Kick my foot once if it's A, if it's B you kick twice, and all the way down the line." I got the kick on all 150 questions. I passed the test. I tell you, I don't know a thing about that subject.

Sports was the only thing that mattered in my high-school days. Even after football practice, we'd go down to Kuntz Park and play tackle. Because we enjoyed football so much. That was the thing to do, go play football in the park and have all the girls come around and look. Like every Christmas and Thanksgiving we had the Turkey Bowl, the Gold Dust Bowl. Everybody knew there was going to be a pickup game on Thanksgiving Day and Christmas. They still have the Turkey Bowl in the Toe, and it's real fun to watch.

It's funny that my brother Roger and I are so different. Studying never bothered him a whole lot. In fact, he kind of enjoyed studying. It helped, I think, that the kids he ran around with were the academic types. They were athletes but they studied, too, and it kind of rubbed off. Me, I ran with Break, who was no student, and Gunn, who could have been a student but had other ideas. That was my crowd. And I didn't concentrate or use whatever ability I had to try and make good marks.

Break and I did everything together. We stole pop together, we worked from time to time at different jobs together, we jocked around, dragged around, and stood in corners, as Linda said, giggling together. Then, when we got out among people, we were always at a loss for words.

We used to go to the drags all the time in Lincoln, which is about fifty miles from Omaha. That '49 Chevy was souped up a little; they even put the shifting power on the left side for me because I'm left-handed. Break claims I almost killed him ten or twelve times on the way down there. I was a reckless driver in those days and I still am a little loose on the road. But Break gained more confidence in me as we went along. "Gale," he said not long ago, "I never saw anybody with more perfect timing. You could drive right now in the Indianapolis 500, no doubt about it."

So it was sports and music and dragging and hanging around—and all at the expense of school. I was pretty bad in high school. I talked, I did everything wrong, I got in trouble in school. In my senior year my counselor wrote my mother a letter that if I didn't pass this English course I wouldn't graduate. The parents got on my back about that. But I didn't worry about it—and I passed. That's the way I was. Nothing ever worried me.

The only time I became aware of studying was after I met Linda. She used to study all the time, at least four hours a day. "What are you studying for?" I asked her.

She said, "I might want to go to college. Don't you?"

I said, "I haven't thought about it." And I hadn't. Nobody had ever said, Why don't you try to learn more for college? Here I was at one of the finest academic high schools in the country. I think, out of four hundred in my class, maybe half got some sort of academic scholarship. And I still got out of that school without learning anything. And I think that's the real tragedy of being a black athlete and coming out of the Toe. You're not prepared for college. When I finally did get to college, it was like someone had picked me up and sat me down in the midst of a foreign country where no one could speak my language.

So I figured I would join the Army or something. I wanted to play football, but college didn't appeal to me. That's why I waited until the last minute before deciding. And, finally, it was Linda who talked me into it. I had decided I wasn't going to college. I had decided I was going to be a bachelor. When I met her, things changed.

At the end of my junior year I got my first letter from a college. It was from Iowa State. After my senior year of football I got over a hundred offers. I visited seven colleges—Iowa State, Northwestern, Notre Dame, Minnesota, Iowa, Nebraska, Kansas—and Break went along on most of the trips. And I ended up signing seventeen letters of intent, saying that, yes, I would enroll at such and such college. We weren't thinking of the college, just of taking the trip. We were young and we just signed and we went to these colleges and we had a helluva time.

We went down to Iowa State first. I felt an obligation to them because they were the first ones to contact me. Clay Stapleton, the head coach at the time, had written me. I liked the school very much and so did Break. They ran the single wing, and Break felt there was room for the small man. I liked what I saw of the campus, and I think we told them we would enroll there. We must have, because there was a letter printed in the Omaha paper shortly after our visit. It read:

"Well, Omaha's done it again. Two more fine athletes have enrolled at Iowa state right under the nose of one of the largest N clubs of Nebraska. . . . To the athletes I have this to say—if you choose to play to a crowd of about 8000 to 12,000 strangers instead of 30,000 friends and neighbors, and defeat Drake instead of the United States Military Academy, that's your business and I bid you cheer loud and long. . . ."

That was but a sample of the letters I would get personally after I made my final decision. But that one was kind of premature. Because Iowa was actually my number-one choice at the time.

One Omaha fellow, Virgil Williams, was at Iowa (I broke his high-school intercity scoring record), and they also had Willie Fleming and Bob Jeter and Randy Duncan at quarterback. They had a wide-open brand of football, with a lot of razzle-dazzle—the kind of stuff we ran in high school. And that's where I wanted to go.

Then I went up for a weekend and became dis-illusioned. The weekend I was there Henry Carr was up there, too. He was a hotshot sprinter and running back (he won a gold medal in the 220 in the 1964 Olympics, then played in the NFL for a few years), and head coach Jerry Burns stayed with him those whole two days. I was with Virgil and I never got to see Jerry Burns once. I said, To hell with it. If they're that much interested in Henry Carr, they can have Henry Carr. Henry wound up at Arizona State.

The most fun Break and I had was the trip to Notre Dame. It was an adventure from the start.

We flew up there. I had just flown for the first time when I visited Northwestern, but Break had never flown before in his life. So he was really nervous. I was too, but I tried to act like a veteran. "Don't worry, Break," I said. "Ain't nothin' to it, ain't nothin' to it." Like I knew all about it, like I had been flying for twenty years.

Our first stop was Cedar Rapids, Iowa. It was snow-ing and the plane was coming in funny, and we were both scared to death. The pilot acted like he had control all the time. But he didn't. He missed the runway and slid off into the rough for maybe 150 feet. Break said he had to go to the bathroom. I sat there like a mummy. Frozen.

Somehow they got the plane turned around and we took off ten minutes later, and in another hour and a half we were in Chicago. Someone picked us up at the airport and drove us to South Bend.

I got to meet the coach, Joe Kuharich, and Jim Snowden, who went on to play for the Washington Red-skins, took me around. I remember Break and I went to a Notre Dame basketball game. I don't know what Break did—he threw something out onto the court, popcorn or something. And they gave Notre Dame a technical foul.

We didn't have any dates or anything and had to hustle back to the dorm because they locked all the doors at ten P.M. And that's when the fun started. Break and I brought back some crackers and put them in all the guys' beds.

They came back at night, took showers, and jumped into bed, into all the crackers and stuff. You could hear the crackling sound all over the dormitory.

A little later that night we started running up and down the hall, knocking on everybody's door and then scampering back into our room. They had put us next to this kid who was studying to be a priest. I was running down the hall in my shorts and Break was in the room, and when I rushed back to the room the door was locked. He had locked me out and he started beating on the wall where the Catholic priest was living. So here I was in the middle of the hall with my shorts on, and out comes the student priest. I hid behind a little corner and the priest didn't see me. When he went in, I went to our door.

"Hey, Break, hey, Break," I hollered, banging on the door. "Let me in, come on, man, let me in."

He said, "I'm not going to let you in."

And he opened his window and started hollering out of it, "Help! Help!" Really loud. All this noise at twelve o'clock at night, when you were supposed to be in your room with lights out.

There was an open transom over our door. The only thing I could do was try to climb through the transom. But Break heard me and put this little rod up where it locked the transom and mashed my hands. I jumped down and Break started hollering some more out the window. He finally let me in, and we wrestled for an hour because I was so mad he had kept me out. We had so much fun.

But I decided against Notre Dame because it was too far from home.

That's one of the reasons I thought I ought to go to Nebraska. It was only sixty miles from Omaha and I could go back easily to see Linda. Of course, I could have gone to Omaha University. It's just a local school, no dormitories, so you stay at home. But they decided to get in the bidding war, too. They called me up one day and said, "Gale, you know we'd like to have you stay in Omaha and you're known here and so forth. It would be a great help to Omaha University."

Then came their offer.

"We'll give you bus fare back and forth to school, and lunch money."

Well, my brother did go there and he did very well. In 1962 he ran against the Russians and was the only man to qualify for three events—the 100, 220, and 880 relays. And Omaha won the small-college nationals and he beat Bob Hayes that year. So he did get the recognition, but it would have been nicer for him to have gone to a bigger college. He would have gotten more recognition. My younger brother, Ronnie, went to Omaha, too, and got enough recognition to be drafted number two by the San Diego Chargers in 1969.

The University of Nebraska came after me a little stronger than Omaha. Right after the football season my senior year, an alumnus gave me a job every Saturday, washing a couple of cars for $25. Sometimes I didn't do a damn thing and they still gave me the $25, just for spending money. Then an alumnus came around and bought me a stereo and clothes and gave me the use of a car. When I drove to Kansas in the summer of 1961 to look over the campus, I drove there in the Nebraska Ford.

Nebraska really kept the pressure on. They got to my mother and father. They promised my dad the moon if I went to Nebraska. And, naturally, my folks thought I ought to go to Nebraska; they were under almost as much pressure as I was. The Nebraska recruiters weren't fooling around. They knew how poor we were, they were trying to make an impression, appeal to my emotions, and maybe make me feel obligated to go to Nebraska.

The whole episode with Nebraska almost cost me $10,000. My rookie year with the Chicago Bears I wanted to average my income back to 1961. And there was a $200 question mark about 1961. If I didn't come up with that $200, I would have to pay $10,000 more income tax. The question was, Had I made enough money in 1961 to buy my own clothes? I wrote a letter to this fellow who had bought my clothes for me. I

said, "Look, can you send a letter to the Internal
Revenue Service that you helped buy me the clothes?
That will save me $10,000." He wrote back and said
he wouldn't. So one of my advisers wrote him back and
said, "If you don't do this we'll have to take you to
court and tell them that Nebraska violated Big Eight
rules. Finally, the fellow said, O.K., you win, and he
took care of it with the Internal Revenue Service, saving
me $10,000.

Break and I visited Nebraska and we weren't too impressed. We felt we could have been treated a little better.

We went down there wearing our letter sweaters.
They were probably the best letter sweaters ever to
come out of the state of Nebraska. We had stars on the
sweaters for different achievements—for making All-
State in football, gold medals in track, etc. The stars
and stripes covered our sweaters. We wore the sweaters
everywhere we went, but we found out we weren't supposed to wear them on the Nebraska campus. They
wanted all recruiting prospects to look alike and act
alike. They didn't want to be influenced by any high
school's reputation. So we walked down there, and a
guy by the name of Willie Ross—he was one of
Nebraska's finest running backs—took offense. He
started hollering at us and he wanted to jump us. Break
and I wanted him to try, too. Another great Nebraska
back, Thunder Thornton, was keeping Ross off us, and
we hollered, "Let him go, we'll get him." Ross was big
and tough-looking, but, between the two of us, we
figured we could get him. Break told me, "You tackle
him low and I'll hit him high." Nothing came of it, but
that left a bad taste in our mouths.

That weekend they put us in this dormitory basement
where the heating pipes run along the ceiling. One minute it was real hot, the next minute it was freezing. And
the pipes were banging all night. Break told me, "I
wouldn't come down to this college if they gave us a
million dollars, man. They came down to recruit us and
they put us in a room like that." What made us so mad
was that there were three or four high-school kids in from

Oklahoma and they all had nice rooms upstairs. "That's it for me," Break said. "I'm ready to go back home now."

But we stayed for a dance at the student union. There were only two black girls there. We found out there were forty-four black athletes at Nebraska and two black girls.

It got into the newspapers that we were unhappy about the way we had been treated, and Bill Jennings, the head football coach, came to Omaha and apologized and took us out for a steak dinner. I'll never forget that dinner. He took us to a fancy restaurant in town. I wasn't much on social graces in those days. I wasn't sure how to cut the steak, and as I was cutting away the steak flew off the plate and onto the floor. But Jennings overlooked that one.

He was an excellent coach and a fine person, and I'm sure he lost his job because he failed to recruit me. He had recruited a tremendous team—Mick Tinglehoff, Bob Brown, Dennis Claridge, fellows like that—and all he needed was one more year. That's all he wanted, because he knew these fellows would develop. But they wouldn't give it to him. Nebraska had finished last in the Big Eight in 1960. Bob Devaney came in and Nebraska won the championship two of the next three years, with Jennings' team. The ironic thing about it was that shortly after, Jack Mitchell, the head coach at Kansas, hired Jennings to be his backfield coach—and, as it turned out, my backfield coach.

Mitchell was a different cat than Jennings. Where Jennings was soft-spoken, quiet, a nice man, Mitchell always had lots of bull going for him. He was a dynamic personality, and I liked him from the first.

Right after the outdoor track season, I announced that I was going to the University of Nebraska (that's when I got the car to drive around). But I still wasn't sure, and Mitchell wasn't about to give up.

First he sent Kansas freshman-football coach, Tom Triplett, to see me, and he was very persuasive; he was Kansas's top recruiter. Then Break and I drove to Kansas and I liked the campus right off. Most people think Kansas is flat, but the school's up on a hill and the town of Lawrence kind of surrounds the school. It's a beautiful campus with a lake in the middle and an eighteen-thousand-seat fieldhouse—the house that Wilt Chamberlain built.

When Break and I got to Lawrence, Mitchell introduced us to some of the athletes there: Bill Bridges, who now plays for the Atlanta Hawks in the National Basketball Association; Curtis McClinton, who, along with Bert Coan, was the team's star halfback. McClinton took me around and told me how much he enjoyed the school. He pointed out too that it was a good school for the black athlete. There were two Negro fraternities and two Negro sororities.

Then Mitchell took Break and me to Kansas City to meet some big people. That was quite a trip. Mitchell loved to chew tobacco. In fact, all the Kansas coaches loved to chew tobacco. Break and I were in the back seat of this car and Mitchell was in the front seat, driving and talking. His window was down and my window was down. And he spat his tobacco juice out the window and it caught me right in the eye. It like to blinded me.

"Coach," I said, "you just lost yourself a halfback."

But he hadn't. The more I thought about it, the more I leaned to Kansas. I began to feel I'd get more recognition from the pros at Kansas than Nebraska, since Kansas was on top and Nebraska was on the bottom. I didn't know then that the pros looked at every college from Pee Wee State down. I had it in mind that I was going to play pro football; that's what I was going to college for. So why not go with the best?

The only thing that bothered me was that it was 180 miles from home. I visited Kansas once more with Linda. In fact, a rich alumnus flew us up in a private plane. And that trip settled it. Mitchell turned it on. He said, "We've got a great institution here. We've got a winning football team and we got some players coming back who'll help us keep winning. But we're going to need a halfback badly because McClinton's going, Coan's going, and you can step right in." Which I could, because they had nothing as far as running backs. So I chose Kansas.

Well, that kind of irritated the local folks. Here it was just a couple of weeks before the fall school season, and I had switched to Kansas. It seemed like I got thousands of phone calls wondering why I chose Kansas. I got a lot of mail, too, some of it of the hate variety. I got letters all the way through school. A lot of the people thought I was out to get as much as I could. But some of the letter writers also attacked Nebraska for not opening the school more to Negroes.

The local writers were bugged, too. I read one item where a Nebraska underground alumni group had allegedly arranged for me to go to Iowa if I didn't go to Nebraska. This one fellow was quoted as saying, "That way, if we couldn't have him, at least he wouldn't be playing against us."

Once, in the fall of my freshman year, an Omaha sportswriter wrote: "Lack of social life for Negroes in Nebraska was one of the reasons cited by Gale Sayers in his decision to enroll at Kansas. Progress report: Gale had a chick on each arm when he showed up for the Iowa State–Kansas game Saturday."

I was so mad I wrote a long letter back and said the "chick" on my left arm was the girl I was going to marry and the "chick" on my right arm was her girl friend. And they promptly put an apology in the paper.

So Kansas it was, and the only regret I had about my choice was that it broke up the old gang from the Toe. Break didn't have the grades to get into Kansas. He went a year to Lutheran Junior College in Wahoo, Nebraska, and got married and then quit. Ardell Gunn went there too and dropped out after a year.

Me? I was just dumb enough to think I could make it in college.

11

A Place That Was Not Home

"What are you doing, Gale?"

I didn't even bother to look up at my roommate, Mike Shinn. By the tone of his voice, I knew he really was saying, What in the hell is he up to now? So I didn't answer.

"What are you doing, Gale?"

"Nothing, man, nothing."

I was sitting at my desk in our dorm room, looking over one of the old KU football programs, looking up all the Big Eight rushing records—most yards gained, most touchdowns, etc. And I cut them out of the program, pasted them on a piece of paper, and wrote under them, before pinning them to the wall: THESE MUST GO.

Shinn took a look and couldn't believe it. Some of the other guys came in, saw what I was doing, and said, "What's this stuff?"

I admit I was kind of embarrassed.

"Ah, you know . . ." I just let it hang that way.

My first year at Kansas I was a lost soul. It seems the only way I could relate to people was by pointing to my ability as an athlete. Like when they first put Shinn and me in together, I would tell him, "I broad jumped 24–10, and I ran the hundred in 9.7, and I scored this many touchdowns." I was compulsive about it because I didn't know what else to talk about and I was down on myself as a person. As a human being, I felt inferior.

Shinn would hear all this bragging—which wasn't really bragging at all—and I'm sure he said to himself, This guy's lying. So the next time I went home I came back to school with my scrapbook, which, I guess, had replaced thumb-sucking as the crutch in my life.

I was pretty damn hard to live with in those days. I don't know how Mike stood it, though he only had to get through the first semester with me. After that he and I joined a fraternity, Kappa Alpha Psi, and he went to live in the fraternity house. But that semester probably seemed like a hundred years to Mike.

In the first place, I was always an early riser. I'd go to bed about ten, ten-thirty at night and I'd get up about six-thirty. Every morning I'd get up at six-thirty, turn on the record player, put on the rock-'n-roll records and stand at the mirror and apply Noxzema to my face. Shinn, trying to sleep, would look over at me, like with one eye open, shake his head, and try to go back to sleep. But he couldn't because the music was too high and the sight of me at the mirror applying Noxzema was too much. Every morning I'd be at the mirror, with Little Richard or somebody in the background, applying the Noxzema. Linda said it was good for the complexion.

And I'd be the first one over to the training table for breakfast, just as I am still the first one to breakfast when we're in training camp at Rensselaer. Just as I try to be the first one everywhere—the first one out on the field before practice and before a game, the first one out of the locker room after a game, the first one on the plane and the first one off the plane. Tommy Dare always says, "Never walk down the street with Sayers because you don't know if you're with him or going the other way. You might be going east and he will be going west. He just drags you along."

There's this tension within me that I can't explain; maybe it's an alarm clock. And it's always ringing: *never be late.* I can't remember any place I've been late. If we're supposed to be at a party at nine—which means it really begins to get going at eleven—I'm there at eighty-thirty. And ready to go home at eleven.

I've always been that way. When I was playing midget-league football, I was always the first one on the field. And when the coach said, "It's time to go," I was always the first one to leave. In high school in the locker room after the game, Break would be at the mirror combing his hair and I'd say, "Break, you better comb your hair, man, if you want to leave with me because I'm getting ready to go. I'm gonna start the car. As soon as it's warm, I'm gone." Break had to move a little faster when we were together.

A lot of people think Linda and I are a sweet little couple when they see us holding hands, walking to the car after a Bears' game. But what I'm saying is, "Come on, I'm going to leave you, c'mon, c'mon, hurry up, let's get out of here."

And maybe I should have called this book *I Am First,* because that's the story of my life, too. I don't know why, but all my life I've had to be the first one everywhere. I think that probably helps explain why I was so taken with the saying *I Am Third* when I first saw it in Bill Easton's office, why it never left my head. That, it seemed to me, was the humble way of life I should be striving for, instead of this arrogant need to be first all the time. What a wonderful thing to live up to—*I Am Third.*

My first semester at Kansas I was *always* in a hurry. Like I would be going home almost every weekend. And while everybody else would cut out on Friday, I would cut out on Thursday. Thursday afternoon I was gone. And when we had Thanksgiving and Christmas vacations coming up, I'd pack all my traveling clothes *two weeks* before going home. And I'd wear one pair of black pants for the whole two weeks. Because I had made my plans and I wanted to be ready to move.

I don't know how Mike Shinn stood it that first semester—he kept calling me some kind of a nut—but he did, and we became close friends. He was my closest friend in college, and today Mike Shinn is still one of my closest friends.

I don't know how they came to put us together, but it was like rooming Albert Einstein with Donald Duck. Shinn came from Topeka, Kansas, from a middle-class family. His father worked for the railroad and two of his older brothers had already gone to college. Mike was extremely intelligent, and he talked well. He was also a helluva football player. He stood six-five, weighed 235, and played tight end in college. He was drafted high by the Green Bay Packers, but he had had an operation on his knee and decided to give it up. He got a fifth year of college free and went into aeronautical engineering. He is doing very well now, working for General Electric in Cleveland, Ohio.

All my close friends, the people I like to associate with, seem to have the same characteristics. They may be opposite to me in personality—Mike is as much of an extrovert as Breakfield—but they all have the drive that I admire in people. It may be that I feel a guy is selling himself cheap if he doesn't have that drive. I think it's because I demand so much excellence of myself that I want my friends to be the same way. I can't stand being around people who try to sell themselves short.

When Mike decided not to play pro football, I was angry. "He has the talent," I said to Linda, "why wouldn't he want to play?" Mike knew I would be disappointed at his decision and he wrote me a letter of explanation. I admit I couldn't understand it at first. I read the letter and said, "Oh, the guy's crazy." But the more I thought about it, the more I understood that he was doing the right thing.

And Mike was one of the guys who saved my life in college.

It wasn't that he could help me with the classwork, because he was taking different courses. But he helped keep my morale up by just being around, being available, being a buddy. Otherwise, I'd really have been lost.

As soon as I got out of high school all that academic jazz slipped from my mind. I didn't think about books or anything. I just dropped everything. Then—boom!—there I was at Kansas, in the midst of a college orientation week, taking all those tests, getting books, and so forth. I was by myself, away from home for the first time in my life. I couldn't handle it.

Here I was, a shy fellow, a shy black boy from the ghetto, thrust into a completely different atmosphere, a strange new world. Kansas had fifteen thousand students, and people came from all over the world to go to the school. You had rich, bright kids who knew exactly how to fit into the situation. You had athletes, like Shinn, who were more sophisticated than I was, probably more study-conscious than I was. Most of the fellows had done very well in high school and studied more. And I was thrown into a situation which I didn't know anything about. I was a poor kid, up from the Toe, unaware of what I was getting into. And I just couldn't fit in. I didn't think I belonged there.

Part of the trouble, I suppose, was that I was going home all the time, visiting Linda. Every time I had to go back to Kansas I'd start crying. I cried because I hated the thought of going back to a strange place, a place that was not home.

Another problem was that I had a lot of trouble expressing myself verbally, I was terrible in English. I had what a friend called "a lazy tongue." The language of the ghetto doesn't translate easily in a university. And it was the same way in writing. I couldn't set down what I really wanted to say, so the writing of quizzes and term papers was almost a lost cause.

Even cheating didn't work for me. I tried it, I cheated a little bit that freshman year, but I never was very good at it.

In college you take your tests in blue books. We were going to have a final in American government and this instructor gave the same test for the first section as the second section that I was in. I knew a girl in the first section and she gave me her test. So I bought a blue book and, using the girl's test, wrote out the whole test in the blue book. Then I went in and took the test—and it was the exact same test. When the instructor went out of the room I simply switched blue books, I put the blank one in my pocket.

I figured, Oh, boy, I got an A in the course. I was about the twentieth one to hand in my blue book, then I went back to my seat to collect my books. As I started to leave the room I looked up at the desk—and *I* turned blue. My blue book was the wrong color blue.

I couldn't believe it. I never knew they made two different color blue books. The instructor had bought his blue book at the same bookstore as I had bought mine, but mine was a light blue, very much a lighter blue than all the others. The instructor got a little mad. He said I was cheating, which I was, and he flunked me.

Linda says I majored in cheating at Kansas, and I did keep trying that first year. I once went into a test with blue ink writing all over my pants, blue ink up and down both legs. But when it came time to use it, I couldn't read the damn writing.

There was another football player who taught me how to cheat, too. He would sit in the back of the room with his book on the floor and his toes moving pages. He had the most educated toes I have ever seen. He was unreal. Another thing he did, he'd get two pencils, cut them to about an inch and a half, and wrap a long piece of paper with the test answers into the two pencils. And he made a scroll out of them. He'd just put this pencil in his hand with the scroll, roll it, roll it with his thumb. It was beautiful, nothing like it. I used it once in a while, but my thumb wasn't as educated as his.

Out of frustration over this, my inability to handle the schoolwork, I did a lot of fooling around. Mike Shinn likes to say that the only reason we stayed in school is that we were lousy poker players.

At the end of the first semester there were big gambling games going on in the dorms—poker, craps, blackjack. We got in the poker games. And it turned out the winners were the losers. The games went on twenty-four hours a day, right during finals week. Mike and I ran out of money right away, so we had to go back and study. A lot of the guys who were playing in that game, and winning, later flunked out of school. They kept winning, and kept playing. We played until we lost, and the only reason, Mike says, that we finished school, that we got to play football, was that we ran out of money and had to quit and go study.

Other times I'd go over to the student union or the fraternity house and play ping-pong. Before I went to Kansas, Break could beat me with his left hand. But after a semester of ping-pong, I went back to Omaha and beat him twenty straight. So I did get that bit of knowledge out of my freshman year.

I also found out I could play college football.

That came easy to me my freshman year. Of course, football had always come easy to me. The only difficult thing in college was picking up the Kansas system. Being a freshman, I didn't know what college football was all about. But I learned fast.

Actually, Kansas had recruited me to play defense. Jack Mitchell figured on me as a linebacker or defensive back, or a combination of the two. But when we started working out that fall, it seemed they didn't have any running backs. Half the fellows there seemed scared to run the football. So I started running the football. I ran almost every day in practice. And they started to take a look at me as a halfback.

We played only two games that year, against Kansas State and Missouri. And after those games the varsity season still had a month to go, so we just scrimmaged the varsity and the second team. We had to go out there every day and play dummy to those idiots. And we just used to kill the varsity. We had a helluva team, with Brian Schweda, who went to the New Orleans Saints, at defensive end, Mike at offensive end, a fellow named Ron Marsh, who came from Omaha and was a strong lineman, and a lot of others. We constantly beat the varsity to death.

Our first game was against Kansas State, and Jack Mitchell took his wife, Jeanne, to see the game. I guess Jack had told her about me, but she was a little skeptical because Mitchell always used to come home with tales about great new freshman players. Well, I got off a fifty-one-yard touchdown run and the local paper reported Mrs. Mitchell as turning to her husband and saying, "My gosh, he got there so quick."

And Mitchell supposedly answered, "He's so fast you don't have time to cheer his touchdowns."

Mitchell once gave a writer a good explanation of my running form, better than I could have ever described it. He compared me with an automobile. "A car going sixty miles an hour doesn't have the maneuverability of one going thirty. But Sayers has the sixty-mile-an-hour speed along with the thirty-mile-an-hour maneuverability."

Anyway, we beat State 21–6, and I scored the other two touchdowns, too, a one-yard drive and a fifteen-yard sweep. I got 160 yards in twenty-five carries.

That's when they started writing about "Gale the Jet Sayers," "Big No. 47," all that jive. I had worn 48 all through high school, but they gave me 47 as a freshman. I got back 48 when I played varsity. Then, when I went to the Bears, Andy Livingston owned 48, so I took 40. The ironic thing about that was that Livingston had worn 40 in high school.

For the Missouri game everyone was playing up the duel between Johnny Roland, the freshman glamour boy of Missouri, and myself. I don't altogether buy these rivalries. As people say now, When you get in there against Leroy Kelly, or whoever's number one, you've got to prove something. I've got to prove nothing. I'm just going in there to try and win. I play offense, Kelly plays offense. I never run against him. If they can stop him, fine.

In a sense, though, there is an element of competition between me and anyone who's up there with me in the yardage race. Throughout college it was Roland and me. And I admit it did bug me a bit. Like if there's a guy who's really tough, who I really respect as a runner, I'll say, "That trick, that trick." Mike Shinn used to rag me pretty good. He'd say, "You know, Roland runs the ball pretty good. He's not too fast, but he runs pretty good."

And I'd say, "Shut up, shut up."

Mike and I were down in New Orleans for the 1970 Super Bowl game and we ran into Calvin Hill, who was my main rival for running leadership in 1969. Hill had something wrong with his toe and he was down there on crutches. I started bad-mouthing him to Shinn: "What the hell is he doing down here on crutches?"

Calvin came over very friendly like and said, "Hi, Gale." I gave him a quick hello and turned my back on him and just kept walking. Now why did I do that? I don't know, except maybe I had taken this competition with Hill a bit personally. He's a trick all right, like all those guys chasing me for the yardage lead. But he's also a guy I respect as a runner.

So they built up this duel in the freshman game between Roland and me. Well, the game ended in a 21–21 tie and Johnny got eighty-seven yards in nineteen carries. I got 161 yards in twenty carries and, again, scored all our touchdowns. I scored on runs of twenty-five, one, and seventy-nine yards.

That spring I wanted to go out for track. I had met Bill Easton and was impressed with him right off. But we had a hard session of spring football drills and they were important, so I stayed with football.

I did well for the varsity right off. I broke off a lot of long runs in scrimmages, and I knew I would start for the varsity as a sophomore. In high school I played at 182 pounds. I was up to 190 now, just under six feet, and in excellent physical condition. Except that, with about two weeks left in spring practice—and the big game coming up with the alumni—I sprained an ankle. I wasn't ready to go at full speed in that game.

The annual varsity-alumni game traditionally climaxes the spring practice season. They had recruited a pretty tough alumni team, including Curtis McClinton at running back and John Hadl at quarterback. And there were eight thousand people there on a Saturday night to watch the game.

It turned out O.K. We beat them 17–6. I didn't play too much, but I went in five yards for one touchdown and I threw an option pass thirty-four yards to our other halfback, Tony Leiker, for the second touchdown. I was so happy about that one I ran into the end zone and hugged Leiker, a demonstration of emotion you won't often see from me.

That ended my freshman year of football and very nearly ended my college-football career. Because I flunked English and I got a bunch of Ds and they put me on probation and told me I'd have to go to summer school to be eligible for football in the fall.

All this time Linda was doing her college freshman year at the University of Nebraska at Omaha. Unlike me, she studied hard to maintain her scholarship and she worked in her brother-in-law's record shop and also in a supermarket. And she thought about our marriage.

We both thought about it. I was ready; she wasn't so sure. And we really hadn't decided that we would get married. It was as bad a year for her, because of her mixed emotions, as it was for me because of my loneliness at school.

We wrote each other all the time and said we missed each other and everything, but we were still kind of undecided about marriage. She still wasn't sure if she should get married, if she was ready, but, she told me later, she was afraid she'd lose me if we didn't get married. So we got married.

She had her finals on June 5. The next day she started making the dresses for the wedding party. She made all the bridesmaids' dresses and she stayed up all night before our wedding making her wedding gown.

It was a pretty big wedding, maybe the biggest wedding a black couple ever had in Omaha up to that time. Roger was my best man, Mike was there, Break was there, Gunn was there—all the football players. It was held in her mother's Baptist church, and Linda's sister—the one who was closest to her in age—boohooed through the whole ceremony.

We spent our wedding night at a motel and we both went right to sleep. Linda was very tired after staying up all night making those dresses. And the tension had got to me, too. I had a U-Haul outside because we were leaving the next morning for Lawrence.

I got up early, as usual, the next morning. Linda was still asleep, so I went out and had breakfast, read the paper, and walked around. I came back and she was still asleep.

I nudged her.

"When are you going to wake up, girl? We're married."

We were married, and it was the best thing that ever happened in my life.

12

"Look at You, Sayer!"

Marriage bailed me out. It was the only thing that bailed me out. I doubt that I would have finished college if I hadn't got married. Marriage helped settle me down. And my grades improved one hundred and fifty per cent. I think Linda was the big factor, because she had determination, she had drive, and she gave stability to my life. As for me, the responsibility of being married and knowing now that I did want very much to go into professional football made me study better.

We moved into a one-room apartment in the married couples' dormitory in back of the campus. We paid $75 a month rent. We knew we couldn't afford babies for a while, so we got ourselves a dog, a Chihuahua. It was illegal to keep dogs in the apartment, but we got away with it for a year. That dog was so small I could smuggle him in and out of the apartment, stuffing him in a pocket or shopping bag. I took him to classes with me and he slept with us, and we used to worry more about him than we did about each other.

They finally caught us and we had to move out of our apartment. We didn't have any money, but we moved into a more expensive place because we couldn't give up Tiny. He is still with us, but now he shares our affection with the children and Red, an Irish setter.

Money was a problem throughout college. The conference gave me $90 a month as part of my scholarship, so Linda had to go to work. She earned $2.25 an hour working on an assembly line at the Hallmark Card factory in Lawrence. She stood there as the cards went by, putting on a feather or a button or whatever. She hated the work, but there weren't too many jobs to be found for women. She stayed with it for two years and then went to work as a secretary.

So we had about $325 a month to live on and we really had to budget the money. But Linda did the job. She was in charge of the budget and she still is today, and I don't know what I would ever do if she decided to chuck it.

Linda put the fear of the dollar into me back in those days, and, as a result, some of my friends think I'm a little cheap today. If I am—and I don't deny it—I owe it all to my wife. Tommy Dare, who, you must have gathered by now, is a close observer of Gale Sayers, once observed that I liked to keep a big roll on me—filled with singles. Which is true. Every now and then I would pull one out, wave it at Tom, and say, "Tom, get yourself something." Then, when he'd go to grab it, I'd pull it back into my pocket.

Tom says, "Gale puts his telephone book and his money down in a certain spot, in a certain way. And he looks at it very carefully. Then he comes in and if he sees it's moved a bit he hollers at Linda or the kids, 'Who touched it, who touched it?' " Sometimes I sprinkle a little powder over everything, too—just to be sure, you know.

The thing is we really didn't need that much money in those days. The movie in town changed every week and it only cost a quarter to get in. I'd borrow a student ticket for Linda to get her into the basketball games. There was always a lot going on at the fraternity house. So really, our social life was great. But Linda was a worrier, and she still is.

I laugh about it now, I laugh about my own personal hangups. But when Gale was in school I used to worry myself sick. I can't imagine what I was worrying about. Now I say, God, what was I worrying about? I have no idea. I'd go to work, and the women who work there, they had been doing factory work for ten or fifteen years and would be doing it for ten or fifteen years more. I'd tell them I was worried about money and

Gale passing his subjects, and they'd say, You got to be kidding, you don't realize the things you have, you really don't. And of course they were right.

I remember the one time we went on a vacation with Mike Shinn and Joyce, his wife. We drove to Colorado Springs, and it cost us about $150 apiece. We spent the whole first day driving around, looking for a cheap motel to stay in. We finally found one that cost us $6 a day. And then we found this place to eat. And it was like $2 for a steak dinner. We really had a ball. But on the way to dinner we got into a discussion about being poor.

Linda started it by saying, "We're poor."

I said, "How are you poor, Linda. You've got clothes on your back, so how are you poor?"

"Well, we are poor."

And Mike and Joyce took my side. "You're not poor," they said.

Linda said, "We are, too. We only got $2.50 in our checking account, don't tell me that's not poor."

So we argued for a while about being poor. We argued a lot in those days, about a lot of things. We had our ups and downs—just by being young and not knowing each other really. We had regular fusses and fights, but they didn't amount to a hill of beans. Looking back, I can't remember much about what we argued about. And we always ended up laughing about it, making jokes about our problems.

I think this goes back to my home life, too. When I was at home I'd laugh about our sleeping with the gas up all night, about having to go out and shoot sparrows because we didn't have enough to eat. This is probably the saver for the poor people, the people living in the ghetto: They can laugh about their conditions of life. If they didn't have the ability to laugh about what's going on, they would be in bad trouble. This is what helps keep them going. They say black people love music. Why? Because they got some music, it keeps them going. Sometimes I think we Negroes have managed to

endure because we are able to laugh at the things that
happen to us.

All in all, we really had lots of fun in Kansas. Those
days in college were probably the best days of our
lives, and when it was all over we hated to leave there.

I reported to the varsity in the fall of my sophomore
year weighing 170. A lot of people figured it must have
been Linda's cooking, but I deny it. She was a helluva
cook then and she is even better now. I don't know
why I dropped twenty pounds that summer; a combination of things, I think. I was going to school, maybe
worrying a little bit about my eligibility, and I was also
working on a tough construction job. I never knew
what I would be doing from day to day. A lot of times
I spent busting up sidewalks with a sledgehammer. One
time I went to work in tennis shoes and my job was to
pour hot asphalt on the street. By the time I got home
my feet were burning and I had no shoes left.

The team doctor thought I might have a salt de-
ficiency so he gave me pills and shots to increase my
appetite, and I did start gaining weight. I must have
gotten up to 185 by the end of my sophomore year and,
as a junior, I played at 207. But I couldn't have
weighed more than 175 for our first game with Texas
Christian.

I don't know whether Jack Mitchell was trying
psychology on me or what, but somebody fed the
Topeka paper (I have the clipping) the following:
"Coaches have applied an antidote for a swelled cranium. Sayers has been demoted to the third team."

Well, Mitchell always graded films of our scrimmages every day and on the basis of the films he would
post those who had made first string that day, second
team, third team. And it would change every day. And
maybe one day I might have been third string because
I missed an assignment or a block or something. That's
all there was to that. And I don't think I ever had a
"swelled cranium." It was never my nature to get big-
headed over my football ability.

The same article also said I was running in high tops with heavy soles and iron stays running up the side. "Coaches hint," it said, "that Gale is not as fast as he was last spring."

Well, I still had some effects from my ankle injury in spring practice, but why the big deal? The high-top shoes are about two ounces heavier than the low cuts. And once the season started I wore low cuts. It was in my junior year that I wore the high shoes. In a spring scrimmage before the junior season my old buddy Mike Shinn hit me. He was ready to throw a block for me but caught me on the ankle instead. I sprained it pretty bad, so I stayed with the highs all season long. But I never missed a game in my whole varsity career.

And I put in a full day against TCU. I carried the ball twenty-seven times (a Kansas record) for 114 yards. I also got in a forty-four-yard kickoff return. But we lost the damn game 6–3.

Most of the TCU players had nice things to say about me after the game, except the quarterback, Sonny Gibbs. He was quoted in this article I saved as saying, "I sure wasn't impressed. It looked like he let up a little. I expected him to be a little more punishing and powerful in addition to having good speed."

One of Gibbs's own coaches disagreed with him in the same article, which was unusual. This coach said, "I don't know how in the world Gibbs would know how hard Sayers hit. Sonny didn't play on defense to speak of. Several other players told me they got cracked pretty good by Sayers. Anyway, that Sayers is so darn hard to catch that you can never be sure how hard he can smack you because you very seldom get him zeroed in well enough to hit."

Maybe Gibbs was right, I don't know. We did start winning after that. We went to Boston and beat Boston U. 14–0, and I gained seventy-two yards on eleven carries. We beat Colorado 35–8, and I scored my first college touchdown in that one. It was an off-tackle run from the fourteen. I saved a photograph showing two men coming up to trap me. One was Bill Symons, who later played defensive back for the Green Bay Packers. The photo shows both of them on the ground and me sailing over them. I carried fourteen times in that game for 112 yards.

Then we beat Iowa State 29–8, and I gained ninety-four yards. So that was three wins in a row, with Oklahoma coming up.

By this time Mike Shinn and I were pretty loose—no sophomore jitters for us. And we kept each other loose. The night before each home game, Coach Mitchell made us go into Topeka, which is twenty miles from Lawrence. We'd stay together, eat together—all that stuff. He was a big believer in togetherness. And I remember a bus ride to Topeka in one of our early home games that sophomore year.

Mike and I were sitting together and he said something to me and I started laughing. And, you know, going up on the football bus the night before the game, you were expected to be real quiet. All the other guys, the older guys, turned around and looked at us and said, "What's wrong with those guys?" I was just cracking up. I don't even know why. Mike said something silly to me—"Look at the coach's head," or something—and I cracked up.

The night before the game Coach wanted all the guys to go to a movie together. And most of them would go. But Mike and I preferred to walk around town a bit and then go back and watch a little TV before going to bed. This one night Coach Mitchell took a head count. "How many of you fellows," he asked, "aren't going to the movie?"

Mike and I were the only ones to stick up our hand.

Mitchell got suspicious right away. "Are you fellows going out to see Mike's family or something?" He knew Mike came from Topeka. But he really wasn't asking that. He wanted to know if we were going out with some girls.

We said, "No, we're not going out to see the family. We just don't like the movies."

And that was the truth. We were a little wise as

sophomores, but we got taken down pretty well after what happened to us in the Oklahoma game.

We had managed to get hold of four tickets to what we knew was going to be a sellout game. We figured we could make some money on those tickets. Somehow, Shinn got in touch with a fellow he knew who wanted to buy the tickets. We expected to make a killing, sell them for $20 apiece or something like that.

That night in Topeka, Shinn's contact called. "I'll be down to pick them up at ten o'clock."

Well, we waited around the lobby, and it was getting to be ten-fifteen, which was when we were supposed to be in our room. We saw Coach Mitchell and, unfortunately, he saw us. So Shinn went up to him. "You know, Coach, I have these tickets for this guy and he was supposed to pick them up at ten and he hasn't shown up yet. So I was wondering if I could wait a couple of minutes until he comes." Coach said it was O.K.

The guy did come about five minutes later. He turned out to be a young fellow and he only wanted to pay the regular price for the tickets. What could we say? We had never come out and told him we were scalping the damn things. So we had to sell him the tickets at the regular price, $4 or $5. And there went our killing.

The next day Oklahoma did the killing. Not really a killing, because we only lost 13–7 and Oklahoma went on to win the Big Eight that year. They had some team —guys like Jim Grisham, Joe Don Looney, Ralph Neely, and Lance Rentzel. They cut off our offense completely. The killing was made mostly at the expense of Sayers and Shinn. We were both terrible. I gained only twenty-three yards all day and Mike let a guy get outside of him on a big play and the man went down and set up a field goal.

Coach saw the films on Monday and he said he was going to make us the dogs of the film and provide a running commentary.

"Ah, ha-ha. You guys with your ticket deals—Mike *Big Deal* Shinn and Gale *Ticket* Sayer [he always called me 'Sayer']. Look at you! Big deal, my ass." He kept flipping the film back and forth, at our mistakes. "Look at you, Shinn! The guy ran right around you. Look at you, Sayer! Look at yourself, cutting the wrong way. That money you made, it'll never amount to what you lost in this game. You'll never forget the football game that you big deals went out and lost." We hadn't made any money on the tickets, not a dime, and still we took this big chewing out. He ran us down.

Jack Mitchell was a tough coach but a fair one. He ran a very tight ship. He was an emotional kind of guy, too. I remember we were playing Syracuse my senior year. They had Floyd Little and he scored five against us—he had a helluva day. We were losing 21–zip at the half and Mitchell came down to the locker room. There was this big blackboard on a stand, and he put his fist right through it. He started cussing, but it didn't do us any good. They gave us our hat that day, 38–6.

Mitchell often used the pep talk. It seemed like in college, unlike the pros, you needed a pep talk, you kind of looked forward to it. And he was good at it. "You been working hard all week," he'd say, "and you should try to go out and win, because it will all be for nothing if you don't win." And he would get very emotional in the delivery.

And after the Oklahoma game he gave me a personal pep talk.

Mitchell always had a couple of pet phrases. One was that his players didn't know the difference between pain and injury. Another was "You can't make chicken salad out of chicken —." I had hurt my hand in the Oklahoma game and I didn't know about playing the next week against Oklahoma State. So Mitchell walked around the block with me and we talked.

He didn't bring out the chicken-salad routine, but he did say, "You got to understand, Gale, that there's a difference between pain and injury. I know your hand is hurting, but we'll tape it and you'll be all right. The only way you can stay out is if you've got a broken bone. You got to remember, everybody plays football with pain."

So I played against Oklahoma State, and I'm glad I did. It turned out to be my biggest day ever in football.

They were ahead of us 17–7 at the half. I had broken a run of sixty-nine yards in the first quarter to set up the touchdown. But I hadn't done much else. Coach wasn't too happy at the half. He came in and said, "You know what you've got to do." And then he walked right out.

In the second half I started knocking off fifteen-, twenty-yard chunks at a time. In the last quarter we were pinned at our four-yard line when we tried a power sweep left. One of the Oklahoma State players caught me close to the side lines, but I feinted left, then hit right with a leaping crossover step. I was able to keep my speed and balance and shake loose. That ninety-six-yard run tied the longest run from scrimmage in Kansas's history.

We ended up beating them 36–17. I carried the ball twenty-two times and gained 283 yards, which set a Big Eight single-game record and is still a record in the Big Eight and will be forevermore. My last fifteen yards gained—the yardage that set the record—were the most fascinating of the whole afternoon.

Late in the game, I was trying to turn a corner when I hit the side lines and this Oklahoma State defensive halfback tackled me ten yards out of bounds. Hell, I had already thrown the ball to the ground and this trick tackled me and jerked my jersey from behind. I just kind of pushed him a little, jerked loose, and shoved him. And he called me a nigger. That started it. We went at each other, and the next thing I knew the whole team was out on the field, on top of me.

As we were going back across the field, some of the Oklahoma State players taunted Mitchell, who was in front of me, "We got your black boy, we got your black boy out."

Nothing like that had ever happened to me in a

high-school game, and that was the only time a racial taunt was ever directed at me in a college game.

I was thrown out of the game (the other kid was, too), but neither Mitchell nor I realized it. On the next play I ran for the ball for fifteen yards. Then the officials told me I had been ejected. But the fifteen yards stood and that was it.

The next week we beat Kansas State and I scored three touchdowns, passed for a two-point conversion, and knocked off 156 yards.

I knew the Nebraska game would cause a lot of static, and it did. Kansas's big rival had always been Kansas State and Missouri, but since everyone from Nebraska thought I was a traitor not to go to Nebraska, they hit that hard. I remember one paper ran a headline: NEBRASKA PLAYS SAYERS OF KANSAS. All this big bull. They made a big thing out of it.

It was a home game at least—homecoming, in fact—so that helped; there wasn't all that pressure on me. I picked up 144 yards rushing, passing, and receiving, but they beat us 40–16. A lot of good those 144 yards did. The fact is our team was scared of Nebraska. They had a big team—big backs like Willy Ross, big linemen like Bob Brown. Our team was scared of them. They ran over us. They killed us.

One thing that game did accomplish: it increased my fan mail. Oh, yes, I was hearing regularly from Nebraska fans, especially when Nebraska lost to Kansas in something. I heard all the time from some trick who lived in the YMCA in Omaha. His letters always said the same thing: "I told you not to go to Kansas, that bum school." And after the Nebraska game the I-told-you-so letters flooded in on us.

I have gotten two kinds of hate mail. One came in college because I chose Kansas over Nebraska. All through college I got hate letters from Nebraska fans. Then, when I chose the Bears over the Kansas City Chiefs, I got hate letters from Chief fans. One Kansas City fan wrote me a hate letter every week—and he put his name on it. That's the way people are, I guess.

We did bounce back and beat California 33–21, though they got a fine passing performance from a sophomore quarterback, Craig Morton. My eighty-one yards gained in that one put me over the 1000 mark in rushing for the season.

Our last game of the year was against Missouri, and naturally they played up the Sayers-Roland rivalry. Johnny was having a good year, too. He was right behind me in rushing in the conference. But he didn't do much in this game. He gained thirty-four yards. I picked up seventy-two. We played to a 3–3 tie.

So we finished with a 6–3–1 record, and I was fairly satisfied with my own performance. I gained 1125 yards for the season, which was first in the Big Eight and third in the country. I believe my 7.2 rushing average was the best in the country. I made All-Big Eight and the Kansas propaganda machine began to grind out releases saying that I was a sure thing All-America in 1963.

We had an older fellow name of Don Pierce, the sports publicity director, who was very good at that sort of thing. He had manufactured a lot of All-Americas in his time, and he started right out on me. He wrote an article about me that received wide circulation. In it he quoted me as saying that the secret of my running was: "I go where my feet go." Which I never said.

But that wasn't all. He also pinned a nickname on me—The Kaw River Gale. That's the river that runs through Lawrence, and there the resemblance ends. When Linda read the article she said she thought she'd die.

I wasn't too happy about it either, because it kind of made me look a little bit like a low-grade moron. And despite my success in football, I still did feel a little inferior, a little out of it, as if I still really didn't belong in college.

Marriage helped me, marriage helped me tremendously, but I knew I had a long way to go and there were things I had to do myself. *Look at you, Sayer!*

Look at yourself. . . . I kept remembering those words of Jack Mitchell. He had used them in a different context, but I took deeper meaning—and understanding—from them.

And I began to look at myself.

13

Exploding Inside

I saw a vast change in Gale those four years of college. Everybody that got to know Gale in college says it was unbelievable, the change in him four years later. Because Gale had been quiet to a point where it was almost weird. He had a hard time in just grasping words to put a sentence together. He almost had a lisp. He just wouldn't talk well at all, so he wouldn't bother talking. He was afraid to make a blunder, afraid to say the wrong thing or do the wrong thing or anything like that.

He used to, like all the time, give me credit for his being a success. I told him, Look, you were born with this God-given talent and you don't have to prove anything to me or anybody. I think he tried hard, because at the time when we were in school I was working very hard and I was maybe the first person who really had a lot of faith and trust in Gale. Maybe that was part of it, but there was nothing he had to prove to me.

One of the people at Kansas I got close to was my speech teacher, Tom Hendricks, who was also the public-address announcer of the Kansas City Chiefs' games. I minored in speech in college, which was kind of a joke, because I had a bad time talking, making myself understood.

I remember the first speech I made in class. It was terrible, just terrible. I think it was the worst experience of my life. I struggled through it, and Tom Hendricks struggled through it with me. In fact, he struggled through the whole semester with me. But by the time it was over I *had* improved. I mean, I wasn't great, but

155

there was quite a contrast at the end from what there was at the beginning.

Another man who helped me with my speech, and with a lot of other things at college, was Jesse Milan.

I had first met Jesse when Break and I went up on that recruiting trip in our senior year of high school. Jesse and his wife had been working with black athletes and black students on campus for a number of years. He is an education consultant for the Lawrence school district today, he teaches on campus, and he is the fraternity adviser for Kappa Alpha Psi. And, right away, I felt he was someone I could trust.

Jesse and I became friends my first year in school, when I was so lonely. I would go over and talk to him all the time, and he was always available. It was at his house that I learned to play ping-pong so well. His door was always open to all the kids in school, and I took advantage of it. We spent many hours in his basement playing ping-pong and talking. Later on we played handball together.

He must have been about thirty-five at the time, and he had never played handball, but he became a good player. He didn't beat me very often because my stamina and quickness would wear him down. But we had good battles.

We just became very close. By my junior year it got to be a ritual that on Sunday afternoons we would do things together. I would come over and he would say, "Gale, would you like to go someplace with me?" Either it was a speech he was making, or a visit to his brother in Kansas City, or maybe to a ball game.

One Sunday afternoon my senior year we went into Kansas City to see the Chiefs play. Linda was with us, too. I had to be back in Lawrence about five because Jack Mitchell had called a meeting. The team wasn't going too well and he was about to put his foot down. "Anyone who misses the meeting," he said, "is going to be in bad trouble."

We left the Kansas City game in time, we thought, to

make the meeting. And, wouldn't you know it, our car broke down—ker-ploomp—right on the highway.

We were standing there when a truck came by and stopped. Jesse said, "You and Linda go to the service station, call Mitchell, and then have them come back to tow the car in."

So we went to the service center (I remember Linda and I talked afterward how bouncy it was in the cab of that truck and wondered how they could stand to ride in it) and I got the guy to come back for Jesse. And I went back with him, without phoning Mitchell.

The first thing Jesse asked was, "Did you call Mitchell?"

"No, not yet."

"Man, you're supposed to be at the meeting."

Well, we all finally got back into Lawrence and I was late for the meeting and Mitchell was a little put out. Jesse talked to him later and told him what happened and Mitchell's response was "Yeah, yeah, yeah." But I didn't get penalized.

Jesse helped me in so many ways in those years. He helped me through my shyness. He had the kind of personality that enabled him to bring even the shyest person out of himself. In our talks he encouraged me to think, to understand that I did have a personality, that I did possess character traits that weren't so bad. He encouraged me to think positively. He never talked negatively. He never said to me, "You can't do this, you can't do that." It was always, "You can do anything you want."

He helped me with my speech, too. Jesse was the one who claimed I had a lazy tongue, and I think that's one of the reasons he pushed me to go with him whenever he had to make a speech. He had a great voice, a cultivated voice. I would listen to him talk, so easy in his delivery, so relaxed, and I could feel that hunger inside of me to be able to do the same. I was like exploding inside; I wished so much that I could project myself the way he did.

Another thing he did. He would sometimes go to

church at seven-thirty and read morning prayer, and I would go with him some mornings as the lay reader. And that helped, too.

And it was Jesse Milan who introduced us to the Episcopal church.

At the time, I guess late in my sophomore year, Linda and I really didn't have any church to go to. So we just went to church every Sunday with him. And we both liked the services. The Episcopal religion seemed very informal; it was in Lawrence, anyway. They would take something that was happening in everyday life and talk about it. I liked this kind of religion. So we started classes to learn about it. We went for about two weeks at night to learn what was going on. And we decided to join.

I went under instructions to be baptized, and I asked Jesse to be my godfather and he said he would. And Linda and I were confirmed in the church.

Though Jesse never taught me in school, he did help me with my studies. He taught me how to focus in and study and how to prepare for an exam. He got me to relax a little, too. He tried to instill confidence in me that I could make it. He knew I would be depressed a lot and he constantly encouraged me.

And I did improve in class. I think my proudest achievement in college was not making All-America in football in my junior and senior years, not setting a Big Eight career rushing record—not any of that jive. It was making a three-point average right before my senior year. I really studied in that period and I came out with the best grades in the fraternity house that semester.

I had been kind of rebellious in high school, but I lost that rebellion in college. I hung around with only a certain type of person in high school. In college I began to broaden my friendships. For instance, I got along well with all my instructors, I respected them. A mark of that respect is that, beginning in my sophomore year, I didn't miss a class in college—except two days in my junior year when I had the flu. That was the only time. I never cut a class or anything.

English was really the only subject that always gave me trouble. I took four psychology courses and I B'd them all the way through. I loved psychology. I enjoyed anatomy, too. That was the most rugged course in the whole school (I had that my first semester my senior year) and I enjoyed it. You had to name all the nerves, the muscles, everything in the body. Like on a test, you had to trace one drop of blood from the big toe on the left foot all the way up to the heart and back down to the little toe on the right foot. And you had to name all the things—nerves, arteries, and stuff—along the way. I always did well in that kind of thing.

I'll never forget the first day of the anatomy class. We had a cadaver—he was a black cadaver. He was all covered up, and the first thing the teacher did was roll back the sheet. This black cadaver had sunglasses on. I thought I'd die. A lot of funny things happened in anatomy.

The only slight regret I have about my college career —actually, it's Linda's regret, not mine—is failing to graduate. I came up ten hours short of getting my degree. Because after I signed my pro contract I started dropping classes. I think that period, from January to June of my senior year, was the toughest go of our married life. Every time I came home I'd tell Linda I had dropped out of another course and she was tied, she couldn't stand me.

"But I'm thinking about next year with the Bears," I tried to explain. "I'm getting my mind ready for football, Linda."

And she would throw up her hands and say, "Oh, no, I don't believe it."

She thinks I wasted my college education, but I don't think I did. And it still is a sore point between us. What good would a degree in physical education do me? Today the world is so specialized, an education degree is nothing. They should throw that out for something specific. I don't regret I didn't get my degree. I got what I wanted in a pro contract.

The only nagging thought I did have at that time was, Well, what if I don't make it in pro football? Then what do I do? Well, I'm sure I would have gone ahead and tried to get that degree. But I did make it.

I've just been lucky as hell. Everything fell into place for me. Like I told my brother, Ron, when he wanted to get married at nineteen. I told him, "Don't get married yet" (he did anyway). "I'm one in a million, Ron," I said. "You don't know what can happen in pro ball. You might get hurt, you might not make it. I'm lucky I didn't get hurt in college. I'm lucky I didn't get hurt in the pros until I was well established. I'm lucky I had the right advisers, the right wife, everything. It worked out perfectly for me." And I told him, "Not many people can be so lucky in this life."

So I didn't get any degree. There's a saying that a good association is better than school. I learned something in college from being around different people, talking to different people. That's an education, a degree right there. You're put in with all these different kinds of people and you learn from them, and you're a bigger person for going to college even if you didn't make your degree.

Another person I learned much from, as I have said, was the track coach, Bill Easton.

I did the hurdles and broad jump in my season and a half on the Kansas track team. And it was through track that I really learned the meaning of work, and other things, too. That saying that stood so proudly on Bill Easton's desk—*I Am Third* . . . it seemed to be calling out to me every time I saw it. When Easton explained to me where the saying came from, I understood its meaning. And I understood it more after I got to know Easton, after I got to know that I Am Third was a philosophy he practiced, he cared about.

I came to admire Bill for his position and stature in the college—he was, at the time, one of the most respected track coaches in the country—and for his strong, positive beliefs about life. When fellows came out for track the first time, Easton tried to explain what he expected from them.

"Work," he said, "is the basis of confidence for a young athlete to perform well. If he knows he's in great condition he's going to have the confidence psychologically to do well." That's the theory he worked on all the time.

And I worked, I really worked at track. Not that I was too crazy about it. I wasn't that interested in track in college, but I knew it would help me become a better football player. Running was the basis of everything I did in football, so running track had to help me in football, especially in keeping me in condition for football.

Also, football came so easy to me that I didn't know my potential, and I may not have been as strongly motivated as I should have been. I learned motivation from Easton.

"We want to give you a little better attitude toward your own ability, Gale," he'd tell me when I might be grousing about something. "You don't realize how good you are yet."

Easton always felt that no matter how well an athlete performed he could do even better. "You don't teach potential," he stressed, "by saying that you *can't* do that." And he worked my tail off, which was the best thing that ever happened to me.

He was very understanding when I told him, after I had signed a pro contract, that I wouldn't be going out for track in the outdoor season of my senior year. I explained that I didn't want anything to go wrong, or hurt my chances of making the pros. I thought he would be mad because he had worked so hard with me to make me a better hurdler and a better jumper and possibly it would pay off for him my senior season. But he wasn't mad at all, just the opposite.

"Gale," he said, "I think when these opportunities come, a young man of your caliber should accept them

and take full advantage of them and work right into
your job."

He asked me how I felt going with the Bears.

"I'm a little scared," I confessed.

"Well, you don't need to be. You have all the equip-
ment to do a great job." He advised me to work every
day on my running and toughening-up programs so
that when I went to camp I would be prepared to perform to the best of my ability.

"You go for broke every time you go," he said. And
that is the lesson of Bill Easton I always tried to follow.

I kept in shape the summer after my sophomore year
with my own body-building program. Four times a
week I'd go over to the stadium—we lived right across
the street from it—and run halfway up each aisle and
back down again. Then I'd run ten 50-yard dashes and
ten 100-yard dashes. You can see the Easton work
formula made an impression on me. I lifted weights, too,
and built my weight up to 207 pounds, which was the
heaviest I've ever been playing football.

The balance of power in the Big Eight had shifted
to Nebraska, although Oklahoma was still strong, too.
I don't know what happened to us, except maybe that
the recruiting fell off a bit. We didn't seem to be picking
up the good players, the real studs, while some of the
other teams in the conference were getting a lot of
good ones.

Even so, we did pretty well my junior year. We were
5–5, but we lost to TCU by four points, Oklahoma by
four, Missouri by two, Iowa State by three. The only
team that really put it to us was Nebraska, and we made
a game of it until midway into the fourth quarter.

We lost our opener to Texas Christian 10–6. We
could have won it 13–10. I got off a forty-eight-yard
run in the final seconds of the game, but the play was
called back by a penalty.

We did upset Syracuse 10–0, and that was probably
our best performance of the year. Syracuse had Jim
Nance and a lot of other strong players and was considered best in the East. But our defense played real

hard-nose that day. I went twenty-eight yards on a screen pass to set up our field goal, then I took one off-tackle and cut back against the grain for a twenty-six-yard touchdown run. I ended up with 122 yards on seventeen carries.

We lost a tough one to Oklahoma 21–18, but at least Big Deals Shinn and Sayers redeemed themselves a little. Shinn had an outstanding game and I think I played one of my best college games ever. I gained 110 yards, scored the two touchdowns, caught two passes, one for a bonus conversion, and completed a pass.

Bud Wilkinson, who was still coaching Oklahoma, had some nice things to say about me after the game. "He has exceptional ability to be absolutely flying when he's running at a ninety-degree angle," Wilkinson was quoted as saying.

We were upset by Iowa State, but we beat Wyoming, Oklahoma State, and Kansas State. And then we played Nebraska, at Lincoln, which was my big homecoming—my first college game in my home state. And the newspapers built it up, built up that Sayers-Nebraska rivalry, just as they had my sophomore year.

After that sophomore game I had been slightly misquoted in the press. They had me saying, "The Huskers didn't hit me very hard. At least I didn't have any bruises." I really hadn't said it that way, but, naturally, Bob Devaney took advantage of the situation. He put that clipping on the bulletin board in the dressing room the week before the game. And one of the Omaha papers said, "So they'll be out to prove that Sayers can be hit hard."

I really wasn't out to prove anything playing Nebraska. You try too hard against anyone and you tighten up. Sure, I wanted our team to beat Nebraska, but not because it was Nebraska. I wanted to beat them because it was a conference game and Nebraska was undefeated in the conference and was one of the best teams in the country.

The week before that game was when I came down with flu and missed two days of school. Actually, I didn't know whether I would make the game, but I felt fine by kickoff.

I didn't feel so fine after a couple of fumbles got us in trouble right away and put us down 10–0 at the half.

Starting the fourth quarter, we were losing 10–3. Nebraska had the ball around midfield but was forced to punt. It went out of bounds on the one-yard line. Actually, it was on the one-*foot* line. The nose of the ball was touching the goal line.

On first down I lined up at right halfback, took a quick pitch, and started around left end. Most of the game they stacked the outside because they had big Bob Brown to block in the middle. This time they bunched in the middle, not figuring on an outside run so deep in our own territory.

I got a good block on the end from our halfback. I sidestepped another man coming up on me at the one, shook off a defensive halfback with a head-and-shoulder fake at the ten, and found myself in an open field, all by myself. That was the longest touchdown run from scrimmage in the history of the Big Eight. I don't know how it'll ever be broken, either, unless they lengthen the field.

That closed the margin to 10–9, but they drove right back for a touchdown, and then Bob Hohn, who had been a rival of mine in high school, in both football and track, intercepted a pass and ran it back for the clincher.

I had 144 yards in eleven carries, not so great if you consider that one run ate up most of the yardage. And they did hit me hard enough to knock me out of the game, late in the quarter, though it also cost them an unnecessary roughness penalty.

And after the game I got double the amount of my usual abuse from the loyal Nebraska fans.

Our last game of the year was to be played on November 23 at home, against Missouri. That was the day after the assassination of President Kennedy, and even though we went into Topeka that Friday night and I put on my game face, I wasn't in any mood to play football. I mean, how can you play football when the flag is flying at half mast for the President of the United States? I wasn't very much on politics in those days, but just talking to Mike Shinn, to Linda (she really made me aware of things going on in the world), reading the paper half the time—I thought he was a tremendous President.

I had gotten my game face all ready and I blew my game face. The game was postponed a week and I suppose it should have been canceled. We lost 9–7.

Mike Shinn made All-Big Eight that year and he deserved it. He had a helluva year. Bob Brown was on that team, Ralph Neely, George Seals, Jim Grisham at fullback. I was named Back-of-the-Year in the conference. I also made most of the big All-America teams.

I ended up with 941 yards for the season and became the first back in the Big Eight to reach 2000 yards in my junior year.

I made All-America again as a senior, even though it wasn't that personally satisfying a year. It was actually a frustrating year. I gained only 678 yards but that set a Big Eight career record (2675 yards). I was hoping we would have a winner, and right up to our last game against Missouri we did have a chance to tie for the conference title. But we blew it and ended up 6–4 for the season.

I think by my senior year I had changed quite a bit as a person. I sensed the change in me, nobody had to tell me about it. One reporter did compare me as a sophomore to me as a senior. Talking about me as a sophomore, he wrote: "He was shy almost to the point of boorishness, completely inarticulate, apprehensive about whether he was going to make it scholastically and as a football player."

And then he said this about Gale Sayers as a senior: "Today he is poised, laconic, instead of articulate, easy in manner, dressed in the best of quiet taste and self-assured."

Well, I did feel more at home with myself. I had a long way to go, I knew, but I was feeling more secure and more self-confident. The contacts I had made, the different people I got close to who worked on me all helped. I think there may have been an explosion inside after all, because I was now aware of my potential—as a football player and as a person.

As a football player, though I fell off toward the last of my senior year, I think I was doing more things than I had my previous two years. Against Iowa State, for instance, I had a total of 212 yards. I had eighty-seven yards in ten carries from scrimmage (including a forty-eight-yard TD run). I completed two passes, I caught one, I ran back punts for ninety-two yards, including a seventy-two-yarder. And we beat Iowa State 42–6.

We also beat Oklahoma for the first time in my career, 15–14, and that was a high point of the season. I made a ninety-three-yard touchdown run in that one that supposedly convinced George Halas, after he saw the films, to draft me. At least that's what I was told.

I have a series of photographs showing me trapped at midfield, three guys converging on me. I don't know what it was I did. Maybe I made a fake for each man. I did fake one of the guys to his knees. I veered right past all three of them, although Carl McAdams got a leg on me. But he couldn't hold me.

Another first for me in college that year was getting hurt for the first time in a game. We played a tough one with Oklahoma State and finally beat them 14–13. Late in the game I was getting ready to throw a block and a fellow ducked and hit me on the leg with his helmet. The outer layer of muscle split open and popped out. I should have had an operation on it to get it sewn back up, but I never did. You can still see the knot in that leg. And I played the next week.

That was the Kansas State game, and it was another milestone. We won 7–0, I scored my last college touchdown, and, at the same time, broke the Big Eight rushing record.

Late in the third quarter in a scoreless game we had the ball on our twenty-three. I ducked in off-tackle. I remember their big end hit me at the line of scrimmage.

I gave him a limp leg and got by him. Then another fellow came up and I gave him a couple of moves and got by him. I don't have the slightest idea what the moves were. It looked like I was stumbling, and I was a little, but I think that helped me because it enabled me to give a convincing leg fake. A couple of other fellows chased me—one dived for me—but that was it.

Up to then I had been held to only thirty yards. I finished with 110 yards on ten carries, and the Big Eight career rushing record.

And of course there was our annual loss to Nebraska. Of all three of the games I participated in, this is the one I will never forget. Because we played a helluva game against them and we might have beaten them—except for me.

They had us 14–7 in the last quarter. Our quarterback picked me up on the Nebraska fifteen. I was clear, the pass was perfect—a sure touchdown—and I dropped it, I dropped the damn thing. I don't know what happened. I was open, the ball was right there, I was bringing it down and my knee hit it and kicked it out of my arms. Ever since then I've always practiced extra hard on catching long passes. I'll never drop another one.

The amazing part of it was that the crowd still gave me a standing ovation. I felt pretty bad when I left the field. In fact, I never felt so bad in my life. But the crowd rose and just applauded me until I disappeared from sight.

They claimed that I had rushed to the dressing room, toweled off, and left without even taking a shower. They didn't realize that I happen to do that all the time, that I'm quick, anyway. I go in and—zoom—I'm in the shower, come out, and I'm gone. I was the first one out of the locker room after that game, but I'm always the first one out. And, yes, I did take a shower.

Of course I felt bad about losing that game, about dropping that ball—the memory will always haunt me —but after the game it was over with. All through college I never really felt that bad about losing. I always played to win of course, but, somehow, defeat didn't seem as crushing as it became in pro football.

It may have been because of the press. Sportswriters never really get on college players the way they do pro players. You can read the paper the day after a defeat in college and feel like you've won the damn game. It helps take the sting out of defeat. In the pros I can't pick up a paper on Mondays after a losing game because I know what's going to be in there. That's what makes losing so much harder in the pros. You read the criticism, Joe Blow reads it, and he'll say, What happened to you guys, why'd you do this, or that? And he'll see you walking down the street and he'll call you a bum because the papers called you a bum. In college ball you just didn't find that, you didn't find that at all.

While I'm at it, let me clear up another myth about me in college. Jack Mitchell always told the press that "Gale Sayers had an *obsession* to be a great football player." I don't think it was an obsession. I was just out there doing what came naturally to me. If I did better, fine, but I never had an obsession on a football field to do something great, you know. If it can be done, I'm going to do it. A lot of people deliberately try harder at something, but I don't. I just go out there and do it.

My final college game was at Missouri and it was kind of an anticlimax. We lost 34–14, and that ended all our hopes for a tie in the conference. It was very cold there and I did nothing. It kind of made a mockery out of a headline that appeared in the Kansas City *Star* the day before the game: SAYERS TURNS FROM PLAYER TO LEGEND SATURDAY. Sunday morning they could have turned it around and said, SAYERS TURNS FROM LEGEND TO PLAYER. But they were kind enough not to.

That weekend was not without its rewards, though. The night before the game I received a telegram from Buddy Young of the Baltimore Colts saying that he wanted to come to Kansas right away to see me.

14

Caught in the Middle

I had vaguely heard the name Buddy Young before. I seemed to recall that he had been a running back in college and in the pros, but I couldn't tell you which teams he played for. He sure didn't explain anything in his telegram. All he said was that he wanted to talk to me about the National Football League and to please call him at a certain number in Los Angeles on Saturday night. I figured he must be calling me on behalf of the Baltimore Colts because he was out in L.A. with Baltimore.

They played on Saturday afternoon and beat the Rams to clinch the Western Division championship. We played on Saturday afternoon and lost to Missouri, and that killed our chances for a piece of the Big Eight championship.

That night I called him. I caught him at a party, the Colts' victory party, and I could tell he was feeling good.

"Mr. Young," I said, "this is Gale Sayers."

"Good," he said. "You're a high-class feller, a man of your word, because you called me back. Call me at this same number tomorrow night, I can't talk now." Bang! He hung up.

So I called him Sunday, and the first thing he asked was, "You haven't signed with anyone yet, have you?"

I said no. He said in that case he would be catching a plane the next morning for Kansas City and for us to meet him at the airport.

And Linda and I got a little uptight, figuring Buddy Young was coming in to see if we'd play for the Baltimore Colts.

By this time things were pretty confusing anyway. I

knew where I stood in the American Football League. Kansas City said I would be their number-one choice. But I didn't know where I stood with the NFL.

Between the times Buddy called and when we finally met him, I received seven or eight telegrams from different NFL teams. They all wanted to know the same thing: "If we draft you, will you sign with us?" Remember, this was in the middle of the war between the leagues, before the merger. I answered every telegram with one word: Yes.

Of all the NFL teams, the San Francisco 49ers seemed to want me the most. They had sent a scout over to see me just before our game with Colorado, which was next-to-the-last on the schedule. The scout said he wanted to take Linda and me out to dinner right after the game. And we accepted.

Then I went out and had a very poor day against Colorado. We won, but I did nothing. It was a bad day all around. And after the game the scout came around and made up some excuse; he said he had to leave early, something had come up, and he canceled out of our dinner.

Linda was really upset when this scout left. "I wonder if we're going to get any offers," she said. Up to then I really thought I would be chosen by San Francisco. But now I didn't know what to think.

Then, soon after, Lou Spadia, the general manager of the 49ers, called and said they were going to draft me number one. I said fine. But something happened. The 49ers took Ken Willard instead. Every time I bump into Spadia now he shakes his head and says, "Gale, we really made a mistake in not picking you." Hell, they did all right with Ken Willard.

So it looked more and more like I was going to wind up in the American Football League.

I had met Don Klosterman, who was then general manager of the Chiefs, in my junior year. He was and is a good man, a fine man. And he came around a lot. He claimed he had seen me play in spring practice after my freshman year and told someone from *Sports Illus-*

trated, "There's a kid at Kansas named Gale Sayers; he's gonna rewrite the record books."

Don got me tickets to the Chiefs' home games. I remember their last game of my junior year. It was five degrees in the stand, and windblown, and I only had on a light coat. Most of the crowd had cut out, but I stayed. I saw Klosterman afterward, and he couldn't believe I had hung in. Maybe that impressed him about me.

I do know not all his scouts were that impressed. He sent one out to the TCU game my senior year. I ran a sweep and fumbled the ball. The scout reported that I just looked at it and never tried to go after the ball. "Doesn't even fight to recover the ball," he said. And his verdict was: Reject.

But Don didn't feel that way about me. In my junior year he was calling me the best runner in college at the time. In fact, he was quoted as saying that the three best runners in football were Jim Brown, Lenny Moore, and Gale Sayers. I don't see how a college kid could have been more flattered.

Don and his wife, Claire, took Linda and me out to dinner one night about a week before the draft. He gave me his pitch for Kansas City. He told me he thought the Chiefs would draft me number one. He said he felt it would be good for me to stay in Kansas City, where I was known, where I had already laid the groundwork, where I could contribute so much to the area. This was a positive factor, he said. He talked about a bank job for me, a job for Linda, said I would be an immediate success in the area. And he said I'd be making a salary at least equal to that of Curtis McClinton. He was one of the Chiefs' stars then and he was supposed to have signed for a good figure. Later, Kansas City offered me $23,500 a year for three years and a bonus of $45,000.

Well, Linda and I did feel we would have a lot of opportunities in Kansas City because we knew the area and had a lot of friends there. It didn't seem like a bad prospect at all.

And then Buddy Young came along. And I got caught in the middle.

He was something else. I thought Jesse Meilen handled himself well. But I had never come across a black man who talked so fast and seemed to know so much about so many things as this little bullet of a cat, Buddy Young.

It turned out that he hadn't come to see me on behalf of the Baltimore Colts, though he was a scout for the Colts. He had come on behalf of the National Football League itself. He was working at the time as a coordinator for the commissioner's office. He was what you would call a field man, representing the National Football League and its twelve teams in its signing war against the AFL.

He said he just wanted to talk about the National Football League. And he talked, and talked, and talked. And I listened, and listened, and listened. Somebody asked Buddy years later whether I had come off as a bright kid to him. Buddy said, "Well, not being very bright myself, how the hell would I know? He could understand English, I'll tell you that."

Well, I *was* trying to understand what he was saying, but he went off in a lot of different directions.

"Gale," he said, "I want you always to keep your contacts with the other people [meaning Kansas City]. It would be injurious to everything I stand for to try and keep you from seeing them. Keep your options open, son, at all times."

Then he proceeded to tell me why the NFL would be better for me than the AFL. He mentioned the pension plan in the NFL, which, he said, was far superior to the AFL's. He mentioned the prestige of the league. Then he brought up something I had not heard before.

"Markets," he said. "The choice you make ought to have to do with markets, markets rather than the name of the football team. That's the important thing, especially for a Negro back of your caliber. Markets." He sounded just like the guy in the movie *The Graduate*, the guy who was always talking plastics to the kid.

He went on and on that way. "We know the AFL wants you," he said, "we know who wants you in the AFL. I just want to open your eyes to the situation. I personally feel you would be a helluva lot better off about leaving yourself free to be drafted by the NFL."

"Well, who wants to draft me?" I was impatient to know.

He brushed that aside. "I don't know. But that's not important now. By the way," he said, "are you sure you haven't signed with the AFL?"

"No."

"I don't want you to lie to me."

"I haven't signed with anyone."

Then he kind of sat back and relaxed. He was smoking one of those big cigars and feeling, I guess, in a philosophic mood.

"You see, Gale, there's something about a youngster twenty or twenty-one years old that men like myself who have been in athletics for years can always appreciate in determining not how good a football player a boy is but what kind of a person he is." Having emphasized the point, he took a big puff on his stogie. "Now a lot of people are what I call bow-wow listeners—they are talking while they're listening. Which means nothing sinks in, simply because they have all the answers. And it's not possible for any boy twenty-one years old to have all the answers. And you're a listener. You are intent. I like that. But it puts me on my guard, too, because it means that everything I say to you you'll remember and that I'll have to make good on everything I've told you."

He smiled that little smile of his, half angel pie and half Cheshire cat. "I really like you," he said. "You're a nice couple. I think you ought to come to Baltimore and have Thanksgiving dinner with my family. You'll enjoy my cooking because I'm a helluva chef."

All this time he never once talked money to us, never once told us which club wanted us, never once really told us a thing we really wanted to know. It was just pensions, prestige, and markets, especially markets.

But he really swamped us with all that jive talk and
we said yes, we'd like to go to Baltimore with him and
spend Thanksgiving with the Youngs.

Before we left, I called Don Klosterman and told
him I was making this trip. Don was very nice about it.
He said, "Fine, I think you should go ahead. You
should hear their story, too."

So we went and it turned out to be an epic journey.
On Wednesday morning we flew into Washington. I
don't know why, but we stayed in Washington overnight. I went out to a Redskin practice that afternoon
and went by the Redskins' dressing room and Buddy
introduced me to Bill McPeak, the head coach, Abe
Gibron, one of his assistants, and I met Bobby Mitchell
and a few of the other players. That night we went to
a basketball game. On Thursday morning Buddy's son,
Henny, came up and got us and we drove to Baltimore.
I kind of got the feeling that I was being held in pro-
tective custody. It sure seemed that way because Buddy
stayed really close to us. But it could have been worse.
I understand that the NFL had stashed away a bunch
of prospects in a Detroit motel the whole week.

We had a much better time at the Youngs', especially
that Thanksgiving dinner. I don't know about Buddy's
being such a great chef, but his wife, Geraldine, did a
job, I'll tell you that. And afterward, at Buddy's request,
I helped with the dishes. "You eat, you work," he said.
Just like home.

The next morning we all took a train into New York,
where the Kodak All-America team was gathering for
weekend festivities. And Buddy Young stayed with us.
He was always around.

Linda began to feel a little disturbed about Buddy,
because wherever she went Buddy would be there, cutting it up with one person or another. And she said to
me, "My Lord, everywhere this man goes, somebody
knows him." It kind of frightened her a little bit. I
think she wondered, Is he staging this? Is he paying
somebody for this?

Later, when she got to know Buddy better, Linda's

fears vanished. It turned out that Buddy Young was to become my closest confidant and adviser. I don't do a thing without him. I ask his advice on everything. We're on the phone to each other three or four times a week. And today he is like a second father to me.

On Friday evening, the night before the NFL draft, we all kicked around together, and then Buddy came back to the hotel with us. He got on the phone and made a series of calls. Beside the phone was a vase full of red roses—compliments of the American Football League.

Finally, he stopped talking on the phone long enough to tell me, "It's between the Giants, the Bears, and San Francisco. It's still a little up in the air. But don't worry," Buddy said earnestly, "they're all big-market teams."

Well, at that moment the markets didn't interest me at all. Linda still preferred Kansas City above all. But she said she wouldn't mind San Francisco because she had a brother living there. New York didn't sound too bad, either. But she didn't say anything about Chicago. I didn't know a thing about Chicago. At that point I just wanted to get the best possible deal.

Apparently, the three teams were getting together among themselves to see whom they would draft. They all wanted running backs and they decided to choose from three—Tucker Frederickson, Ken Willard, and myself. In those days of the war the NFL teams worked pretty closely together; it wasn't the cutthroat kind of competition it is today. Same in the AFL, which allowed Kansas City to draft me without competition.

At three o'clock in the morning we got a call. San Francisco had decided they were going to take Willard. The Giants were going to take Frederickson. The Bears, who had three number-one draft choices, decided I would be one of them (the other two were Dick Butkus and Steve DeLong, who was picked off by San Diego).

I wasn't too excited about the Chicago Bears, but Buddy, who came from Chicago, seemed really happy. "This is the best thing in the world for you," he said.

"I know about that town, I was born and raised there. I know what it's all about, and the guy that owns that club is a great guy, and the town is waiting for a guy like you. And one more thing . . ."

"Yeah, I know," I said wearily.

"That's right," he grinned. "Markets."

The thing is I always wanted to play in the National Football League. I told Buddy early in our relationship that in order to better yourself as a football player, you've got to play with and against the best—and the best was in the NFL at the time. I really felt that way. All my life I've had something to prove to myself. And to prove my true worth as a football player, I knew I should play in the National Football League.

The bargaining started in that hotel room at three in the morning.

Buddy was on the phone constantly, talking back and forth to George Halas. It was just Buddy and me. Linda was fast asleep.

They offered me, I think, $23,000 a year for three years. I told Buddy, "Look, I'll sign for $25,000 for four years and a $50,000 bonus." I gave him the figure I wanted.

Buddy picked up the phone. "Hold on," he said. There was a pause, then he cupped the receiver. "Gale, he offered you $24,500."

I said, "Buddy, if he gives me $25,000, I'll sign."

Buddy sighed. "I'll give you the phone and you tell him that."

So I picked up the phone and said hello.

George Halas's first words were, "How are you, my boy?" I found out later that his favorite saying was "How are you, my boy?"

He said, "You know, we want you as a football player."

"Look, Mr. Halas," I said, "if you give me $25,000 a year for four years and a $50,000 bonus, you have yourself a football player."

There was a moment of silence . . . then, "O.K., fine."

That terminated our conversation. That did it. It was all over.

At four o'clock on Saturday morning, about six hours before the start of the NFL draft, I woke Linda and told her, "I'm going to sign with Chicago."

"Chicago?" She groaned. She couldn't believe it. She like turned up her nose. She wasn't too happy about that.

The next day we went down to where they were holding the draft and Buddy brought me $500. Five hundred dollars! "Here, go buy yourself something," he said. Linda and I went on a little shopping binge.

The only thing that bothered me now was that I hadn't told Don Klosterman anything. I felt bad about that because I think he was pretty sure that I would go with Kansas City.

On Sunday evening the All-America team appeared on the Ed Sullivan show and right afterward we were supposed to go to a party at the New York Playboy Club. Then something happened that really kind of turned me against Kansas City.

Just as the Sullivan show was ending, Jack Steadman of the Chiefs pulled me off stage.

"Lamar Hunt wants to talk to you," he said.

"Look," I said, "I'm with my wife. We're going to the Playboy Club."

"We'll get you out in time."

I barely had time to holler to one of the All-Americas, Tom Nowatske, to take Linda over to the Playboy Club and tell her that I would see her there later.

We went to Lamar Hunt's hotel. I had met him before. He was an unassuming man, a quiet man, he never said too much. He just sat there and told me what they would pay me. They offered me $27,500 for three years and a $50,000 bonus. But I wasn't paying too much attention. I just wanted to get back there to Linda at the Playboy Club.

I didn't say much to them. I told them I was going into Chicago that night to meet with the Bear officials on Monday. Lamar Hunt said they would go with me.

At this time (I found out later) Don Klosterman was in New Orleans signing a couple of draft choices—Frank Pitts and Gloster Richardson. And Lamar Hunt called him from New York in a panic. "Gale won't talk," he said. And Klosterman said he would fly to Chicago to see me.

So late that night we all flew to Chicago. And as soon as we got into our hotel, which was conveniently across the street from the Bears' office, the phone rang. It was Don Klosterman.

"How you doing?" he said. "What's up?"

I said, "I'm here to talk to the Bears tomorrow morning."

"Just do me one favor, Gale. Don't sign until you talk to me."

But I couldn't really talk to him, because I had made up my mind. I had given the Bears my word. I went over to the Bears' office and met Muggs Halas, George's son. We worked out the details. When I got back to the room that afternoon I called Klosterman.

"Don," I said, "Linda and I decided we want to play in Chicago."

"Have you signed?"

"I'm committed."

"Gale, would you take $50,000 right now?"

I said, "No, Don, I can't."

That was it. There was a big press conference late that afternoon. Buddy was there, and I met George Halas for the first time. I saw this old man walk toward me and it kind of shocked me. I don't know why, but I thought I'd see a younger man. I found out later that he was still a young man inside.

Under the glare of television cameras, I officially signed my contract.

That night Linda and I were at the airport on our way back to Kansas City. As we were walking down the concourse, I spotted Don Klosterman behind me. He had his head down. I think he had seen us and was pretending he hadn't. He was as embarrassed as I was over the whole thing. But he had seen us. He told me later than I made the greatest move in my life that I jumped fifteen to twenty feet in the air and ducked into an alcove. Which I had, because I felt really bad.

Wouldn't you know it? We were on the same plane. And the takeoff was delayed. So Linda and I finally went over to his seat and tried to explain why we had chosen the Bears. He said he understood, there were no hard feelings. But it was a strained situation, a clumsy situation for everyone. I'm happy to say we got through it and remained friends. And we both value Don Klosterman's friendship today.

Why did I do it? In the end it wasn't money. It was, as I said, a combination of things. Buddy Young had sold us on the National Football League and on Chicago. I felt Buddy was right about markets. I was concerned about the lack of opportunities for black people in Kansas City. I felt there would be more opportunity for me in Chicago. I think at the time there was some racial trouble in Kansas City. I felt, as a black man, I would get a better break in a big city like Chicago. There were better job opportunities, and a black man could find a better place to live.

I got caught in the middle again late in my senior year.

School could have been an anticlimax after that— after I had fulfilled my greatest dream—but it wasn't. I went back to Lawrence and, though I kind of pulled out of some classes—and got Linda very mad—I was active in school affairs. More active than I ever had been before, in fact. And in March 1965 I was arrested, along with over a hundred other students, for taking part in a sit-in on campus.

I had found Kansas to be generally a very progressive school, a little more progressive, I think, than most other schools. Black-white relations were always very good (three-quarters of those arrested in that sit-in were white). Kansas, like a lot of colleges, has had some trouble in recent years. But when I went there, it was really a healthy situation.

Up to that March arrest, I can remember only a couple of incidents that upset me a bit, but they had nothing to do with the school itself. The summer of my junior year I worked for a paper company in town. My job was packing or burning paper. And the factory had segregated locker rooms, one for blacks and one for whites. Only our locker room was nasty all the time and the white locker room was always clean.

One day I was talking about this with Sims Stokes, another Kansas football player who was working with me. And this fellow whom we called a white Uncle Tom heard us. We called him a white Uncle Tom because he was always going back to management, telling them what black employees were saying.

What Sims and I were saying was that we were going to write our Congressman a letter about conditions at the paper company, comparing our locker room with the white locker room. We were going to let our Congressman know about this, we said.

So this fellow got very upset. He went back and told the management what we had said. The next day they let us go. "We don't need you any more," they said. And we were fired.

The other thing that bothered me quite a bit was that at the football awards dinner in my senior year the team's Most Valuable Player award went to a defensive back and a fellow who kicked field goals—a white fellow.

Well, I had led the team in five of seven offensive departments my senior year. I had made most of the All-Americas for the second year in a row. I had won two of our games with long touchdown runs. I really couldn't understand why this other fellow was picked ahead of me and it hurt me quite a bit. Right away I thought back to my senior year in high school, when I wasn't named the top high-school athlete of the year in the state, when a white kid was.

Was it racial prejudice? I have to think it was a factor. All through college some of my black friends had said that there were people at Kansas prejudiced against me. And I always said no, no, it's not like that at all. And then, after this fellow was voted Kansas's MVP, my friends were saying, "Well, why did that happen, Gale, why did that happen—because you *were* the most valuable player on the team?"

I don't know why it happened. My personality might have had something to do with it. As I said, I have always looked down on inferior players or guys I felt never gave their best effort. I have had close friends on the Bears and they've gotten me so damn mad because they didn't put out on the field. And our friendships have come to an end because of that. And I'm sure I was that way to a lot of my college teammates.

But I don't think personality should matter when you're voting for the Most Valuable Player. Performance is the only thing that should matter. And I had to think that the main reason I wasn't voted Most Valuable Player my senior year was that I was black.

I've never forgotten it, either. The last time Mike Shinn was in town, it came up. "So-and-so," I muttered the guy's name. "So-and-so. How do you like that?"

In my freshman year at Kansas I had participated in a very casual way in a small demonstration. We were protesting the policy of some fraternities and sororities of banning blacks from even trying to pledge. We also had a problem about off-campus housing for blacks. One apartment in town had a FOR RENT sign in the window, but if a black went there they said, "We can't rent it to you."

Someone came up to me that year and said, "Gale, why don't you come along?" So I did. We just marched down Jayhawk Boulevard. But there were no arrests or anything. It was all very calm.

That was the first time in my life that I had been active in any way in civil rights. But after our marriage Linda kept telling me to get off of cloud nine. "Why don't you think about something concrete," she'd say, "instead of daydreaming so much?" So when I was asked to go along on another demonstration that spring of my senior year, I decided to get involved. A lot had happened in the civil-rights movement in those four years, and I felt it was time for me to know the issues and take part in some of these problems.

The problem at Kansas was the same old one—fraternity and sorority discrimination and housing discrimination. The housing situation was the most serious. The student newspaper would carry a list of apartments to rent in town, and half of them were segregated. They didn't want black people to live in them. When black students would answer an ad for an apartment it would always turn out that the place had just been rented or that there was some mistake, they didn't have a room after all. So we were protesting against (1) the university paper's carrying ads which discriminated against blacks and (2) the fact that black students couldn't rent houses offered in the ads.

About one hundred and ten of us went to Strong Hall, to the office of the chancellor. We asked to see Chancellor W. Clark Wescoe. We wanted him to hear our grievances, but he wouldn't see us. We said we were going to stay until he saw us.

Then the vice-chancellor came out. "If you're not out of this building by five o'clock, you're going to jail." We stayed.

There were a few athletes in the group. Mike Shinn was there, Walt Wesley, who was the star of the basketball team, was there, along with some of his teammates. Kansas's faculty representative to the Big Eight came by. He said to Walt, who still had eligibility, "Look, if you don't get out of here, you're going to be off scholarship." So Walt cut on out. A couple of more athletes cut on out, too, because they had a year to go. Shinn and I and some of the others said the hell with this. We stayed.

And a couple of busses came and took us to jail.

It was all very peaceful. We walked right into the station to be booked. I remember Mike Shinn pulling a fast one. There were people lining a path for us as we stepped off the bus, and Mike simply stepped off to the side and acted as if he was one of the people watching the students go to jail. So they didn't arrest him. He thought he was sharp and he kept walking around outside, waving at us. He and another fellow who was on the bus just stood outside the jail, joking with everybody, ha, ha, ha, laughing it up.

All of a sudden a policeman came up to Mike. "You were on that bus, weren't you?"

Mike said, "What, me? No."

"Yes, you were. Come in here." And he grabbed Mike by the arm and shoved him into the jail.

They put twenty of us to a cell that normally holds about three. And we were there a couple of hours. It wasn't bad. We were singing and all.

During this time the Kansas athletic director came over and talked to the athletes. "What are you guys up to?" he said. We told him. Jack Mitchell called down, too, and said we could call our parents and let them know everything was all right if we wanted—the school would pay the bills.

Then we all went over to Chancellor Wescoe's home. We marched around the house, picketing and singing, until he came out and finally agreed that he would meet with us.

The next day he did meet with the leaders of the group, while the rest of us paraded outside Strong Hall. He said he would look into the sorority-fraternity thing, but that the problem was with the national chapters, not the local ones. And he said he would try to do something about the housing situation.

We were all suspended from school. But we knew they wouldn't kick us out of school, not for that, because there were too many people involved and we really hadn't done anything wrong. The suspensions were quickly lifted.

I wish I could say the housing picture lifted as easily. The only thing that came out of it—in my time at Kansas, at least—was that these bigots were forced to stop advertising in the school paper.

But it was a good experience for me. I think it did me a lot of good. Our complaints were legitimate and they were not far out. This was not one-millionth of a per cent of what Martin Luther King was doing at the time in Selma, Alabama. But it was something, at least.

I think too my participation made people aware that I was more than just an athlete. I think a lot of people up to then were accepting me as a football player, not as a black man. When my black brother goes to look at a house and they say it's all filled up, it affects me. Because I'm black, too. And I know if I weren't an athlete I'd be in the same boat.

And that was a lesson that has stayed with me ever since, and it helped me when I went up to Chicago to start a new life.

Part Three

15

Who Needs Seven Touchdowns?

Everything would have been all right if I could have reported to the Chicago Bears right away in July 1965, stayed in camp, and started to learn about professional football. But there was the Chicago All-Star game at Soldiers' Field, matching the college All-Stars against the champions of the National Football League (the Cleveland Browns, that year). That game got my career off to exactly the opposite of what I had planned.

Up to the Chicago game, I had enjoyed all the All-Star games I had participated in. I had played in the East-West Shrine game at San Francisco. It was a rainy, muddy day, and Roger Staubach of Navy was named the MVP. The thing I remember about that game is that Dick Butkus twice centered the ball over the punter's head. The West got two safeties as a result and beat us by two points.

Then I went to Hawaii for the Hula Bowl and I did well in that game. I gained about 120 yards in ten carries. Larry Elkins, the Baylor end, and voted the MVP.

In June 1965 I played in the All-America game at Buffalo. Dick Butkus did not center the ball over anyone's head. Instead he almost took off my head.

Butkus was with the East and I was with the West. It seemed that he was keying on me every play. It was the first time I really noticed a person keying on me. In college no one man keyed on me that much. We played basically a five-four defense in college, and they didn't stack defenses. The Buffalo game was the first time one man keyed on me. And it had to be Butkus.

I scored one touchdown in that game (Ken Willard gained about 150 yards and was the Most Valuable

Player), but Butkus was really all over me. I had never been hit so hard before in my life. He gave me a raking over. That's when I first got to appreciate him as a football player. And I appreciated even more the fact that he was going to be my teammate, not my opponent.

We gathered as teammates for the first time at the Bears' rookie camp at Soldier's Field. The Bears always held a ten-day camp for the rookies prior to the time the veterans report. It was a good rookie camp. We had, among others, Dick Gordon, Jimmy Jones, Butkus, Ralph Kurek, and Brian Piccolo.

Before the first day of practice George Halas came over to me. "How are you, my boy?" he asked. "How do you feel after the game you played at Buffalo? Good to have you here." He looked a lot younger, more vibrant, out in the field than he did when I first met him at my contract signing.

We barely got into camp when Butkus and I had to cut out for the All-Star game at Northwestern. And that was a great camp, a tremendous collection of college players. There was Willard, Tucker Frederickson, Craig Morton, Bob Berry, Staubach, Jack Snow, Clancy Williams, Junior Coffey, Ralph Neely, Malcolm Walker, Larry Elkins, Fred Biletnikoff, Bob Hayes. Great players. Everybody who was there made the pros. The class of 1965 was a helluva class.

And I was starting all the way. I was starting at halfback, and Willard, I think, was the starting fullback. And then we went over to Rensselaer to scrimmage the Bears.

On my first play of the scrimmage I was throwing a block for Willard. As he went by, he kicked my right leg.

I didn't know exactly what was wrong. I guessed I had wrenched the leg or sprained my knee or something. Anyway, I came out. I was in one play and I came out.

I tried to run on the sidelines. Then I told our head coach, Otto Graham, "I can run straight ahead fine, but I can't cut at all."

The next day I went to see the doctors. They checked the leg over but couldn't find anything wrong with it. I went back to camp and didn't practice for a couple of days. Three days before the game, we were having a banquet. I don't remember who it was, but one of the players came up to me.

"I heard that Graham thinks you're dogging it," he said. "He thinks you're ready but don't want to play."

Right after the banquet I went up to Graham. "Is it true that you think I'm dogging it," I said, "that I'm not hurt?"

Graham looked right through me. "That's right. I don't think you're hurt."

I said, "Why don't you think I'm hurt?"

"We sent you to the doctors twice and they can't find anything wrong with you."

I don't know what I said to him then. Maybe, O.K., fine. But I know I said the hell with it to myself and just walked off.

After that I went to practice and didn't do a thing. My leg was fine by then. At the time of the game I was ready to play, and Otto Graham knew it. But I didn't get in for one play. I just sat there in the rain, sat there and got wet. After the game I went home, and the next day I drove to training camp at Rensselaer.

And it got into the papers, Graham's saying, "This boy has great natural talent. But unless he changes his attitude, he'll never make the Bears, because George Halas won't have him."

That really hurt me. People had started sniping at me during my senior year in college when I tailed off near the end. "He's not tough enough," they said. "He's too meek for pro football. He's not putting out, he's saving himself for the pros." And after the All-Star game that kind of talk spread.

Well, anyone who knew me then knew that kind of talk was totally in error. If I was meek, it was because of my shyness for so many years, because I didn't say anything, didn't talk to people. But on the football field I wouldn't call myself meek.

I went into camp, and of course George Halas asked me about it. "How are you, my boy?" he said. "How do you feel?" This time he really wanted to know.

"I'm fine," I said. "I'm ready to play now."

He said, "Forget about the All-Star game, don't even worry about it. Maybe it's better you didn't play in it, anyway. I'm going to judge you by what you do here in camp. That's all." And that was the end of it.

Or almost the end of it. I still felt the incident had left question marks in the minds of my new teammates, at least some of them. There was a coolness there at the beginning, I could feel it.

It was not the natural kind of coolness you get between rookies and vets. A lot of pro teams have a regular hazing routine for rookies, but the Bears don't believe in it. The only kind of initiation is that about a week before we break camp the veterans get together and try to get the rookies drunk. In my rookie year Doug Atkins was with the Bears, and he used to drink 110-proof Fighting Cock whisky. He would take it all day long. And he just made us drink Fighting Cock. "Chug-a-lug," he said. My Lord, it was so strong. Somehow, I managed to survive that.

You expect that kind of thing to happen to you if you're a rookie, but not what was happening to me on the field. We had two fellows in our camp at the time named Billy Martin, a white Billy Martin and a black Billy Martin. The black Billy Martin was a halfback. Now, the rookie backs go out early to catch punts. And one day the big defensive end, Ed O'Bradovich, was out there on the practice field. And he was fielding some of the punts. Billy Martin the halfback pointed to me and said to O'Bradovich, "If you don't watch out, this hundred-thousand-dollar rookie will get you cut."

O'Bradovich mumbled something—I could tell he was pretty teed off—and we almost got into it right there.

We were getting ready to run the ropes, and I asked O'Bradovich, "What's the matter with you?"

He said, "Just stay in line."

"What do you mean, 'Stay in line'?"

He started running the ropes so he didn't answer, and I didn't say anything else after that.

And it wasn't until after our third exhibition game of

the season in Nashville, Tennessee, against the Los Angeles Rams, that I felt the fellows on the team started to accept me.

We had a 7–0 lead when the Rams punted and I caught the ball on our twenty-three-yard line. I cut for the sidelines, found daylight, and went in for the seventy-seven-yard touchdown run.

Later I had a ninety-three-yard kickoff return, and I threw an option pass to Dick Gordon for a third touchdown. We beat the Rams 28–14.

After the game O'Bradovich came up and smiled at me. That was all. He just smiled. But it made me think I was beginning to be a part of the team.

I had another good exhibition game against the St. Louis Cardinals, but when the season started Jon Arnett was the starting halfback. I don't know why I didn't start. I never asked Mr. Halas. I guess he just wanted to go with experience. And Jon had the experience.

Down in training camp, I could see that if I didn't get hurt I was going to start sometime or other. With all due respect to Jon Arnett—I think he was a helluva back; I never saw anyone pick a hole better than Arnett—I could see he didn't have what I had in natural ability. Hell, he was thirty-one years ond then and had been in the league ten years. I knew it was only a matter of time before I would start. Things had to go right for me.

In our season opener we got beaten by San Francisco 55–24. I carried the ball only once in that one. We lost our second game to the Rams in Los Angeles 30–28. I was in for only one play, and I scored a touchdown.

It started out from the Rams' eighteen as an option pass play. I ran laterally to my left—it is easier to throw from my left since I am lefthanded. But the Rams must have smelled out the play or remembered the pass I had thrown against them in Nashville. The receivers were covered, so I reversed field, turned the corner near the right side lines, faked out a couple of the Rams, and went in for the score.

Our third game was scheduled against the Packers in Green Bay. George Halas had a policy of never telling anybody until just before the game who was going to start. Just before the game he named his starting lineup. And in the locker room at Green Bay he called out the lineup—and up popped my name. I was very much surprised. I didn't think I was going to start. It didn't bother me, though. The tension before a game started for me in Wrigley Field the next week, when we played the Rams, when I knew I was going to start. From that time on that year, I was never able to keep anything down before a game.

We lost our third straight 23–14, but I earned a starting job.

In the third quarter, the Packers leading 20–0, "Gale Sayers burst from his rookie cocoon and came alive like the Pepsi generation." That's the way a Milwaukee writer put it, which was a little idiotic, since all I did was score on a six-yard touchdown run. It started as an off-tackle play, but the hole was plugged so I slid laterally toward the end, found a glimpse of daylight, then just put my head down and bulled over the goal with four Packers holding on. The thing I liked about that run is that it showed people I could go inside, that I had some power, that I wasn't just a scatback.

Late in the game I caught a pass from Rudy Bukich for a sixty-five-yard touchdown. I came out of the backfield and curled inside and the Packer linebacker, Lee Roy Caffey, closed in, thinking it would be a short pass. Then I turned on the speed and was all alone when Bukich hit me. I caught five passes that day and gained eighty yards in seventeen carries.

But it wasn't all that easy. The Packers had a really tough club. I remember one time I carried on a sweep around left end and Willie Davis, their All-Pro defensive end, shed blockers and came up on me. And, right alongside him, was another All-Pro, middle linebacker Ray Nitschke.

I decided I'd better just duck my head and hit into them.

The next thing I knew I was four feet off the ground.

Davis had my left leg and Nitschke my right leg. And Davis was saying, "O.K., Ray, make a wish, baby."

We played our home opener against the Rams, and I didn't do a thing from scrimmage. I carried nine times and gained twelve yards. But I did do some damage.

Early in the game I took a screen pass on our twenty. I took it on the left and cut back across the grain. Rosey Grier, who weighed 300 pounds, hit me once and spun me around, but he couldn't hold me. ("I hit him so hard," Rosey said afterward, "I thought my shoulder must have busted him in two. I heard a roar from the crowd and figured he had fumbled, so I started scrambling around looking for the loose ball. But there was no ball and Sayers was gone.") Another Ram, Chuck Lamson, leaped on my back, but I shook him off. That was it. I went in eighty yards for the touchdown.

Later in the game I hit Dick Gordon on the option pass for a twenty-six-yard touchdown. Best of all, we won our first game of the year 31–6.

By this time I was really beginning to get the feel of professional football. I began to evaluate the difference between college and pro ball, and I didn't find that much difference. The players were bigger, of course, and a little bit faster, and the defense was much more complicated. Where we played a standard five-four defense in college, the pros had a basic four-man line, but with all kinds of variations. You had to pick up their different defenses, pick up their different red dogs and stuff like that. And that took a while to learn. And they chopped at you at the line of scrimmage. In college ball when an end went out for a pass they never tried to take his head off. So you had to learn to absorb that kind of punishment on the line.

I didn't find the Bears' system hard to learn. It was odd numbers to the right, even to the left, with colors indicating formations. That's all you had to memorize. You did have to be alert on audibles, the quarterback's signaling a change in the play at the line of scrimmage.

Once I got all that down, the big thing was learning how to use my blockers. I know several times I ran past them or too close to them, so that if a defensive back was close to the line to take out the blocker, he'd take me out, too. And the blockers had to learn to adjust to my speed, too. With most backs, the blockers can slow down a little bit. But with me, as soon as the blocker comes up off his stance he's got to be rolling because I'm right on him. It was a matter of adjustment on both sides. I had to contain my running a little better, let my linemen get out in front of me.

Still, I really hadn't proven myself as a pro. I hadn't done anything special. And there remained plenty of doubters around. The week before our game with the Minnesota Vikings their head coach, Norm Van Brocklin, said something to the effect that I was just another fast scatback. He said I hadn't really been hit yet and that my roommate, Andy Livingston, was the better runner.

I think that game against the Vikings established me in the pros.

Again, I didn't have such a great day rushing, sixty-four yards. And I didn't score a touchdown in the first half. But in the second half I scored four. And the best thing about that was that I scored the last two when we needed them.

It was a real see-saw game. We led 17–13 at the half. I caught touchdown passes of eighteen and twenty-five yards in the second half, but with two minutes to go in the game the Vikings scored and took the lead 37–31.

We set up a "return left" kickoff. I was in the left receiver's spot, and if I got the ball I would veer left into an alley opened up by a wedge of four Bear blockers. Of course the Vikings knew what we intended to do, and we could hear Van Brocklin hollering from the side lines, "Plug the lane on the left. Don't give it to him."

I took Fred Cox's kick on the four. I got three beautiful blocks and was gone. Nobody touched me. I remember looking back and hollering, "Don't block, don't block!" I didn't want a clipping penalty. I got back to the bench and the players mobbed me, and that made me feel good.

After the game Viking linebacker Lonnie Warwick

was interviewed and he said, "It was the fastest I've ever seen a guy run through a hole. I was trying to break their blocking wedge, when suddenly Sayers cut to my right. He really turned it on and he was past me in a second."

We still weren't finished. Dick Butkus picked off a pass and carried it down to the Viking eleven. I plunged in between guard and tackle, ran over a couple of guys, and took it in. I didn't go like a scatback on that one.

Before I could leave the field, George Connor, the color man for CBS, grabbed me. It was the first time I had ever been interviewed on national television. Connor sounded very excited. He said. "This really must have been something for you. Was this the highlight of your career?"

"Nope." That's all I said. "Nope."

Connor was so startled he didn't know where he was. He got out of there as fast as he could. Well, hell, I was thinking back to my college days, to the game against Oklahoma State when I was a sophomore, to the good game against Oklahoma. I wasn't that excited out there. I was just doing my job (that's got to be *my* favorite expression, like Mr. Halas's, "How are you, my boy?"). The old man was paying me to run the football. That's what I was doing.

But I did feel good when I got back to the dressing room and co-captains Bob Wetoska, Mike Pyle, and Mike Ditka presented me with the game ball. And the whole team sang the traditional serenade: "Hooray for Sayers, he's a horse's ass. . . ."

I felt a little bit like one when I stepped off the plane and my good friend, Paul Patterson, met me. He gave me hell for not being kinder to George Connor over the microphone. "I don't care what's happening, man," he said, "you don't leave him hanging like that."

I sputtered, "What do you mean? Hell, I'm just running. They're blocking and I'm running."

Paul Patterson played football with Buddy Young at Illinois and Buddy introduced us to Paul and Shirley Patterson the day I signed my contract. They were really the first people we met when we moved to Chicago. They got us settled in an apartment and they've been our closest friends every since.

Paul would advise me about different business deals in those days. He told me to be careful with my money, not to be extravagant. I remember I had invested part of my bonus in some stocks. And one day I got my first dividend check and didn't know what to do with it. I went down to the store Paul was running at the time and showed him the check.

"Paul, what's this?"

He said, "Any time you see something at the top that says *pay*, it's a check."

Shirley loves to cook, and she used to invite us over every week for dinner. They just made us feel at home until we got to know the town. It was especially helpful for Linda, because she really didn't know anybody and I was away all day at practice or doing something and she was by herself all the time.

From a bad start, the year turned around completely for us.

After losing the first three games, we came back and won nine of the next ten. And we should have won ten straight. Baltimore beat us 26–21 on a disputed call. Raymond Berry was in the end zone when he caught the ball. Dave Whitsell hit Berry, and he fell out of bounds with the ball. And no part of his body was in the end zone. But they gave it to him. No way we should have lost that game.

Still, we had a shot at the Western Conference title going into our last game against Minnesota. The Rams were playing Baltimore on the Coast on a Saturday, and we'd be alive if the Rams could win. And they should have. But they blew it. They had the winning touchdown on the Colt goal line and Gabriel threw a pass and somebody intercepted it. He could have run it over.

That let us down, of course, because it eliminated all our chances. And the Vikings beat us the last game of the season 28–13. Still, it was a great turn-around season. And a satisfying rookie season for me.

After my four touchdowns against the Vikings, we beat the Lions. And the only thing I got in that game was a headache. I was running a kick back, going down the right side lines, and Wally Hilgenberg was coming up the right sidelines. Only I didn't see him. I don't know why. Maybe I was looking away. And he clotheslined me. (A "clothesline" is a forearm extended into a runner's path; it catches you in the Adam's apple at full speed. It's like running in the dark in your back yard and hitting . . . a clothesline.) Hilgenberg nearly took my head off, and I was groggy most of the rest of the game. That was the toughest shot I took all year long.

The next week we played Green Bay again. They came in undefeated, they had won six games in a row, they were heavy favorites. And we stopped them 31–14. It was probably our best effort of the year, a helluva team effort.

I didn't play an exceptional game. Jon Arnett was the big gun for the Bears. I did pick up sixty-two yards in sixteen carries. I scored one touchdown from the ten. I also returned a punt sixty-two yards. Junior Coffey got hold of a leg in that one and slowed me down, but I was able to pull loose. Two other Packers lunged at me, one from each side, but I slipped past them and they knocked into each other. I got hauled down from behind on the fifteen.

After losing that disputed game to Baltimore that we should have won, we beat St. Louis, Detroit, and New York (I ran for 113 yards against the Giants, my first 100-yard day; I also scored my thirteenth and fourteenth touchdowns of the season, a Bear record, and a record for rookies in the NFL).

We went into Baltimore, who were now leading the West, and we beat them 13–0. It was a tremendous effort by our defense. I rushed for 118 yards and got away on a sixty-one-yard touchdown run. After the game, one of the Chicago papers quoted George Halas as saying that I proved I was for real on that run.

Well, I didn't think it was anything special. It was just a pitchout and Bobby Boyd came up. Soon as I got the ball he was there. I faked to the inside first, then to the outside, then went inside of him. He grabbed my leg, and I cut back away from him. And that was it.

The game everyone associates me with, to this day, was the San Francisco game, our next-to-the-last of the season.

The night before, Buddy Young called me at home. "You got a shot at Rookie of the Year," he said, "but they're pushing Bob Hayes and Tucker Frederickson. You have to have a good day against San Francisco."

I said, "I'll see what I can do for you."

I went out and scored six touchdowns to tie a National Football League record. I set a single-game record of 336 total yards—rushing, receiving, and returning kicks. Buddy called me back that night.

"I wanted you to have a good day," he said, "but not that good a day. That was ridiculous."

Most people seem to think that was my greatest day as a pro. As far as setting records, it was the best, but I still feel the Viking game was better because we needed my touchdowns to win it. This one wasn't even close. It was a game we couldn't lose. Everything went right for us. We just put points on the boards almost every time we got the ball (we beat them 61–20). There was no way in life they could keep up with us that day.

It had rained the day before the game and the field was muddy. Mr. Halas had us put on nylon spikes. They're longer than rubber and they grip better. Actually, the footing was pretty firm under the surface. I didn't have any trouble cutting.

The first time we got the ball, on our twenty, Bukich called for a screen pass to me. I took the ball in a crowd but found a slit of daylight, stepped through, and broke into the clear. That was the toughest touchdown of the whole day because of the traffic. On the others, the blocking was just fantastic.

My second one was a twenty-one-yard sweep. My

third one was a seven-yard sweep. My fourth one was off a pitchout at the fifty. There was daylight from the start, and I just sprinted in. Number five came late in the third quarter, a one-yard pop over the center.

Midway in the fourth quarter they punted to me at our fifteen. It was a low line drive. I went straight upfield, cut to my right, made a quick move, and got away from the first wave of tacklers. They started chasing me upfield, but they ran into my blockers coming back downfield. I was touched one time, by Ken Willard. He was chasing me from behind, and I was cutting back to the left against the grain to avoid some men. Willard got a hand on my leg, but I made a little move and took it away.

I must admit I lost my cool on that one. When I crossed the goal line I tossed the ball into the air, clapped my hands together, danced a few steps, and ran back to the bench where a couple of my teammates lifted me off the ground. I don't know why I did it. The other five I just gave the ball to the officials, as I always do. I guess I was a little excited on this one because it was something I had never done in my life.

I might possibly have made a seventh touchdown, too. Mr. Halas took me out after my sixth TD. We had a big lead and he didn't want to see me get hurt. We drove on the 49ers once more. The crowd was hollering, "We want Sayers! We want Sayers!" But Jon Arnett stayed in and scored from two yards out.

I did have one more chance, the last play of the game, when I took a punt on our nineteen. I started running straight ahead, then angled to the left and into the lane opened by my blockers. I saw open field then and cut back, but I slipped a little and they brought me down around midfield. Another step and I might have gone all the way.

But as I told Tommy Dare some time later when we were talking about that game, "Who needs seven touchdowns?"

I got into the dressing room and the Bears broke a precedent. They presented me with the game ball. That was the first time ever that any Bear player had received two game balls in one season. And they sang me that sweet song again: "Hooray for Sayers, he's a . . ."

I had never received so much attention in my life. That locker room was unbelievable, full of reporters and cameramen. There was no way I could be the first one out that day. While reporters were talking to me, George Halas was telling people it was the greatest performance he'd ever seen on the field by one man.

Naturally, the writers wanted to know, "Was this your greatest thrill in football?"

"One of the greatest," I admitted. I gave them that. At least I didn't say, "Nope." It *was* a thrill because that gave me twenty-one touchdowns for the year, and the next week in our last game I scored another, and the twenty-two was a new NFL record and also beat out Jim Brown by a touchdown for the scoring title. I had 132 points to his 126. Which made me the highest single-season scorer in Bears' history.

While I was dressing and talking to the writers, the telegrams started coming in. I saved two for my scrapbook. One was from Ernie Nevers, who had set the six-touchdown record in 1929. He said, "Congratulations on the greatest one-man performance I've ever witnessed on a football field. Your brilliance will long be remembered in this sport. With every good wish to a player who has only begun to contribute. . . ."

The other telegram I saved was from my high-school coach, Frank Smagacz. It read: "It's about time you cut loose."

16

Looking Somewhat Like a Man

I think Linda felt a lot more excited than I did about
my rookie season, about leading the league in scoring
and touchdowns and making Rookie of the Year and
the All-Pro team alongside Jim Brown and playing in
my first Pro-Bowl game at Los Angeles. She told me,
"You've been deserving of things before but never
gotten them. Now you have."

The recognition made me feel good, of course, but
really not overwhelmed. People have always asked me,
"Gale, what have been the highlights of your career?"
What do I tell them? I tell them I don't have any highlights, and that lets them down. But it's the way I feel,
it's the way I am. As I have said over and over—and
will say here for the last time, I promise you—I'm getting paid to do a job, and if I do it better, fine. If people
want to write about me, fine. The only highlight I get
is when another player comes to me, from an opposing
team, and says that he saw the movies of me and saw
me put some move on so-and-so. That makes me feel
good. And after a game when somebody praises me,
that satisfies me. The six touchdowns, hell. It's just
something I did, that's all. I'm just trying to do the
best job possible.

The biggest satisfaction I received after my rookie
year came in a meeting with Coach Halas. Every year
he calls his men in. He and his son Muggs make it a
point to talk to all the players before they go away. The
Halases will go over the season with the player—how
he did, what is expected from him next year, and so
forth. They'll tell the player to stay in shape in the off
season, and they'll just generally wish the player well.

When George Halas called me in, I wasn't prepared for what he was going to say.

"You had a fantastic year, my boy." He smiled and said, "I'm giving you a little bonus." He handed me a check for $10,000.

I was so surprised I didn't know what to say. Because I wasn't expecting a damn thing. I was happy to get my salary. I was happy to know I was doing a job. I guess I muttered my thanks and said, "I hope I can come back next year and do the same thing."

And each year after the season George Halas has had this little talk with me and given me a sizable bonus. Even in 1968, when I missed five games, I got a big bonus.

I know the reputation Mr. Halas has in the press and among some players. He's supposed to be cheap, a tightfisted owner. Well, he doesn't pull any punches with you, that's for sure. He tells you exactly how it is. And he will fight you over $500 at contract time. But is this being tight? I think the man has gotten an undeserved reputation. I think he probably pays his players the salary they deserve. I only know this: The only way I can judge him is on what he's done for me, and there is no way I can knock him.

He's helped me in so many ways over the years. He's introduced me to prominent people, like Sam Lizzo, vice-president of the Northern Trust bank, who has become a valued friend and business adviser. Mr. Halas helped us find the house we bought in 1966. We wanted to borrow some money so we could make a larger down payment and not have as large a mortgage interest. We didn't have the money handy, so I went to Mr. Halas and borrowed the money—without interest. And there was no hesitation at all on his part. I think any Bear player can borrow money from him, with no interest. And there aren't many owners who will do that.

I always respected him as a coach, too. He was very stern, a bug on detail. He wanted to get everything right. We might practice an hour and fifteen minutes or we might practice an hour and forty-five minutes because he wanted to get it down exactly right. That was fine with me. A lot of players bitched about it, but if we had to do it, we had to do it.

And I have never believed what a lot of people have said, that football has passed Halas by. There are only certain things you can do in professional football, and we run the same offense as anybody else in the league and the same defense. He is an old man in age but he has always surrounded himself with relatively young aides, men of imagination like George Allen and Jim Dooley, and he has always been open to new ideas. That's the thing. Although he is old, he is always open to new ideas.

As I say, my relationship with Mr. Halas may be a little special because of my value to the team. Also, I think it developed a little into a father-son thing between us. He likes people who are loyal to him and I think I always have been. It's a matter of mutual respect. The only thing he asks of you is that you meet him halfway—sometimes, I admit, a little more than halfway.

In my rookie year I owned a Corvette, a real cool car. I have always liked to drive small cars, fast cars. I still do. One day we were driving back from an exhibition game against the Packers in Milwaukee and I opened it up a little bit—110 miles an hour. Naturally, Mr. Halas was driving along the same road—going a lot slower, I might add—and he spotted my car on the highway. This wasn't hard to do, since my license plate was GS40. About two days later he called me into his office.

"Gale," he said, "you know what? They could arrest you for murder."

"What do you mean?"

"Well, for one thing you were driving too fast at 110, and if you killed Linda that would be murder. You would probably kill yourself, too. So I think, my boy, you better get rid of that Corvette."

I decided to give in to his wisdom.

The same thing happened to me between the 1967

and 1968 seasons when I was tooling around on a Honda motorbike. I was just driving it around the neighborhood and he found out about it. He told me to get rid of it, and I did.

In the winter of 1969–70, I was playing with the Bears' basketball team. We had a bunch of exhibition games scheduled and we got paid for playing. I received a call from Mr. Halas in Phoenix, Arizona, where he has a winter home. His spies had been active. "I hear you're playing basketball," he said.

"That's right."

"Retire."

He didn't want to see me risk an injury because of some has-beens and never-weres who think they're just as tough as football players and go out on the court and try to prove it.

So I retired.

Maybe you would call Halas paternalistic, but it works both ways.

In one of my early years with the Bears I got Mr. Halas to agree to give my brother Roger a tryout. Mr. Halas offered Roger $12,000 if he made the club. Well, he didn't make it, he got cut. He stayed with the club for about three weeks, and the old man cut him and still gave him $6000. That was done out of respect for me.

In the summer of 1968, before the Presidential election, somebody put in the papers that I was supporting Richard Nixon. And I wasn't. George Halas, who is a Republican and contributed heavily to the Republican campaign and was for Nixon, told them to take my name out of the paper and print a retraction. "If you're not for him," he told me, "you're not for him." And that was that. I think generally that Mr. Halas's philosophy is that he's going to treat each of his players with respect and he wants the same respect.

I looked forward to my second season in the pros for many reasons. For one thing, I was more relaxed. In 1965 I had to make the team, I had to prove myself. Now that was over with. Secondly, our home life was becoming more stable. Buddy had told me that I absolutely had to live in Chicago in the off season. And that was fine with me. I got into the Sears Roebuck training program and did a few other things. And when Linda became pregnant, we decided to buy a house. We reached this decision right after the Pro Bowl game in Los Angeles.

That was the one good thing that came out of the game. I have played in four Pro Bowls and been named Most Valuable Player on offense in three. But that year Vince Lombardi didn't let me play much; he just had me run back kickoffs. The East beat us badly and Jim Brown was named the Most Valuable Player. And a little while later he announced his retirement from pro football.

I don't know whether that made me feel better or not. Brown had won the rushing title in 1965 with over 1500 yards. I was second with 867. So there was a lot of competition out of the way, just like that. I always had tremendous respect for Jim Brown. It was just unbelievable how he ran. People like to compare us, but he was a completely different kind of runner from me. He was much bigger, much stronger. I'm a little faster than he was, a little quicker, too. Not that he wasn't quick. He had a lot more speed than people realized. You never saw him running over too many tacklers. He was so big at 230 they thought he ran over them. But he didn't. He kind of slid off, and then he'd outrun people. He was the kind of man who could carry the ball forty times a game, and I wasn't that kind of man.

If I carried twenty times a game in my early years with the Bears it was a lot. If it was ninety degrees out there and I ran a lot of sweeps at the beginning of the game, I might get tired after twelve carries. I have always preferred to start by hitting off tackle, hitting up the gut a couple of times to get used to carrying the ball, get used to people hitting me, and dragging me, and falling on top of me. You start running sweeps, you run ten yards laterally and maybe gain only two yards. Running sweeps at the beginning of the game takes a lot out of you.

And in 1966 I didn't run as many sweeps. I was running up the middle more. People said I was stronger. I may have been. I had gained a little weight; I think I played at 205. I had started working out that off season at the Lawson Y under madman Woit, so I was in shape when I reported with the rookies ten days before the veterans came to camp.

Another reason for running inside more was that in 1966 Green Bay introduced the "jet-eye" defense. And that helped cut off the sweeps. The way it works is the defensive ends line up outside the two tackles and come down across the face of our tackles, toward the center, and their tackles do the same thing. They converge across the face of the guards. This knocks off the pulling guard so he can't get out. So when a runner gets out there, he's all by himself. This brings the linebacker up, and here comes the defensive halfback forcing. And it kills the sweep.

The thing worked very successfully, and a lot of other teams adopted the system. So we started running more plays up the middle. And we had good blocking off the line—we always had good blocking off the line. I felt we had a really fine line, but they never got the credit they deserved.

Off our 1965 finish I thought surely we'd have a championship contender in 1966, but the team never got off the ground. Before we got started we were two-and-three, just as we had been in 1965, just as we would be in 1967, 1968, and 1969. We just had a history of not getting off the ground quickly enough. So we were out of the race before the season was even half over. And we ended up with five wins, seven losses, two ties.

Rudy Bukich was the quarterback and he had a terrible year. Mike Ditka was playing out his option and he had an off year. Nothing went right. Finally, Coach Halas, after we knew we couldn't win it, told our line, "We can't win anything, so be sure to go out and try to help Gale win the rushing title."

He designed special plays for me to carry the ball, to utilize my blockers, to get yardage. And fellows like Ronnie Bull, George Seals, Bob Wetoska, Mike Rabold, and Jim Cadile really did the job.

I have often been asked, "Does it hurt the ball club when it comes down to one guy instead of a more balanced attack?" More than likely it does, but what do you do when the quarterback can't hit his man? You've got to give the ball to somebody who's going to get you the yardage, get you the touchdowns. Do you think I like to lose? I do not. I'd rather win a championship than a rushing title any year. The only goal I have ever set in football is to win a National Football League championship, to try and help the team win the championship.

Anyone who has the smallest amount of pride in himself wants to try and win, try and *earn* that money instead of collecting a paycheck. You've got to admire the athlete who plays the game because he loves it and is really trying, and not just for the money. I've known many pro football players who just tried to hang on, make the top forty so they could get the money. I don't think that's the attitude to take in professional football.

I have learned to accept defeat over the years, but that doesn't mean I have learned to *love* it. In my early years with the club it was really bad. I used to blame all our defeats on me. If I didn't have a good day I'd say, Well, *I* lost the game. And I really worked hard to come back the next week to have a better game. But now I have learned to accept defeat. If the hole's not there, I'm not going to go through it. If Roger Brown's standing there, I'm not going to run over Roger Brown. So I learned to look at it in a different light and say, Hell, I did my best—if I really have done my best. I just want to do the best job and come out of this game looking somewhat like a man.

That was my attitude in 1966, even as we were losing. And I think I did come out of that losing season looking like a man.

The last five games of the 1966 season I gained 486

yards on sixty-two rushes, 139 yards on five pass receptions, 183 yards on seven kickoff returns, 164 yards on twelve punt returns. And I scored twelve touchdowns in those five games.

I had one big game against Atlanta in which I gained 172 yards. That was my third 100-plus game of the year. The next week I got only thirty-eight against Baltimore, then only thirty-nine against San Francisco. Our last game of the season was against the Minnesota Vikings. Cleveland had played on Saturday and Leroy Kelly, my closest competitor for the rushing title, had gained only nineteen yards. But I still needed ninety-seven yards to beat him, to win the NFL rushing title.

Leroy Kelly had moved right in for Jim Brown at Cleveland, and he immediately became my biggest rival as a running back in the league. There's no question about it, he's a great runner. Again, like Brown, he's a different kind of runner from me. I depend a lot on my moves. I do a lot of faking—head, arms, legs, and all. But Kelly hits a hole and kind of hesitates a little bit, relaxes, and then breaks off. A lot of times you think you have him and you don't. It's not a glide like Brown's. It's a more subtle kind of style, and he's very successful with it.

That Viking game meant a lot to me in other ways, too. My mother and father had come to Chicago for the game. This was the first time they had seen me play pro football live. It was a very cold day and my mother went into the ladies' room at half time and never came out. But my father stayed with it and joined me in the dressing room after the game.

It all broke right from the start. I returned the opening kickoff ninety yards for the touchdown. I scored another on a three-yard sweep. I set up two others with a thirty-eight-yard off-tackle run and a twenty-six-yard pass completion. And I helped put us in field-goal range twice with runs of forty and fifty-four yards.

We swamped the Vikings 41–28, and my teammates really got behind me. The blocking was tremendous. I had the NFL rushing title all locked up before the first half ended. We went into the dressing room leading 31–14, and I had run for 120 yards.

I finished with 197 for the day. I wasn't even looking for 200 yards. I figured, if it's gonna come, it's gonna come (it did come, against Green Bay, in 1968). The 197 yards, the 339 total yardage for the day, was enough to set four Bear records: most yards gained rushing in a day, most yards gained rushing in a season (1231), most total yards, and most total yards in a season (2440). That last one was a league record, too. And I ended up leading the National Football League in rushing and also in kickoff returns.

I also ended up with the game ball, which made me feel very good, especially since my father was in the dressing room when they presented it to me.

There must be something about playing against the Vikings. In 1965 I had that four-touchdown day. Now this. And our earlier 1966 game with the Vikings turned out well, too. We were losing late in the fourth quarter. The score was 10–7 when we got the ball on our forty-five.

I ran for seventeen yards, then for nine yards. And on the next play Mike Ditka carried a Bukich pass through three defenders for the winning touchdown.

I'd have really been down if we lost that one. For that night when I returned from Minnesota I took Linda to the hospital. The next day she gave birth to Gale Lynne. That not only helped make my season complete. It made our life complete.

17

The Subject Is Relaxation

One thing about a woman, a woman never stops arguing. She talks and talks and talks. I don't care how big a man you are, a woman thinks she can whup a man. And she just keeps on coming, you know.

I think the thing with a woman is that she finds it difficult to keep things in. She will cry and all. But the man, most of his emotions are kept in. A woman likes to have her say and get it over with.

Evening.
Linda is sitting on a chair in the den holding the baby.
Gale is slumped back on the couch, staring out into space. Music is coming from the record player.
LINDA: What are you thinking about?
GALE: Thinking? If I've got my music on, I'm thinking? You say I'm not relaxing, you say I'm thinking about things.
LINDA: But you are.
GALE: Am I relaxing when I have my music on?
LINDA: Like me, when I'm sitting down in the evening, I'm—
GALE *(annoyed):* Different strokes for different folks.
LINDA *(remaining calm, but with a hard edge coming into her voice):* Most people find something to lose themselves in.
GALE: I lose myself in my thoughts and my music, and you should accept that. You should accept the fact that people relax in different ways. And that's the way I relax, and you say I'm not relaxed. If I say I am, why do you want to say I'm not relaxed? You don't know . . .

LINDA: Some people don't want to tell themselves the truth.

GALE *(becoming sarcastic):* And you say I'm one of those people, huh?

LINDA: You are.

GALE: Who told you that?

LINDA: I've been living with you for seven years. I can tell when your nerves are on edge. I don't mind your wanting quiet. That's one thing I will accept, not wanting to talk and all that. But this pensiveness, this always thinking deep, deep thoughts.

GALE *(rises from the couch and moves around the floor):* And what's wrong with it?

LINDA: Last year—don't tell me you weren't thinking and worrying about your leg a lot.

GALE: Why shouldn't I worry about my leg?

LINDA: I know you should, but why put yourself through that emotional strain?

GALE: You know I didn't want to be bothered, so why did you bother me?

LINDA: I wasn't bothering you, honey, that's why I was under emotional stress, trying not to.

GALE: This is something you have to accept.

LINDA: I have accepted it—now you must admit it— I do accept it well. But, Gale, you put a lot of unnecessary pressures on yourself.

GALE *(back on the couch):* Now you're getting off the subject. We're talking about relaxing and thinking; you're talking about something else.

LINDA: You're saying that I don't let you relax, that if I would let you relax you'd keep your mind clear.

GALE: I keep my mind clear.

LINDA: But you put it on me.

GALE: No, I don't.

LINDA: Yes, you do.

(Pause.)

GALE: Just because I sit around the house and think, you think I've got to be thinking of something. What do I think about? To be truthful, I don't know. I think of millions of things. Sometimes so many things are running through my mind, nothing makes sense. I imagine most of it is about football. Nothing specific. When I listen to music I just listen. While I listen I might be thinking about something, but this is the way I relax. I don't want to be doing anything. A lot of people daydream about nothing, you know.

LINDA *(in a resigned tone):* Honey, from my observation—and I've observed you for seven years—you can sit for hours and hours—

GALE: Well, so what? What difference is it how long I sit?

LINDA: But you should realize that I'm a wife, that I'm totally, completely dependent on you in every kind of way there is. . . . I don't like to see you like this all the time.

GALE: This is like you studying for a big exam. Do you want to be bothered? No, you don't. It's the same way week after week. I don't want to be bothered. Week after week I got a big exam, every Sunday.

LINDA: Gale, I'd accept that during the football season but not during the off season.

GALE: Off season is different, Linda.

LINDA: No, it's not. Not the last two years. Because in '67 you had somewhat of a bad season. . . .

GALE *(voice rising, full of disbelief):* Had what? That was no bad season. I made All-Pro.

LINDA: Yes, you did. But you thought it was a bad season.

GALE: I won Outstanding Player of the Pro Bowl. How could that be a bad year?

LINDA: Why was it? Because in '67—that was when you worried so much about getting a slow start—you had a couple of bad games. Like against Los Angeles you carried the ball thirteen times for thirteen yards. You had a good game against Detroit. The week after, you couldn't play in Cleveland. Then you came back and had another bad game. Well, as a result, you got sick, your stomach bothered you.

GALE: No, don't blame that for my getting sick.

LINDA: I do, because there was nothing wrong with you at that time.

GALE: I had diarrhea.

LINDA *(her voice rising):* Gale, your stomach was upset.

GALE *(his voice rising):* Linda, I had diarrhea.

LINDA: You had gastritis. You will not admit it, but that week you had a bad case of gastritis.

(Pause.)

GALE: What's gastritis?

LINDA: That's inflammation of the stomach.

GALE: What's it caused by?

LINDA: By nerves.

GALE: What else?

LINDA: Nerves.

GALE: Oh, come on.

LINDA: Nerves, period. It wasn't from eating rich foods. You do not eat rich foods. I do not feed you rich foods. We do not eat—

GALE: I tell you, I had diarrhea the whole week.

LINDA: I'll tell you what. After that Detroit game you hurt your knee. Remember, you stayed up all night long worrying about your knee. All that week you were wondering if you would be able to play.

GALE: Why shouldn't I worry about it, Linda?

LINDA: I know you should, Gale, but you shouldn't extra worry.

GALE: Extra worry? That's my livelihood. Extra worry. *(He snorts.)*

LINDA: I know that, Gale, but to the point that you weren't sleeping. And then the next week when you—

GALE: How many hours of sleep do I get a night? Five? Four and a half?

LINDA: Yes, but you were staying awake all night most of those nights. You were. Why don't you admit that you worry?

GALE: If I didn't worry, Linda, I wouldn't be a football player.

LINDA: I know you wouldn't. But I just think you should do something to relax a little bit more.

GALE: I relax. *(Pause.)* I'm going to take up the guitar.

LINDA: Isn't it right that you didn't play that game in '67 and came back and had a couple of more bad games.

GALE *(greatly irritated):* Linda, don't say *bad* games.

LINDA: I think you came back and—

GALE: I was third in the league in rushing.

LINDA: I know you were.

GALE: All right, dear, don't say "bad."

LINDA: Gale, Gale, it wasn't bad, but it was bad for you, and you thought it was bad. I kept telling you, Gale, you're not having that bad a season, why are you upset? I can remember those words, me telling you—

GALE: So you wanted me to say, "Well, O.K., it's not bad." Well, I'd just go ahead—

LINDA: You kept saying, "Well, it's not too damn great." I said, "What do you expect? The Bears are losing as usual, what do you want?" You don't remember that time, you don't remember it being a bad time?

GALE: No, I don't think it was.

LINDA: I think it was. I know I was worried to death about you. I wish I were like some people who couldn't care less. I wish I were that way because I worry lots, I worry lots about you. I mean, I care about you.

GALE *(gently, almost under his breath):* Let me do the worrying.

LINDA: Well, I worry about you because there's no way a woman can live with a man and not worry about his emotional well-being. That's all there is to it. And I can't accept your torturing yourself.

GALE: Why do you say I torture myself?

LINDA: Well, you do.

(Pause.)

GALE *(in a tone of resignation):* What's all this got to do with relaxing?

I'm not really easygoing at home. Sometimes—during the season especially—I seem to stay on edge all the time. But when I'm at home I like to relax. I don't like to do anything. Linda thinks I'm supposed to do something, which of course I am. But when I want to relax, I want to relax—and not do anything.

I can say that in seven years of marriage we really never had a serious, serious quarrel. We've had discussions, we've had arguments, about just totally unnecessary, ridiculous things. I mean, most people argue about money—I don't know what they argue about; but we haven't really had anything serious to argue about.

When Gale and I were first married—even a few years ago—I misunderstood him a lot. I understand him now a lot more than I did. I really do. I mean, I can understand a lot of his feelings. He doesn't think so, but I do. At first, I didn't think he felt deeply about many things. But I learned, and I would say, Boy, I was really wrong about Gale because he is a person with lots of depth. He has a sensitivity about things. I used to think he didn't have any foresight and things, but he does. But it's still hard for me—I guess for any wife— to see her husband go through this mental anguish.

Linda has made me more conscious of the things I do and say. And it's probably helped me grow.

18

Paying the Price

Maybe Linda is right, maybe 1967 was a bad year, maybe I was extra worried about it. It certainly wasn't the best year of my career. And things happened to me that had never happened before.

Like in our first game of the season, against Pittsburgh, I gained two yards rushing, *two* yards. And the way it started, I thought we would wipe them out.

They kicked off to us. I ran the kickoff back 103 yards for a touchdown.

We kicked off to them. They got the ball and Rosey Taylor intercepted a pass and ran it in. And we're two touchdowns ahead.

They kicked back to us. On the first play from scrimmage I gained about twelve yards. Only we were called for holding. From then on it was all downhill. From then on I couldn't get to the line of scrimmage and they just stomped on us.

We couldn't do anything right. One play I was open in the flat for a pass. There was nobody near me. And our quarterback, Larry Rakestraw, didn't see me. Later our other quarterback, Rudy Bukich, threw behind me when I had an open field.

Here we had jumped off 13–0. What did we think to ourselves? Why, that we've got an easy game today. And they beat us 42–13. Certain things happen. You think, What else is going to happen?

The next week we played Green Bay. We intercepted them five times, we recovered three of their fumbles. And they beat us. . . . Certain things happen.

Finally, we won a game. We beat the Vikings, and I had my first good game, gaining seventy-three yards against them. But then Baltimore handed it to us, and I bruised my left leg, my Achilles tendon, in that one. I sat out part of the game but returned in the second half.

The leg didn't feel too good most of the next week, but by Friday I was running full speed and it seemed to be holding up O.K. We played Detroit in the rain at home, and I had a really good day. I gained 142 yards, and we beat the Lions 14–3.

On Monday, our day off, I felt fine. On Tuesday I came to practice and ran hard, as I usually do. When I got up Wednesday morning I couldn't walk, I couldn't even put any pressure on the leg.

I think in the Detroit game somebody must have kicked my Achilles tendon. But I didn't feel it at the time. I guess I just ran too much on it on Tuesday and maybe even stretched it a little bit more. I went to see Dr. Fox before practice. He gave me a cortisone shot, which hurt at first more than my foot did. I had had shots before, but not like that one. The Achilles tendon is about the strongest tendon in your body. And he shot me right in that tendon, and I thought I would die, the thing hurt so much.

And it was up in the air whether I would be able to play against Cleveland.

The business of injuries to professional football players is a tricky one, with all kinds of complications. You really have to leave it up to the team doctor. I have always found Dr. Fox a man I could rely on, a man I could go to if I had problems. My philosophy about aches and pains is to get them checked out, to be sure they're not going to impair your performance. I have never faked an injury or thought that I've had an injury when I haven't. Everything that I go to see the doctor about is something I feel might hinder my play. Like if I sprain my neck: If it doesn't feel right, I'm going to see Dr. Fox and ask him why it doesn't feel right. And if he says there's nothing wrong with it, then that's fine.

In my rookie year, when I wasn't all that sure of myself or my own capacity, I may have overdone it with

the doctor. After a ball game I'd have an ache here or
a pain there and I'd want him to check it out. Finally,
he gave me his lecture for beginning running backs in
professional football who are annoying their doctor.

"Gale," he said then, "now I've been taking care of
professional athletes for over twenty years, and there's
one thing I've learned. There are two kinds of athletes
that come to the Bears: One is the athlete and the other
is the pro."

I wasn't sure what he was talking about, but he kept
right on going.

"I'm the first guy who knows the guy who's going to
be the pro and is going to be great, and I also know
the guy, the athlete, who's going to be average, medi-
ocre, and may not make it at all. I can tell you how I
know this." He shook a finger at me and continued.

"This is a brutal sport, a collision sport, and you're
going to have bumps and bruises. My job is to tell you
when you have an injury that is going to keep you out
of one game, two games, three games, or four games.
Mr. Halas has kept me on this team as orthopedic
surgeon because he knows that I have been able to keep
the players playing; by treating them for their trivial
injuries I keep them playing from week to week. But he
also knows that when I say a player can't play, that I
won't let him play, he will not play. My first responsibility is to protect the man, then the team.

"Now, you have to trust me, Gale. If you're hurting
in a way that you can't play or it's going to make you
worse, or it's going to damage you in some way, I will
not let you play. No amount of pressure from anybody,
Mr. Halas or the coaches—anybody—is going to let me
allow you to go on that football field if you're really
hurt. But if you are hurting and I judge you're able to
play, you've got to be the pro and have the heart and
the motivation and the guts and what I call the X-
quantity [Dr. Fox loves that formula—the X-quantity
elevates a player one plateau: it makes a star out of an
average player, a superstar out of a star, etc.]. You've
got to be able to go out there and do your best even

though you might have a pain in your butt or a pain in the neck or a pain in the head or a pain in your big toe. As long as you have confidence in me, as long as you realize I know what I'm talking about—that I consider you as a patient and a person first and a football player second—I think everything is going to be all right."

End of lecture. I finally understood what he was driving at. Many times in high school or college if you were bruised you might not play (though I always played). But here you've got to play. It's part of what they call, in pro football, paying the price.

Paying the price means that when you're so tired and you can't go on any farther, you've just got to give a little bit more, make that one more block, carry the ball one more time. Paying the price is working to get that knee in shape, the one that was operated on. Paying the price is playing when you're hurt, too, playing with injuries. I think most football players are willing to pay the price. The ones who aren't take the easy way out. It hurts a little bit, so they say they can't play and they won't play. That's wrong. If the doctor tells you you can play, you can't hurt what you've got any more, it might pain you but you can play—you play. You just have to go out there and do your best.

In 1966 I was at the San Francisco goal line, running an off-tackle play, and a big tackle jumped on my back. And as I was going forward, trying to hit that goal line, Kermit Alexander came up and hit me. He smashed the front of my right knee and it felt as if I could hear gristle popping. Oh, it hurt badly. I stayed in the game, and Ronnie Bull carried for the touchdown. When I came out I could hardly walk on it.

I told Dr. Fox that the knee felt like hell. He said, "Well, try to walk on it and it'll be all right." So I pranced up and down the side lines and it was sort of bad. He took the cold stuff and sprayed the knee.

This was before half time. I went back out and played the rest of the game and wound up with eighty-seven yards.

We were playing Green Bay the next game. I didn't

practice the whole week. I couldn't even walk until Thursday. Dr. Fox shot me almost every day with cortisone. He said, "Well, you can't do anything else to it. It's going to pain to run on."

I started jogging on Saturday. On Sunday I couldn't even bend my damn knee. He gave me a shot and I played. I started and played the whole game. We lost 13–7. I couldn't cut well, but I carried the ball twenty times and gained sixty-eight yards. I think that's what is meant by paying the price.

So I personally thought I'd be able to play against Cleveland. Wednesday at practice I couldn't do anything. Thursday I couldn't do anything. Friday I tried it, and Saturday I started running a little bit.

At that time every National Football League team had to submit an injury report to the commissioner's office on Tuesday. Well, on Tuesday I was ready to go, so they didn't list me as a doubtful or anything. Friday I was running and Saturday I could do a little more. I thought surely I'd be able to play.

That Saturday we got on the plane for Cleveland. George Halas came over to me and said, "I don't think I'm going to let you play." I guess Dr. Fox had talked to him. The Achilles tendon is a tricky thing. It's what a runner pushes off on. If I reinjured it, or it wasn't properly healed, I might have to miss four or five games or maybe the rest of the season. So he probably advised Coach Halas not to play me.

And I didn't bother to put on my game face.

Gale puts on his game face every Friday. That means he gets evil. And he doesn't realize this transformation that comes over him. It happens on Friday. All week, through Thursday, he is almost human. But on Friday he gets very solemn. And on Saturday he becomes just completely oblivious to everything that's going on around him. Like the house could fall down and he's not too concerned about it. And then Sunday morning he's just awful. I walk around all Sunday morning with a lump in my throat. I remember one morning we got

*into an argument because I cooked him Cream of Wheat
and didn't have toast to go with it, and he always has
two pieces of toast with his Cream of Wheat. He
stomped around in a rage because he didn't have that
toast. "You know I can't eat Cream of Wheat without
toast." I learned long ago not to say anything to him on
Sunday because he's really so keyed up.*

On Sunday morning Coach called me. "Gale," he
said, "I want you to get a couple of shots and play."

I said, "O.K., I will." I don't know what changed
his mind; maybe he felt we needed the game. I really
don't know. But I did think I could play. Even though
my game face wasn't on.

Then I got on the field. I saw Dr. Fox. "Coach wants
me to play," I said, "give me a couple of shots in my
leg." I meant the usual combination of cortisone, the
quick healer, and Novocain, the pain killer.

He said, "No, I won't give you a couple of shots. It
might last during the game, but you'll be in so much
pain afterward it'll be unreal."

So I went on the field and I was taking exercises and
I started running and it seemed like I pulled or stretched
it a little more. So I told Dr. Fox.

He went over to Coach Halas and said, "Look, Gale's
out." Dr. Fox has the last word. He told the old man
that a shot would hurt me more than help me. That was
it. I sat out my first football game.

Paul Wiggin of the Browns said afterward, "It was
like going to a Harry Belafonte show and Harry Belafonte isn't there."

But we played a strong game. It was 0–0 at the half.
Mr. Halas came up to me in the dressing room. "Gale,
don't worry about it. Just tell the reporters you hurt the
leg again." Cleveland finally beat us 24–0, but we
stayed in pretty tough.

The next day there was a big furor in the papers. The
game had been taken off the boards by the bookies in
some cities three or four days before the game and the
Bears were accused of concealing my injury.

We were six- or seven-point underdogs against Cleveland and taking it off the boards meant you couldn't bet on the game, the bookies wouldn't touch it.

I don't know where they got the information that I wasn't going to play. Somebody said I was spotted limping in practice. Well, if that was what they were looking for, they could have seen that almost any time we practice. I'm always gimping around the week before a game. Hell, when I walk normally it looks like I've got a limp. And there was no indication until game time whether I would play or not play. I felt it was a big stink about nothing.

But someone from the commissioner's office came over, had lunch with me, and asked me what happened. I told him, and that was it. Cleveland made a big thing out of it, but I don't think anyone else did.

Of course gambling is a constant worry in pro football. People ask me if I've ever been approached by a gambler. I have to say I don't know. I talk to a lot of people. I don't know who's a gambler and who's not a gambler. You talk about football, you don't know if your best friend could be betting on games. People ask me, "What do you think about Dallas and Cleveland?" And you just give them your opinions. "I think so-and-so is going to win." They want to bet on it, let them go head. It's very tough to stop gambling in football.

By Tuesday of the next week I was running on the leg again. It felt fine. And I was looking forward to coming back and having a good game against the Los Angeles Rams. And I went out there and carried the ball thirteen times, and gained thirteen yards. And we lost 28–17.

That's when I became a little depressed, a little worried. And I came down with diarrhea or gastritis or the flu or whatever you want to call it. All I know is I lost about twenty-five pounds; I weighed about 180 for the Green Bay game.

I do remember that our regular physician, Dr. Braun, called me and told me that I was all right physically, I was just probably upset over my playing. And Mr.

Halas called Linda and asked her what it was. And then one night that week—it was about twelve o'clock—he called me.

Really, all he said to me was not to worry. The club was going bad but it wasn't my fault. We had quarterback problems, injuries on the offensive line. He told me just to go out there against Detroit and play my game.

And I did.

The second time we had the ball I broke around left end, reversed field twice, and carried sixty-three yards before they caught me on the one. Quarterback Jack Concannon took it in from there.

The second quarter I fielded a kickoff and went down the left side lines ninety-seven yards for the touchdown.

I gained sixty-four yards in eight carries. We won the game 27–13, and the fellows gave me the game ball afterward.

Still, things weren't going right. Here it was, coming up to the eleventh game of the season, and I was down thirteenth among the NFL rushers, the lowest I'd ever been in the pros. Some people were a little critical of my performance. One writer devoted a whole column to the subject of why the Bears should trade me. "By trading Galloping Gale," he wrote, "the Bears would have a better team without him than they have with him." That made me feel really good. But I figured I'd go out there and try to do my job.

Our eleventh game was against the Packers, and I gained 117 yards, including a forty-three-yard touchdown run.

The next week against San Francisco I gained only thirty yards on the ground. But I scored one touchdown on a fifteen-yard run, another touchdown on a ninety-seven-yard kickoff return, and a third on a fifty-eight-yard punt return. That last one I remember very well.

Steve Spurrier, the 49ers' quarterback, had kicked the ball. It was kind of a high kick, and I caught them a little by surprise by returning it instead of calling for a fair catch. On a high punt when they think you're going to call a fair catch you can sometimes catch them napping. They can't hit you until you catch the ball, so sometimes they start to slow up ten yards away when they think you're going to raise that hand and signal fair catch.

I caught the ball, just made a little move, and that was it. No one touched me. Spurrier was waiting for me on the ten, but I made a quick move, cut by him, and went into the end zone.

Then we tied Minnesota 10–10, and I rushed for 131 yards. I set up a field goal with a thirty-eight-yard run and carried twenty-one yards on two carries for our only touchdown.

Our last game, at Atlanta, I scored two touchdowns on a thirty-yard pass reception and a fifty-one-yard run. I gained 120 yards for the day, so I ended in third place in the league, behind Leroy Kelly and Dave Osborn of the Vikings.

It was kind of a disappointing season, but when you lose early and come back strong (we won five of our last seven, and tied one) it kind of lifts you up. It's always good to go out with a victory. So I think Linda was a little wrong. It wasn't an altogether bad season. Sure, it could have been better—I wanted it to be better —but it didn't turn out to be that bad.

Right after the 1967 season I went back to school.

I don't mean I went back to Kansas to get my degree in physical education. I went to New York City to take a ten-week course that, I hoped, would earn me a license as a stockbroker.

Up to then I really hadn't done too much in the off season. After my rookie year I accepted about ten speaking engagements, and, as I've mentioned, I started in the Sears Roebuck training program. I was in training to be a buyer, but I discovered it could be a very long process. Lots of times when you got to be an assistant buyer there was quite a lag until the time you could become a buyer. It could be one year, it could be twenty years. It all seemed to depend on fate. If somebody died, or somebody moved to a different department, then they'd say, Well, you're a buyer now. And it's a salaried job. I enjoyed the opportunity they gave me at Sears, but I don't think I'm the type to be a salaried man.

Jon Arnett was the first person to talk to me about becoming a stockbroker. He was a very successful broker in Los Angeles. The more he talked the better it sounded. Being a stockbroker, he said, there's always something new and exciting happening. If you don't sell one customer, you've got somebody else you can go to. And you aren't tied down to doing one certain thing, doing it all the time.

I called Buddy Young for advice. I said, "Do you think I ought to go into the stock-market business?"

Buddy said, "Will you work at it?"

"Yes."

"Well, sure," he said, "go ahead."

I talked to Coach Halas about it, too. He said it might be a good thing to get into. I visited several of the houses on LaSalle Street, which is the Wall Street of Chicago. A lot of them just won't accept part-time brokers, you had to be full-time all the way. Then I went to Paine, Webber, Jackson & Curtis and I was impressed. Coach Halas did business there and he thought it was a fine firm. And I liked the people I met. I barely knew what a stock was until I walked into a broker's office, but I've always felt that I can do anything I set my mind to. So I became a trainee in Paine, Webber's Chicago office.

It was like a new world. They have the largest office stock-quotation board in the country in there. It's so big it scares you. It's like the manned-flight control headquarters at the Houston space center. It took me a while to understand how to read the board—and to understand a lot of other things. I went from department to department, just trying to learn the ins and outs of the operation. And the following year, after the 1967 season, I went to school in New York.

It was a very tough course. They don't give away licenses, that's the one thing they don't do. Because you're dealing with other people's money. Teachers would come in from different universities, lecture on the law, teach about tax problems, municipal bonds, mutual funds—the whole round of brokerage business. There were twenty tests in that ten-week period, with the big final exam at the end, the test that would determine if you got a license or didn't.

It was a little tougher on me because I had to miss a whole week when I was out at the Pro Bowl game in Los Angeles. When I came back I was really behind. They gave me a tutor and it still was tough, trying to make up what I had missed and keep up with the class at the same time.

It all came down to our final examination. I took it a week later than the others because of the time I had lost. I *had* to pass the test. One of the reasons I had to succeed was that I would become the first black broker in Paine, Webber. If I flunked the course in New York, I'd be embarrassed coming back. I knew I had to do it.

I remember when he first went into the brokerage business, I was kind of afraid. Maybe because of the black-white situation, because I felt he might have a hard time attracting customers—or white men—that would have confidence in him, give him their money to invest. That bothered me quite a bit. I didn't think he was going to play his job cheap, because Gale's not the kind of guy who plays anything cheap when he wants to do it, but I didn't know how it would work out.

I took the test on a Friday and I knew I passed. So I called Linda right away and said, "I'm in." But I wouldn't know officially until Monday. And Saturday and Sunday, the more I thought about it, the more I started to feel, Well, maybe I didn't pass it. I thought, Maybe I missed a few more questions after all. That weekend was really a trial. Other guys, who had taken the test earlier, knew they had passed, and they were partying every night. I couldn't.

On Monday morning I found out I had passed.

Paine, Webber has helped Gale become lots more responsible, because before he wasn't that much responsible to anything but football. I remember when he was in New York. I worried, really worried. Not that I didn't have any confidence in him. But I knew him, and he had never before really applied himself to study. He finished number twenty-two out of a class of sixty-seven. To me, that was his greatest accomplishment. That was my proudest moment.

Football does come easy to me. I don't have to work for that. Getting my broker's license was an experience. That was one thing I really had to work for, and I'm proud I passed.

But that was only the start. I still had an awful lot to learn (and I still do), and a fellow named Dan Reske, who is the research manager of the Chicago office, has been of tremendous help to me.

I was first introduced to Dan when I was in training at Paine, Webber. I would come to him with questions, all sorts of questions. And he was always patient enough to take the time to answer them. And we became good friends. When I report to camp in July, I'm sort of automatically suspended from the exchange. I can't actively solicit business until I come back full-time again. The first summer I went off to camp one of the partners called Dan in and asked him if he would be willing to assume my accounts. Dan said yes, and he's been taking care of my business ever since when I go off to football. I trust his judgment and I trust him as I would a brother.

So far I've got about two hundred accounts. I'm not kidding myself about the reason for my modest success. When I'm out looking for customers it does not hurt to be recognized as Gale Sayers, running back for the Chicago Bears.

One day I was downstairs by myself having lunch. This fellow saw me, came up to me and asked me for an autograph for his son. So I gave him one and he gave me his card. He was the president of a big company. The next day I wrote him a note: "I want to thank you for coming up and asking for my autograph because I think athletes owe something to kids," and so forth. About two days later he called me. "Come on down and let's have lunch together."

I went downstairs and had lunch with him and he said, "I've been doing some business with some brokers, but I'd like to help you out." He is now my biggest client.

You don't get those too often, but you sure can look for them. Right now, since I work only half a year, I feel I can't really go out and look for the small man. I have to go after the big man. Like, now only one-half of one per cent of my clients are black. They just aren't educated about the stock market. The money's there but most of them keep their money in savings-and-loan institutions. I don't care what you say about the stock market—they're not going to take it out of savings-and-loans. But when I retire from football, I think I'd like to try and educate the black man about the market.

There are some things, of course, that won't wait for my retirement from football. The issue of race in this country is one of them, and I have tried to involve myself as much as possible without compromising what is my primary job in life: football. And it is very difficult.

You can hardly touch on the race issue today without upsetting somebody. You're either frightening white people who become offended by your getting involved. Or you're offending black people because you're not involved enough. There is no happy medium, but I try to do enough things to show that I'm concerned. Because I am concerned.

For the past few summers I have been coordinator of Mayor Daley's "Reach Out" program. The phrase means just that—to reach out into underprivileged neighborhoods for kids, bring them out of the ghettos, and try to work with them. From May until I go to camp we work with kids in the Toe; we hold football clinics, sports competitions, the kinds of things we hope will keep them off the streets.

In 1966 I became co-chairman of the Sports Committee of the Legal Defense Fund, which raises money for legal work for the NAACP. When I make a speech my fee goes to the Legal Defense Fund.

In 1968 we started the Gale Sayers Foundation to provide clothes and scholarships for newspaper boys. It had gotten to a point where newsboys were just afraid to hand out the papers in certain neighborhoods. They were getting robbed or beaten up, and you tend to lose incentive when you have to face such situations. So the Chicago *Daily News* and *Sun Times* formed this Gale Sayers agency. They put my name on bags. If a kid brought in a new order, he'd get a Gale Sayers sweatshirt. If he brought in five orders, he'd get a portable record player. We tried to give them incentive. Half of the kids who carried papers were poor, so we bought them clothes, bought them books if they needed them, got them to football games, and established scholarship programs. And it worked out pretty well. Robberies were down, and in some of the worst neighborhoods new subscribers jumped fifteen per cent.

During the football season I would speak once a week to the newsboys. We'd just talk about school or about newspaper routes or any troubles they might be having. It's tough talking to them, I tell you, because the new generation is different. Attitudes have changed. I know when I give talks I can see that no one is listening. You say, What the hell, what am I doing here? You try to get off your feet as fast as you can. It's so difficult to communicate with the kids, but you've got to keep trying. You keep trying, and once in a while something you say hits and they become interested. If you're able to change the direction of one kid's life, it's worth all the other failures.

In the winter of 1969 Mayor Daley appointed me a park commissioner of Chicago. There are five commissioners and we meet once a month. Not many years ago in Chicago you used to be able to go around the city and see the whole family in the park. But nowadays you don't see anybody in the park because the parks are unsafe, and you don't have any programs to draw people to the parks. That's one of the things I want to see changed. I want to see the parks made safer, I want to see better programs in the parks, I want them to build more parks.

The park commissioners also approve contracts for building and repairs and landscaping and various other jobs. Although they say there's no discrimination, I think the black construction workers, carpenters, etc., should be informed of these different contracts that are being put up by the city so they have a chance to bid on them. So I got hold of a list of all the black construction companies and tree trimmers and gravel companies and the like. Now the park commission will at least let them have the opportunity to bid on jobs.

I also work closely with Jesse Jackson's Operation Breadbasket, which has been a tremendous success in Chicago. Just about anything Jesse asks me to do, I do for him. I think most black people respect me for this, and many white people know that Jesse is trying to do a good job and they respect him, too.

Still, there are some white people who don't want you to identify with the black movement at all. They want you to keep hands off. You just have to be their kind of person. Which is impossible in this day and age. I once had a sticker on my car that read BLACK IS BEAUTIFUL. One of my white teammates saw it and put out the rumor that I was a militant.

I've played with this fellow since I came to the Bears, and I can't figure him. There was a time when I was in line to get a couple of franchises for a national fast-food chain. And the fellow in charge wanted to know what kind of person I was. He knew this veteran player and asked him. And the player, my old teammate, said, "Sayers is a militant, he's always causing trouble."

This came back to me through a close friend. And I heard from him also that the same player had made several other remarks, like he definitely didn't approve of the younger players associating with "niggers" too much.

The franchise people turned kind of cold on me when they got this fellow's recommendation. But they talked to some people at Paine, Webber who said, "It's not true. Gale's no militant. Besides he's one of the brightest young fellows we ever had in our firm." But that hurt me. This teammate of mine had always seemed like a helluva dude.

I think you have to say that paying the price is not a term that is associated exclusively with professional football. A lot of people in our country today, because of an accident of birth, are paying the price every day. And they do willingly. And, damn, they carry on, they endure. And seeing that gives you hope.

19

A New Day

As long as I live I'm going to try to change. Change is an indication of life.

—Rev. Jesse L. Jackson

I am sitting in the Capitol theater this Saturday morning, a week after the 1969 football season has come to an end with the Pro Bowl game in Los Angeles. This huge old movie house, with the blue-sky ceiling that is now flecked with cracked-plaster clouds of white, is located in the middle of the inner city and it is filling up rapidly. You see young blacks, middle-aged blacks, old blacks, whites (mostly students), and even a dozen journalists from Soviet Russia.

A big banner is strung across the stage and it reads DECLARE HUNGER ILLEGAL. And underneath, in smaller letters, SCLC OPERATION BREADBASKET. It is Jesse Jackson's baby. The Reverend Jackson is the national director of Operation Breadbasket, which is the economic arm of Martin Luther King's Southern Christian Leadership Conference. Jesse has done so much good in helping to feed the poor and opening up job opportunities. There are now Operation Breadbasket programs in about thirty cities across the country.

Jesse is a year older than I am, and we have been tight for some time. When I was trying to get my knee back in shape he would go out to the park and run with me. I think he's in a very difficult position. He's young and yet, because he's a leader, he's always thrown in with older persons. And he's not only ostracized by many whites, but he's also ostracized by many blacks because they are afraid of this movement. And he's

232

bothered constantly by leeches, people who just want something from him. So he seeks friendship with a person his own age, someone he can come around to and laugh and joke with. He has this hunger to make a solid friendship with someone he has things in common with, and we've become good friends. And, last week in Santa Monica, California, Jesse and I went under the spotlight—the same spotlight, mind you, that they used to throw on the Academy Award winners—and received our awards as two of the Junior Chamber of Commerce's ten outstanding young men of 1969.

There we were rubbing noses with people like John D. (Jay) Rockefeller IV, who is the Secretary of State for West Virginia and who also received the award. Jesse went up to Jay Rockefeller, who seemed like a regular guy, and he had this trophy in his hand and he pointed to the inscription—"The hope of mankind lies in the hands of youth and action"—and he chided Jay Rockefeller. "It ain't gonna get any better," Jesse said, "if you act like your daddy."

When he made his acceptance speech, Jesse said he didn't deserve the award. It should have gone to whoever in the last twelve months received the smallest amount of food; or whoever survived Vietnam and had his leg shot off and came back and couldn't get housing. And twenty-five hundred people in that auditorium listened, and listened with respect.

Now one of the Reverend Jackson's assistants is addressing the crowd. There must be two thousand people in the movie house, and I wonder what the Russians are thinking. "Let us bow our heads, let us think . . . stop . . . and listen. Wherever man is, God is. Whether his station be of wealth or amongst the poorest of the poor. And our mind reflects that where God is, man is. The psalm says that whatever station man finds himself at the turn, whether rich or poor, that His eye is on the sparrow . . . and it is also on me. Therefore I cannot hate, I must love. I cannot let racism enter my consciousness . . . I must love somebody. In love He watches me."

And then a soloist comes on stage and, with the backing of the choir, sings, *You Know My Heart*. Some announcements follow and Jesse Jackson comes on out and starts talking—and this is a young man who talks. I mean, he can really light fires. And he introduces me. "Down there in L.A.," he says, "I was Gale's rooting section. Gale hadn't played with a team all year, you know. . . . Last week he played with his first quarterback, Roman Gabriel. And look what happened. He ran wild, he caught passes, and he was the Most Valuable Player."

And I stand up and take a bow. I try to come to Operation Breadbasket meetings whenever I'm in Chicago, just to try and set an example. I believe it is a very good program. A couple of years ago I picketed with Jesse and a group in front of a supermarket. They had promised jobs to blacks, then backed down. The place was filthy, too. The same hamburger meat you'd buy in a white neighborhood for $.82, say, would cost $1.02 here. We got that changed. This is just one of the functions of Operation Breadbasket, and I give the program as much support as I can. I try to show them that I am on their side and concerned with what they are fighting for.

Jesse Jackson talks on. . . . "Is pollution the number-one enemy? No, it is the polluter, it is the man who allows this contamination. . . ." And while he talks on, I think back to what I said at Santa Monica.

I wish I had the eloquence of a Jesse Jackson. Hell, it's taken me years to stand up and talk to people. I started out life shy and withdrawn, and I'm still that way, though less so. I don't push anything on anyone. I don't talk much. I like to listen. I learn more listening than talking. There's a saying, "It's better to appear stupid than to speak out and remove all doubts." I know I'm not stupid, but I like to listen. I'm not a talker, I never have been a talker.

But I tried to say something meaningful at that Jaycee award night. My little theme was that I was fortunate in having been instilled with motivation and having received opportunity. I said, "It's a combination of the two that is so vital. For opportunity without motivation is a waste. And motivation without opportunity is a shame."

Then I read a poem that had been sent to me by Don Klosterman when I was in the hospital. He was with the Houston Oilers at the time and he sent me a thoughtful get-well letter and enclosed this little saying that he thought would be appropriate. It is called "This Is a New Day," and I recited it out there in Santa Monica.

"God has given me this day to do as I will.
    I can waste it or use it for good.
    What I do today is very important
    Because I am trading a day in my life for it.
    When tomorrow comes, this day will be gone forever
    Leaving behind something I've traded for it.
    I want it to be gain, not loss . . .
    Good, not evil . . .
    Success, not failure . . .
    In order that I should never forget
    The price I paid for it."

And I ended by saying, "As for myself, this is a new day."

And, driving home from the Operation Breadbasket meeting, I think to myself, Another plateau. Ten years ago I was nothing. Five years ago I was nothing. Now I'm one of the ten outstanding young men of the country. And five years later I'm going to be Mayor of Chicago. . . . No way, no way. I'm not that type of person. I'm not that responsible a guy. I like to be free and easygoing. I like to stay at home, and when you're into politics, you've got to go here, go there. That's not my type of living. But I might change. By the time I'm thirty-six I might have a different attitude.

How it all changes! Just since the knee injury I know I have changed to some extent. I mean, I had always taken things for granted too much before it happened. Because things had come easy for me. I never had experienced any real adversity. In college I was pampered for four years. When I came to Chicago I was an instant success in football. Then I was having a big season in 1968 and, all of a sudden, it's over. And I stopped taking things for granted. You begin to realize it can't go on forever, it's going to end. So I have tried to become more dedicated to things outside of football.

I think his knee injury kind of changed my life, in that up to then I never realized how much I enjoyed being married to a professional-football player of Gale's stature. I had always said, Well, this is not important to me. But at that moment I realized that I really was enjoying it. And I suddenly realized that one of the reasons I was enjoying it so much was that, through Gale, I was considered somebody. And I just decided that that was no good because basically you aren't anybody. That was a false attitude I had taken. I never admitted it to myself until that moment.

Since the injury I have tried to become more aware of what's going on in the world. Before, I lived in a world where the only thing that mattered to me was playing football and coming home and just sitting and spending the evening with my family. That's the only thing that meant anything to me. Now I'm just beginning to realize that there are other things. I think reading books has helped, and I might never have started reading if it hadn't been for my injury. With books, you begin to see that there are other things in the world besides football. That there is a world out there outside your own dimensions.

How it all changes! Back in Omaha as a kid, I was a nothing. Everybody called me stupid or dumb. I told Break that when we went back there for our tenth anniversary reunion in 1971, Break and I, we would go back in a limousine. We'd get the longest Cadillac and wear fancy tuxedos and smoke the longest cigars. And we'd sit in the back seat with a white chauffeur driving us to our high-school reunion. That's right. I really mean that, because to all the people in Central, it was "old dumb Gale."

I have never to this day forgotten the morning I was sitting in an assembly at our high school. Some students from Omaha University came out to speak, and my brother Roger was one of them. I was sitting behind a couple of girls. And when he was finished talking one girl turned to the other and said, "How come Gale is so dumb and Roger is so smart?"

Quiet as Gale is now, he was ten times quieter when I first met him. I mean, it was unbelievable. He had absolutely no self-confidence at all. He was like almost ashamed of himself. The only thing he had in his whole life was his football ability. Now, I didn't keep his scrapbooks. He kept those himself. The only satisfaction, I think, he got out of anything, was sitting and reading the scrapbooks. And he would do that three or four times a week, three or four times a week he would just get out his scrapbooks and read them. And that was his only way of expressing himself to all of us—on the football field. Then he had no identity as a person. Now he's come out more as a person, not just a football player. And he found himself, after he began to change, wanting to prove to himself and to me and to everybody that he was really going to be something.

Linda says she feels like I'm having an affair with football during the season. She says I don't belong to her, or to my family. And she is right, up to a point. Linda knows that during the football season I don't want to do things, and a lot of times she gets mad. But that's the way it's got to be. That's the way it's going to be until I retire. Football is one game where you just cannot put half of yourself into it. You've got to put your whole self into it if you want to be any kind of a football player. I like to think that I'm the best right now at my position. I like to think that. If I didn't think that I wouldn't be as good as I am. But I know that I cannot remain the best unless my whole self is put into football.

And yet I'm not that extreme any more about football, and our home life is different. In the fall of 1969, in the midst of everything, we went out and adopted a baby.

After I signed my first pro contract we decided we could afford to start a family. We went three years and we thought we weren't going to have any children. So we talked to Coach Halas about adopting and he put us in touch with an agency. And it was in the final stages when Linda got pregnant. So we canceled the adoption.

After Gale Lynne came along we decided we'd wait two years and have another child. And in two and a half years Linda got pregnant again. But then she suffered a miscarriage. So we decided to adopt again. We didn't want Gale Lynne to grow up without a playmate, or to be too old when another child came along. We wanted them to be like brothers and sisters. Linda had been the youngest child in her family and her brothers were like uncles to her because they were so much older. And we had always talked about maybe adopting a baby after we had our own. But then Linda said, "Why wait until it's the end of us having children? Let's adopt them in the middle."

We were planning on adopting a girl. We had read a lot of literature about adopted children and how they try harder to please their parents. We didn't want a boy growing up thinking he had to be a football player.

We waited for about eight months and the lady from the agency came to our house and told us they didn't have any girls or any expectant Negro mothers. But she did say they had a two-month-old boy. So we said we'd go look at the boy.

And we drove down to Evanston, to the Evanston Cradle Society, about twenty-five miles away, and we were nervous wrecks. We were just small-talking and everything in the car. We didn't know what to say to each other. And we were kind of having second thoughts about it.

I said, "What are you going to do if it's ugly?"

"What would we do," she said, "if we had a kid of our own and he was ugly? If you have a baby of your own, you take what you get. So why fool around here?"

When we got to the Cradle Society we had to scrub up and everything, in case we said no. We could have looked at him and not taken him. They would have had to put the baby back in the nursery, so they made us scrub up and put on the gowns and masks and everything. And they brought this baby out and handed him to me.

He was at that age when he was just starting to recognize voices and look around. Maybe I was the first male that he'd been around, except for the doctor, who had seen him maybe once or twice. Plus he hadn't been around anybody as dark as I am. Anyway, he started looking at me, really looking.

I couldn't stand it. I said, "Take this mask off me and let me kiss my baby."

We felt good from the start. That drive home from Evanston was beautiful. This is our baby. We felt that from the first. It was a really good feeling.

And this is the way it was. It was October 3, Gale Lynne's third birthday. We had told her she was getting a baby brother, and Linda brought her home from school and told her that we were going to get the baby and to take her nap so she would be wide awake when we got back. And when we came into the driveway, Gale Lynne was looking out the kitchen window and she screamed. She screamed for about two hours. She just couldn't believe it. She said that it was her baby.

I know two-month-old babies don't do very much, but Scott Aaron was the most sober baby I'd ever seen in my life. He just lay there, period. But slowly he came around. He began to laugh and seemed very happy. And Linda says she's looking forward to the day when she tells him that he's adopted. She says, "I just want him to think, God, I've got great parents. Not to worship us because we did adopt him, but to know how easy it was for us to love him."

And when people come to the house and they say, "Oh, that's really a lucky baby," we just look at them. A lucky baby? We're the lucky ones.

Gale Eugene Sayers

RUSHING

Year	Games	Attempts	Yards	Average	Touchdowns
1965	14	166	867	5.2	14
1966	14	229	*1231	5.4	8
1967	13	186	880	4.7	7
1968	9	138	856	*6.2	2
1969	14	236	*1032	4.4	8

PASS RECEIVING

Year	Completed	Yards	Average	Touchdowns
1965	29	507	17.5	6
1966	34	447	13.1	2
1967	16	126	7.9	1
1968	15	117	7.8	0
1969	17	116	6.8	0

SCORING

Year	Touchdowns	Points
1965	*22	*132
1966	12	72
1967	12	72
1968	2	12
1969	8	48

* League leader.

100-YARD GAMES

Opponent	Attempts	Yards
1965: New York	13	113
Baltimore	16	118
San Francisco	9	113
1966: Baltimore	18	106
Detroit	21	124
Atlanta	19	172
Minnesota	17	197
1967: Detroit	22	142
Green Bay	18	117
Minnesota	20	131
Atlanta	19	120
1968: Washington	15	105
Minnesota	16	108
Baltimore	15	105
Minnesota	18	143
Green Bay	24	205
1969: Los Angeles	15	109
Minnesota	20	116
Pittsburgh	28	112
Cleveland	20	126

NATIONAL FOOTBALL LEAGUE RECORDS

Most Touchdowns One Season—22 in 1965 (14 rushing, 6 pass receiving, 2 kick returns).

Most Touchdowns Rookie Season—22 in 1965.

Most Touchdowns One Game—6 vs. San Francisco, December 12, 1965 (tied Ernie Nevers and Dub Jones); 4 rushing, 50, 7, 5, 1 yards; 80-yard pass reception; 85-yard punt return.

Most Touchdowns Kickoff Returns, Career—6, 103 yards vs. Pittsburgh, September 17, 1967; 97 vs. Detroit, November 5, 1967; 97 vs. San Francisco, December 3, 1967; 96 vs. Minnesota, October 17, 1965; 93 vs. Los Angeles, October 23, 1966; 90 vs. Minnesota, December 18, 1966.

Most Points Rookie Season—132 in 1965.

Total Offense One Season—2440 yards in 1966: 1231 on 229 rushes; 447 on 34 pass receptions; 718 on 23 kickoff returns; 44 on 6 punt returns.

Total Offense Average One Game—19.76 vs. San Francisco, December 12, 1965. 336 total yards, 17 attempts; 113 on 10 rushes; 89 on 2 pass receptions; 134 on 5 punt returns.

Kickoff Return Average—30.56.

CHICAGO BEARS RECORDS

Kickoff Return—103 yards vs. Pittsburgh, September 17, 1967.

Most Yards One Season—2440 in 1966.

Highest Average One Game—19.76 (336 yards in 17 attempts) vs. San Francisco, December 12, 1965.

Most Yards One Game—339 vs. Minnesota, December 18, 1966 (197 on 17 rushing attempts; 116 on 2 kickoff returns; 26 on 1 pass reception).

Highest Average, Career—5.4 (4866 yards in 955 attempts).

Most 100-Yard Games, Career—20.

Most Yards One Season—1231 in 1966.

Most Attempts One Season—236 in 1969.

Most Touchdowns One Season—14 in 1965.

Most Yards One Game—205, vs. Green Bay, November 3, 1968.

Most Kickoffs Returned for Touchdown—6.

Most Kickoff Returns—81.

Most Yards Punt Returns One Game—134, vs. San Francisco, December 12, 1965.

Most Yards Kickoff Returns One Season—718 in 1966.

Most Yards Kickoff Returns One Game—170, vs. Minnesota, October 17, 1965.

ging through my mind, nothing makes sense. I imagine
... of ... about football - nothing sensible. While I
listen to ... hear I hear listen. While I listen I might be
thinking ... bout something but this is the way I solve
... I don't ... able be doing nothing. A lot of people day